Deciding to Decide

Thomas J. Wilson Prize

The Board of Syndics of Harvard University Press has awarded this book the twenty-first annual Thomas J. Wilson Prize, honoring the late director of the Press. The Prize is awarded to the book chosen by the Syndics as the best first book accepted by the Press during the calendar year.

H. W. Perry, Jr.

Deciding to Decide

Agenda Setting in the United States Supreme Court

Harvard University Press
Cambridge, Massachusetts, and London, England 1991

This book is printed on acid-free paper, and its binding
materials have been chosen for strength and durability.

Library of Congress Cataloging-in-Publication Data

Perry, H. W.
    Deciding to decide : agenda setting in the United
    States Supreme Court / H. W. Perry, Jr.
        p.   cm.
    Includes index.
    ISBN 0-674-19442-X
    1. United States. Supreme Court.   2. Judicial process
    —Research—United States. 3. Certiorari—United
    States. I. Title.
KF8742.P3365   1991
347.73'26—dc20
[347.30735]   91-14002
                                                        CIP

*To my parents, Hersel W. Perry and Dorothy F. Perry,
and my sister, Gail D. Perry*

Acknowledgments

If it is true that one thing in life better than learning is to know you have taught, then the people listed below ought to be very fulfilled. I have learned from them all, and they have been very good teachers.

I am indebted to my informants, especially the justices, for teaching me about the Supreme Court. These lawyers and judges are very busy people, who are fiercely protective of the Court's integrity. I am most appreciative of their time and willingness to be interviewed. I am especially grateful to "C1." She helped me get my foot in the first few doors and taught me an immense amount in that initial interview, making future interviews much more profitable. Thanks also go to Jeffrey Morris for directing me to the first few informants.

Many people contribute to the successful completion of a book—some by their ideas and others in different but equally important ways. My extended family of Stephensons and Perrys provided love, humor, and perspective. The influence of Ruth P. Morgan and Willis M. Tate on me intellectually and personally is inestimable. Jerry and Rochelle Gedaly, Marlene Gedaly, John and Donna Goodwin, Patrick Hobbs, Phillip Leach, Scott and Bet Marshall, Collen McGee, Steve and Lou Pontius, Laura Starks, Bill Wallace and Beth Fagan, and especially John Sewell gave me support and encouragement. The extensive interviewing would have been impossible but for the extraordinary generosity of Mabel and Elbert Peterson. They opened their home and cupboard to me when I was in Washington, and they also sustained me with their friendship. Several other people and institutions made this project easier. Martha Derthick and the Brookings Institution kindly provided me with office space. The Earhart Foundation and the Horace H. Rackham School of Graduate Studies at the University of Michigan provided support in the earlier phase of my research. I appreciate the efforts and good advice of Aida Donald, Elizabeth Suttell, and especially Elizabeth Hurwit at Harvard University Press.

My students are frequently my teachers. Several have worked tirelessly and good-naturedly on parts of this project: Mark Dreyer, Steven Fradkin, Susan Kirkpatrick, and Linda Nathenson at Washington University; and Joel Kaplan, David Kennedy, and Todd Lochner at Harvard. I appreciate their ideas, conscientiousness, and good humor. Some day, scholars will probably be interviewing them.

Many people assisted me in ways too numerous to specify: Scott Ainsworth, Joshua Blatt, Shaun Bowler, Evie. Feinberg, Vod Hatch, Heemin Kim, Mark Lange, Jan Leighly, Jay McCann, Marilyn Schad, Natalie Sekuler, and Maggie Trevor. Thomas Anton, Charles Franklin, Tom Gais, Mark Gibney, Nina Halpern, Phillip Henderson, Brian Humes, Cathy Johnson, Liane Kosaki, Larry Margolis, Carol Mershon, Tom Rozinski, Barbara Salert, Arlene Saxonhouse, Carmine Scavo, Rob Simmons, Rick Sloan, and Paul Warr were sources of intellectual stimulation. Kate Sears helped as both a colleague and a friend. One group lived with this project almost as much as I: I am particularly grateful to Michael Hawthorne, Martha Abele MacIver, and Barbara Smela for their ideas, encouragement, and friendship. I thank all of my colleagues at Washington University for their ideas and the intellectual environment, including Kautsky's "lunchroom," but I am particularly appreciative of their patience, support, and understanding. My colleagues at Harvard have also been supportive. Thanks especially to Robert Keohane, Stephen Macedo, Douglas Price, Robert Putnam, Judith Shklar, Sidney Verba, and Margaret Weir.

Several people played an important role in the intellectual development of this project. M. Kent Jennings and Lawrence B. Mohr spent hours discussing this project with me. Time spent with them is always profitable and pleasant. Lucius Barker, Larry Baum, Nelson Polsby, Marie Provine, and Ken Shepsle all read portions of the manuscript, and I profited greatly from their comments. Evelyn Fink and Susan Lawrence were the source of many of my best ideas. As always, Mark Peterson has been there from the first to the last as a friend and colleague. He gave me standards to aspire to and help to achieve them. Without the enthusiasm and support of Vincent Blasi, I might not have pursued this topic. He provided wise counsel and helped me get my first interview with a justice. George Grassmuck insisted that I get a command of the basics, but more important, when my spirits were low, he was always there to lift them. Few people cut to the heart of the matter quicker than Jack Walker. He blended intellectual rigor with creativity and passion. I wish he were here to see the project completed, but I can imagine that famous Walker grin. John Kingdon taught me how to be a political scientist. I am grateful for his high standards and guidance over the years, but especially for his contribution to this book. Milton Heumann taught me how a political scientist should think about courts and the law. People who know Milt know that one could not have a better friend and mentor. He has been a source of inspiration and encouragement at crucial points in my career generally and for this book specifically. I shall be forever grateful to him.

When I began this project, I could never have imagined that before I completed it, I would have found and married someone like Meme. Her love, encouragement, generosity, spirit, and advice helped make this book a reality, but even more important is the fulfillment she adds to my life. I feel very privileged to have her as a partner with whom I can share the pleasures and difficulties of research and life. And now, as the project ends, we share the joy of Lauren Minette Perry, who no doubt will teach us in ways we have not yet imagined.

Finally, I thank my parents, Hersel and Dorothy Perry, and my sister, Gail. I owe them so much. They have provided me with wonderful opportunities and instilled in me the desire to pursue them. Their love, unselfish support, and unwavering faith have made my formal education possible. Ultimately, though, my parents and sister have been my most important teachers. I dedicate this book to them.

Contents

You know, they say that the British acquired the empire in a fit of absentmindedness, and speaking for myself, I sometimes think that is the way we create our own agenda.

U.S. Supreme Court Justice

1 Introduction

The empire was acquired, however capriciously, and the U.S. Supreme Court does manage to create its own agenda. The question is how. The justice offers one perspective. Witness three others—one from another justice, and two from former law clerks:

> *Justice:* It is really hard to know what makes up this broth of the cert. process.

> *Clerk:* You know when you are riding home on the subway in New York and you want to pick up a magazine, there are hundreds that are all about the same. You pick the one that has something that stands out and grabs your attention. That's kind of how you pick a case for review.

> *Clerk:* How does a case get chosen? Serendipity.

After the last remark, it takes great restraint not to entitle this book *The Nine Princes of Serendip.*[1] Yet any social scientist would be skeptical of claims that the decision process is so mysterious or serendipitous, or that Supreme Court justices are that absentminded. In fairness, those quoted do not seriously believe that the process is quite so haphazard either; but they and many of their colleagues do tend to

---

1. With all apologies, of course, to Horace Walpole.

think that the decision process is impervious to meaningful generalization. Rejecting such a premise, this work represents an attempt to examine systematically how the U.S. Supreme Court sets its agenda.

The desire to explore the topic of agenda setting in the Supreme Court grew out of the intersection of two personal intellectual concerns: first, the belief that political scientists ought to be doing more and better studies of the judicial system and, second, the belief that political scientists ought to be doing more and better studies of how agendas are set. Of course, every topic "cries" for more and better research, but obligatory plaintive pleas notwithstanding, these two areas genuinely deserve more attention by political scientists. Hence, this effort.

The judicial system and political science. Political scientists might not be able to analyze politics with the precision we would like, but politics and political institutions can be studied rigorously. The discipline has developed research methodologies that are particularly well-suited to studying the way institutions function and how individuals behave. Yet political scientists have not brought the full force of their expertise to bear upon the courts. To be sure, there is a long, rich tradition of public law scholarship by political scientists with excellent works on law, courts, and judicial behavior.[2] And there is exciting work currently being done by many bright scholars. But few would argue that the body of good scholarship on courts by political scientists equals in quantity or quality that on other areas of American politics such as Congress or voting behavior. Moreover, we do not draw upon the knowledge gained in these areas as often as we might to aid our understanding of courts. This study, in its design and analysis, is an attempt to employ some of what we already know about other governmental institutions and behavior, and what we know about how to study such institutions, in an effort to understand the agenda-setting process of the U.S. Supreme Court.

Aye, there's the rub. The Supreme Court is at once a political institution and a legal institution. Although this statement is neither new nor profound, we continue to have a hard time accepting it and dealing with it. The issue is sometimes dodged, in fun, by waxing eloquent. Political scientists will point out that all questions are ulti-

---

2. One important contributor to the tradition, who blends public law and political science more broadly, has written an overview of our knowledge about courts. See Martin Shapiro, "Courts," in Nelson Polsby and Fred I. Greenstein, eds., *A Handbook of Political Science* (Reading, Mass.: Addison-Wesley, 1981). For a collection of articles evaluating the subfield, see John B. Gates and Charles A. Johnson, *The American Courts: A Critical Assessment* (Washington, D.C.: CQ Press, 1991).

mately political and will quote David Easton saying that "politics is the authoritative allocation of values." Since that is precisely what the Court does, it is a political institution and, as such, should be studied just as any other political institution. The Court may be unique, but since one could argue that every institution is unique, studying the Court need not cause special concern. Lawyers retort with equal grandiloquence, quoting Tocqueville, who noted, "there is hardly a political question in the United States that does not sooner or later turn into a judicial one." They then insist that only those who know how to "think like a lawyer" and understand the intricacies of the law can truly understand the Supreme Court.[3]

Such feigned and overdrawn differences between political scientists and lawyers would be heard only at a boring party. Organizations such as the Law and Society Association and the best work in both disciplines belie such extreme parochialism. But even though we claim to be "teasing," we know that people often tease on the truth. Moreover, as with any caricature, the political scientists and lawyers described above are based on some degree of reality. Political scientists do often over-politicize the Court, disregarding many of the very real constraints upon it. Herman Pritchett, a political scientist, put it well:

> Again, political scientists who have done so much to put the "political" in "political jurisprudence" need to emphasize that it is still "jurisprudence." It is judging in a political context, but it is still judging; and judging is something different from legislating or administering. Judges make choices, but they are not the "free" choices of Congressmen . . . Any accurate analysis of judicial behavior must have as a major purpose a full clarification of the unique limiting conditions under which judicial policy making proceeds.[4]

It is precisely the lack of appreciation of the nature of the courts, the law, and the legal system, that makes lawyers and legal scholars so derisive of, or worse simply ignore, the work done by political scientists.

On the other hand, legal scholars of all stripes often seem to think that they can account for the behavior of the Court with legalistic explanations as long as they acknowledge legal realism, positivism,

---

3. And of course, how many times have we heard law professors say that they have to teach their students to "unlearn" what is taught about law in an undergraduate political science course.

4. C. Herman Pritchett, "The Development of Judicial Research," in Joel Grossman and Joseph Tanenhaus, eds., *Frontiers of Judicial Research* (New York: Wiley, 1969), p. 42.

hermeneutics, or the tendency of the law to reinforce the bourgeois status quo. They often ignore with impunity what social scientists know about group behavior and decision making. I am not alone in this assessment. In an otherwise glowing review of Alexander Bickel and Benno Schmidt's *History of the Supreme Court of the United States*,[5] Greg Caldeira notes:

> At the risk of seeming overly defensive of our own discipline's *bona fides*, I do think that Bickel and Schmidt could have benefited . . . from some exposure to the better work of political scientists. That the text should reflect no contact with Walter F. Murphy's *Elements of Judicial Strategy* and David J. Danelski's work on the chief justiceship in coverage of internal politics, or with Henry J. Abraham's *Justices and Presidents* and Danelski's *A Supreme Court Justice is Appointed* on the politics of appointments simply mystifies me.[6]

This parochialism has been challenged in many different contexts. Note the remarks of the executive director of the American Bar Foundation: "Lawyers generally fail to appreciate the utility of systematic empirical research on legal phenomena . . . One reason . . . I think, is that lawyers have excessive confidence in their own intuitions."[7] Many lawyers are not only certain of their own judgment but also confident that social scientists have little to offer. Again, according to the foundation director:

> Scholars who do social science research on legal systems are not quite as well off as the snail darter. Both are endangered, but the snail darter at least has advocates who defend it, who justify its existence as an essential link in the food chain. Social scientists are a part of the food chain too, but not many professional advocates take their part, and the scientists themselves are not especially skilled at advocacy. This is a pity, be-

5. Alexander M. Bickel and Benno C. Schmidt, Jr., *History of the Supreme Court of the United States*, vol. 9, *The Judiciary and Responsible Government, 1910–21* (New York: Macmillan, 1984).

6. Gregory Caldeira, review of *History of the Supreme Court of the United States*, in *American Political Science Review* 79 (June 1985): 520.

7. John P. Heinz, "Executive Director's Report: Why Study Law among the Tiv (or among the Los Angelenos)?" in *Annual Report, 1984* (Chicago: American Bar Foundation).

> cause they are in need of defense . . . social scientists who
> study the law are often asked to justify their existence.

The disciplines of law and political science are properly interested in different things leading to different research agendas and different research methodologies. But studying the Supreme Court, whether it be by lawyers or political scientists, requires more than a tip of the hat to the concerns and knowledge of the other discipline. Coming to terms with the Supreme Court's legal and political nature is not easy, but to ignore or understate one or the other generally leads to an incomplete understanding of the Court.

Determining how individuals and groups act, when they act one way and when another, and why they behave as they do, are workaday tasks of social scientists. This book attempts these tasks and posits an understanding of the agenda-setting process of the U.S. Supreme Court. It comes from a social science perspective, but I have tried diligently to incorporate and appreciate the ethic and constraints under which the legal system functions. I hope that my research, evaluations, and conclusions will strike both political scientists and lawyers as intellectually and intuitively satisfying. Such a test is probably a good reality check on any essay about the U.S. Supreme Court.

Agenda setting. The disciplines of both law and political science acknowledge the importance of agenda setting. Social scientists note that outcomes are determined by the availability and ordering of alternatives and that the setting of an agenda usually defines and orders the alternatives. Legal scholars say much the same thing in a different way. They stress the importance of a particular case or a particular fact situation, suggesting that these often predetermine the outcome and scope of a judicial opinion. Though scholars have noted the importance of agenda setting, work on the topic has not been commensurate with its importance.[8] In addition to any inherent interest in agenda setting, if we are to address intelligently several empirical questions of behavior, and many normative questions central to democratic theory, it is necessary for us to understand something about

8. There are important works, however. For examples of agenda-setting studies that are not court related, see Roger W. Cobb and Charles D. Elder, *Participation in American Politics: The Dynamics of Agenda Building* (Boston: Allyn and Bacon, 1972); John W. Kingdon, *Agendas, Alternatives, and Public Policies* (Boston: Little, Brown, 1984); Paul C. Light, *The President's Agenda: Domestic Policy Choice from Kennedy to Carter* (Baltimore: The Johns Hopkins University Press, 1982); Nelson W. Polsby, *Political Innovation in America* (New Haven: Yale University Press, 1984); Jack L. Walker, "Setting the Agenda in the U.S. Senate: A Theory of Problem Selection," *British Journal of Political Science* 7 (October 1977): 423–445.

who sets agendas, how they are set, and how access to this process is achieved.

The need to examine the agenda-setting process is particularly relevant to the United States Supreme Court, an institution that has virtually complete discretion in setting its own agenda. When the Court hands down a decision, the impact often reaches far beyond the litigants and those similarly situated. A decision may set the agenda, or a large part of it, for political, social, and legal institutions for years to come. A seminal opinion often opens the floodgates for future litigation, legislation, and social reform. Even less than seminal decisions can be important and have widespread impact. But before the Court can render a decision, it must decide to decide. We know little about how the Court does this.

Treatises on the impact of an important case abound in scholarly works, sometimes in popular works as well. Legal scholars fill volumes with textual exegeses. The typical analysis attempts to answer questions such as: "Was the opinion a proper interpretation of the relevant constitutional clause?" or "Where does this case leave doctrine?" or "What if the opinion had included this phrase or excluded that phrase?" Social scientists discuss the normative and empirical implications of a decision, and its legislative and judicial progeny, upon society. Typical of the questions they address are: "What are the social and economic impacts mandated by the decision?" or "How has this case changed the authority to allocate values?" All of these questions are quite important, but the question that seems equally important though it is less frequently asked by lawyers or social scientists is: How does a case come to be on the Court's argument calendar in the first place?[9] After having ignored an issue for years, why does the Court choose to resolve or finesse a constitutional issue at a particular time with a particular case? Conversely, why does the Court refuse to take a seemingly important case? Or, why does the Court sometimes take a case that is of very little importance? While one might look at any given case heard by the Supreme Court and offer plausible reasons why that particular case was or was not reviewed, there is a need for a more systematic examination of the agenda-setting process of the

9. There are notable exceptions to my point, among them: Richard Kluger, *Simple Justice* (New York: Vintage Books, 1975), outlining the history of Brown v. Board of Education; and Anthony Lewis, *Gideon's Trumpet* (New York: Vintage Books, 1966), on Gideon v. Wainright. These studies, of course, explain a particular case. For examples of more general studies of particular areas, see Lee Epstein, *Conservatives in Court* (Knoxville: University of Tennessee Press, 1985); Susan E. Lawrence, *The Poor in Court* (Princeton: Princeton University Press, 1990); Clement Vose, *Caucasians Only* (Berkeley and Los Angeles: University of California Press, 1959).

Court at the institutional level, just as there is of any of our other political institutions.

Research Design

There have been several studies on case selection, but their contributions differ from what I believe to be the strengths of this effort.[10] Earlier studies are primarily associational, focusing on the extent to which the presence of certain characteristics in a case predicts review. Or they are attempts to predict how an issue might cause blocs of justices to vote. These studies examine those things that correlation, regression, factor analysis, scaling, and other statistical procedures are

10. See, for example, Lawrence Baum, "Decisions to Grant and Deny Hearings in the California Supreme Court: Patterns in Court and Individual Behavior," *Santa Clara Law Review* 16 (1976): 713–744; Lawrence Baum, "Policy Goals in Judicial Gatekeeping: A Proximity Model of Discretionary Jurisdiction," *American Journal of Political Science* 21 (1977): 13–35; Lawrence Baum, "Judicial Demand-Screening and Decisions on the Merits: A Second Look," *American Politics Quarterly* 7 (1979): 109–119; Saul Brenner, "The New Certiorari Game," *Journal of Politics* 41 (1979): 649–655; Gregory A. Caldeira, "The United States Supreme Court and Criminal Cases, 1935–1976: Alternative Models of Agenda Building," *British Journal of Political Science* 11 (October 1981): 449–470; Gregory A. Caldeira and John R. Wright, "Organized Interests and Agenda Setting in the U.S. Supreme Court," *American Political Science Review* 82 (December 1988): 1109–1127; Peter Linzer, "The Meaning of Certiorari Denials," *Columbia Law Review* 79 (November 1979): 1227–1305; William McLauchlan, "An Exploratory Analysis of the Supreme Court's Caseload from 1880 to 1976," *Judicature* 64 (1980): 32; Richard L. Pacelle, Jr., "The Supreme Court Agenda across Time: Dynamics and Determinants of Change" (Ph.D. diss., Ohio State University, 1985); Jan Palmer, "An Econometric Analysis of the U.S. Supreme Court's Certiorari Decisions," *Public Choice* 39 (1982): 387–398; Doris Marie Provine, *Case Selection in the United States Supreme Court* (Chicago: University of Chicago Press, 1980); Glendon Schubert, "The Certiorari Game," in *Quantitative Analysis of Judicial Behavior* (New York: Free Press, 1959); Glendon Schubert, "Policy without Law: An Extension of the Certiorari Game," *Stanford Law Review* (March 1962): 284–327; Donald Songer, "Concern for Policy Outputs as a Cue for Supreme Court Decisions on Certiorari," *Journal of Politics*, 41 (November 1979): 1185; Joseph Tanenhaus, Marvin Schick, Matthew Muraskin, and Daniel Rosen, "The Supreme Court's Certiorari Jurisdiction: Cue Theory," in Glendon Schubert, ed., *Judicial Decision Making* (New York: Free Press, 1963), pp. 111–132; Stuart Teger and Douglas Kosinski, "The Cue Theory of Supreme Court Certiorari Jurisdiction: A Reconsideration," *Journal of Politics* 42 (August 1980): 834–846; S. Sidney Ulmer, William Hintze, Louise Kirklosky, "The Decision to Grant or Deny Certiorari: Further Consideration of Cue Theory," *Law and Society Review* 6 (May 1972): 637–643; S. Sidney Ulmer, "The Decisions to Grant Certiorari as an Indicator to Decision 'On the Merits,'" *Polity* 4 (1972): 429–447; S. Sidney Ulmer, "Selecting Cases for Supreme Court Review: An Underdog Model," *American Political Science Review* 72 (September 1978): 902–910; S. Sidney Ulmer, "The Supreme Court's Certiorari Decisions: Conflict as a Predictive Variable," *American Political Science Review* 78 (December 1984): 901–911.

designed to measure. When done properly, they tell us things we need to know and their value goes without saying. From such information, we can speculate about a decision process, but there are more direct ways to determine the process. A better understanding of the decision process will, in turn, enable us to develop better hypotheses for predicting case selection and for confirming what we think we know about how decisions are made.

In the methodological tradition of Richard Fenno, Milton Heumann, Ralph Huitt, John Kingdon, and others, I decided to examine the decision process of the U.S. Supreme Court by asking those involved what they do and how they make their agenda decisions. Elite interviewing is a well-developed tradition in social science. As with any methodology, there are things it can and cannot tell us, and there are pitfalls. Done well, it is particularly useful for developing general understandings of processes, and it highlights assumptions that can be tested empirically. Though I would not want to push the point too far, I have a sense that we political scientists have sometimes put the cart before the horse when it comes to studying the Court. Our empirical tests have yielded unstable results and sometimes do not contribute to our understanding of reality because we misperceive certain operating presumptions at the Court. The primary reason for this gap in our understanding—a gap filled beautifully by Dexter, Huitt, Fenno, or Kingdon on Congress—is probably not so much our own fault but is mostly attributable to the ethic of secrecy that surrounds appellate courts, particularly the U.S. Supreme Court. Nevertheless, I suspect that the notable absence of the research methodology of elite interviewing in our subfield is not solely because of the difficulty of access but also has to do with the preference of scholars.[11] My point is not to criticize the prevailing approaches but rather to suggest that we often have not brought to bear the full range of our expertise to the study of appellate courts. I hope my effort is complementary.

Methodology

This book uses several data bases including a random sample of petitions for certiorari (or, cert., the formal request sent to the Supreme

11. Again, there are notable exceptions. Just to name two: Milton Heumann, *Plea Bargaining: The Experiences of Prosecutors, Judges, and Defense Attorneys* (Chicago: University of Chicago Press, 1977); J. Woodford Howard, Jr., *Courts of Appeals in the Federal Judicial System: A Study of the Second, Fifth, and District of Columbia Circuits* (Princeton: Princeton University Press, 1981).

Court asking it to review a case), information obtained from U.S. *Law Week* on dissents from denial of certiorai, workload statistics provided to me by the Clerk of the Court, data from the *Harvard Law Review*'s annual summary of statistics, and other sources here and there. The primary data, however, are personal interviews. Most notably, I was granted the rare opportunity to interview five U.S. Supreme Court justices. I also interviewed sixty-four former U.S. Supreme Court clerks, sixty-one of whom clerked during the October terms 1976–1980; seven judges on the D.C. Circuit Court of Appeals; four U.S. solicitors general and four important attorneys in the Office of Solicitor General; and one Court employee quite knowledgeable about the Court's functioning. The interviews with the justices ranged from one hour to one hour and forty-five minutes. The modal time for the interviews with the other informants was around one hour and twenty minutes.

My original intention was to deal only with the October 1976–October 1980 terms of the U.S. Supreme Court. The boundaries were set for both intellectual and practical reasons. The time period was that of a "natural court," that is, the same nine justices were on the Court for the entire time span. The October 1976 term was Justice John Paul Stevens's first full term, October 1980, Justice Potter Stewart's last. Practical considerations such as time, money, and availability of materials like certiorari petitions required that some bounds be set. As the study progressed, however, I did interview three clerks from other terms.

The sixty-four clerks interviewed came from all nine chambers. For the October terms 1976–1980 there were a total of one hundred and sixty-one clerks. Unfortunately, cost constraints kept me from interviewing nationwide. Most former clerks, however, are located in Washington, D.C., or New York, with several others located in Chicago and at various law schools. I did all of my interviewing in these three cities, or at law schools located elsewhere. As such, there may be some selection bias, but I suspect that it is not important for the way I use the data. I did not try to sample clerks randomly. I interviewed anyone who would talk with me.

Although I asked standard questions in the interviews, most of them called for open-ended responses. Consequently, the interviews were conducted in a conversational rather than a survey research manner. An overwhelming majority refused to allow me to tape-record them, so I took notes on all informants and as soon as possible dictated a transcript of the interview onto tape. Frankly, I used to be skeptical of Kingdon's or Fenno's ability to reconstruct interviews and to remember quotes. To be sure, my first interviews are spotty. But one soon learns many tricks, particularly the ability to get important statements verbatim; and after awhile, one becomes very proficient at reconstruction. I mention this here because I treat my informant's statements as direct quotations. There may be a misplaced "and" or "the," but the important words are the informant's own.

When I began this project, I doubted that I would receive many interviews. I expected the work primarily to be an empirical analysis of petitions for certiorari. As my comments suggest, I thought that there was a need to interview those involved with the process, but common wisdom suggested that the chances of getting interviews were remote. Virtually everyone told me that I would never be allowed to interview a justice. Some suggested that few former law clerks would be willing to talk to me, and the ones that would probably had an axe to grind.[12] I still thought talking with clerks would be a worthwhile venture if I could talk to enough. I could at least come away with a sense of how clerks perceived the process and perhaps some insight into the behavior of the justices.

There was, however, a major problem—a book called *The Brethren.*[13] The book was published in 1979, and its primary sources were a few former clerks, some of whom reportedly felt "burned." Though I was not planning to interview any clerks who would have been at the Court during the terms covered by *The Brethren,* the damage had been done, with the result that few clerks ever wanted another book to be traced back to them. Thanks to the help of some of the people mentioned in my acknowledgments, however, I got my foot in a few doors. Once that occurred, the barriers began to fall. My typical approach was to write clerks letters explaining my research and then call them to try to arrange an interview. With one clerk, no sooner had I begun to explain my project than he responded, "I know who you are. You don't do something like this in Washington without everybody knowing about it. I've already heard that you are okay."

Other than interviews, the primary data used were the petitions for certiorari. A stratified sample was drawn from all paid petitions for certiorari and jurisdictional statements presented to the Court for the October terms 1976–1980. I.f.p. *(in forma pauperis)* cases could not be included because it was impossible to obtain denied petitions. Since the overall denial rate is so high, I oversampled selected cases. In some of the tables in the text, therefore, I had to use weighted data. Given

---

12. A good interviewer knows how to control for problems in elite interviewing such as grudges and self-aggrandizement.

13. Bob Woodward and Scott Armstrong, *The Brethren: Inside the Supreme Court* (New York: Simon and Schuster, 1979).

how the data are used, however, this should cause no problems. Research assistants helped me code the petitions; while they coded for matters such as which circuit the case came from, the number of pages in the petition, and so on, I coded for anything that required a substantive judgment.

An Overview

In studying how the Supreme Court sets its agenda, my assumption, of course, is that the Court does in fact set its own agenda and that the only question is how. The "textbook" argument, however, asserts that the Court is a passive institution that can set its agenda in only the most limited sense. While it is true that a legitimate case or controversy must exist and be appealed, this requirement is not really much of a constraint if the Court does not want it to be. Virtually any issue the Court might wish to resolve is offered to it.[14] Indeed Tocqueville's aphorism that all political questions turn into judicial ones is even more relevant today. Moreover, if a case does not arise naturally, the justices often invite cases via their written opinions and by various other means.[15] During the course of this project, however, I did not assume that the Court was entirely free in its agenda-setting ability. Nevertheless, my research tends to bear out the common wisdom as opposed to the textbook notion, though as shall be seen, there are important caveats to this freedom.

That the Court has a panoply of cases to choose from is not entirely a blessing. The amount of reading required for the relatively few cases that are granted each term is substantial, yet in sheer number of pages it is minuscule compared to the workload presented by petitions for certiorari. Review in the U.S. Supreme Court is sought for over four thousand cases a year. Court rules allow a petition to be a maximum of thirty pages, but this limitation does not include the appendices that may number in the hundreds of pages. Material in an appendix, such as the opinion from the court below, is frequently more important and must be examined more carefully than the actual petition. In short, the amount to be read is staggering. Common sense alone would tell us that there must be some shortcut used to sift through this material.

14. See, e.g., Pacelle, "The Supreme Court Agenda across Time"; Stephen L. Wasby, *The Supreme Court in the Federal Judicial System* (New York: Holt, Rinehart and Winston, 1978).

15. My interviews also confirm this point; see Chapter 5. Also see Pacelle, "The Supreme Court Agenda across Time."

But we need not rely on common sense. We can investigate the decision process.

To the extent that the Court's agenda process has been examined by Congress, the legal profession, or the Court itself, the focus has generally been on "the workload crisis." That is not the focus here, although certainly it is integral to the decision process that has evolved and is thus addressed indirectly. I have not attempted to update the more thorough studies on workload.[16] I do argue, however, that the Court's decision-making procedures are such that the perceived "crisis" is overstated, and that control of the problem is essentially within the Court's hands.

A Review

Most studies on Supreme Court agenda setting by political scientists have been associational. Additionally, many of these studies have an underlying assumption: that votes on certiorari are preliminary, strategic judgments on the merits. In other words, deciding whether a case deserves review depends upon: (1) whether the justice believes that the case was correctly decided in the court below, and (2) whether a strategic calculation leads the justice to believe that he will win on the merits should the Court agree to hear the case. A brief look at a few studies will illustrate the prevalence of this approach.[17]

To my knowledge, Glendon Schubert was the first social scientist to deal specifically with the certiorari process.[18] Aware of how justices voted on the merits for Federal Employers' Liability Act (FELA) cases, he used game theory to try to predict how certain justices voted on cert. for FELA cases, arguing that a bloc of justices voted strategically. There was no real way to test his assertion, however, because certiorari votes were secret, and in fact, a subsequent study by Marie Provine cast serious doubts upon his findings.[19] The next major study on

16. See Samuel Estreicher and John Sexton, *Redefining the Supreme Court's Role: A Theory of Managing the Federal Judicial Process* (New Haven: Yale University Press, 1986); Federal Judicial Center, *Report of the Study Group on the Caseload of the Supreme Court* (Washington, D.C.: Administrative Office of U.S. Courts, 1972); Gerhard Casper and Richard Posner, *The Workload of the Supreme Court* (Chicago: American Bar Foundation, 1976).

17. Other fine studies are omitted here. This has nothing to do with their importance or quality and simply reflects the fact that I am trying to demonstrate certain approaches.

18. Schubert, *Judicial Decision Making.*

19. Provine, *Case Selection.*

certiorari was conducted by Joseph Tanenhaus and several colleagues.[20] He argued that the presence of certain "cues" in a petition are associated with cases that are granted review. I discuss Tanenhaus's study in Chapter 5 and so will say no more about it here except to note that for some time it and Schubert's study were virtually the only articles by social scientists addressing agenda setting on the Court.

Because certiorari votes are secret, the testing of hypotheses has been difficult, which probably accounts for some of the lack of interest by political scientists in the cert. process. The lack of data has required artful assumptions and procedures. Something happened to mitigate this problem slightly. The papers of Justice Harold H. Burton were made public after his death in 1965. Justice Burton sat on the Court for the 1945–1957 terms. Burton kept copious notes of conference proceedings including records of how each justice voted on certiorari. These voting records have made possible sophisticated statistical analysis and have served as the data base for many subsequent studies on certiorari.

Sidney Ulmer has done several important studies using data obtained from the Burton papers. In an early study, he found a relationship between a justice's vote on cert. and his vote on the merits.[21] In a later work, he developed a formal model of case selection that he labeled the "underdog model." Ulmer noted that he was not trying to explain all cert. behavior; rather, he was seeking "to determine the extent to which a restricted model will contribute to explaining variations." He demonstrated the "propensity of certain justices to favor or disfavor sociopolitical 'underdogs' in the cert. process."[22] The model suggested that for cert. decisions, a justice will vote according to his predilection toward upperdogs or underdogs, except that this is tempered by a potential unwillingness to appear biased to the brethren.

Saul Brenner posited a "new certiorari game."[23] He, too, suggested

20. Tanenhaus et al., "Cue Theory."

21. Ulmer, "Merits." Ulmer could confirm that such a relationship existed at the .05 significance level for eight of the eleven justices. When controlling for subject matter (i.e., Schubert's economic enterprise "E" cases and civil liberty "C" cases), he found the associations reconfirmed generally, though less strong when subject matter was controlled.

22. Under his definitions, government and corporations are the "upperdogs" because they are viewed as having more status or power than the "underdogs" (labor unions, employees, minority group members, individuals, aliens, and criminals). A "liberal" justice is one who supports underdogs, and a "conservative" justice, one who supports upperdogs. The model is operationalized examining the splits in cert. votes during the Burton period.

23. Brenner, "The New Certiorari Game."

that justices act strategically on cert. votes, and he hypothesized that justices calculate the odds of winning on the merits. He found that when justices can control a case's acceptance, and there is a desire to affirm, justices act strategically; but when they can control votes to reverse, they do not vote strategically. Brenner suggested that justices' failure to calculate in the latter instance is rational since most cases are reversed anyway. He, too, used portions of the Burton data to test his hypothesis. In justifying his operationalization, Brenner stated what I argue is the underlying assumption of most of case selection studies by political scientists: "Indeed it is possible that some justices usually vote to grant cert not because they seek a particular disposition, but because they believe that the Court ought to hear and decide the case. But most justices on most occasions vote to grant certiorari mainly because they desire a particular outcome."[24]

Marie Provine's excellent book on case selection also used the Burton data as a basis for statistical analysis. She concluded that "justices' perceptions of a judge's role and of the Supreme Court's role in our judicial system significantly limit the range of case selection behavior that the justices might otherwise exhibit"—that is, their inclination to vote on the merits.[25]

Larry Baum has done theoretical, interesting work on agenda setting in state supreme courts.[26] He has written a series of articles based on decisions in the California Supreme Court. Baum developed a model "based upon the premise that judges' responses to petitions for hearing are based solely on their policy goals."[27] He tested the model by using criminal cases and a proximity scaling procedure. His tests supported his model.

Gregory Caldeira has examined empirically the effect of filing an amicus brief at cert. and has convincingly demonstrated its importance when controlling for other variables.[28]

My summary of these works does them a great injustice by oversimplification. Most authors, especially Provine, acknowledge that sometimes the cert. decision might be more than a preliminary, strategic vote on the merits. But I think it is fair to conclude that most of these authors tend to see such situations as rare or of little consequence; or perhaps they simply are not interested in the times when nonstrategic

24. It is unclear to me how Brenner draws this conclusion. He simply asserts it, cites Ulmer, and in the footnote suggests that he recalculated Ulmer's data using a different method.

25. Provine, *Case Selection*, p. 6.

26. Baum, *Patterns*; Baum, *Gatekeeping*; Baum, *Screening*.

27. Baum, *Gatekeeping*.

28. Caldeira, "Organized Interests."

factors might predominate. I think this is a mistake. First, because my findings suggest that this bias has most good political science focusing on the "man bites dog" scenario; and second, even in cases where the man decides to bite the dog, the focus distorts our understanding of how this atypical decision was made. In the course of my research I have found at times that previous studies offer profound insights that seem to explain the behavior of the justices quite well. Other times, however, they just do not fit with what I was learning from my informants. Moreover, some of the authors' suggestions are counterintuitive, most certainly to lawyers, but they also should raise the eyebrows of political scientists, given what we know about decision making in other institutions.[29] That conclusions are counterintuitive does not mean, of course, that they are wrong; but it suggests the need for further and different kinds of examination.

Decisions on cert. often have nothing to do with a calculation of an expected outcome on the merits. Oversimplifying and generalizing, most political scientists have seen behavior at cert. as a strategic vote on the merits that may from time to time be mitigated by other factors. I argue that they have it backward. Cert. votes are primarily not the result of strategic calculations about outcome on the merits. At times they are, but even then the strategic behavior must be viewed in the context of the usual process. I am arguing not that previous studies are wrong but that they are incomplete or missing perspective. I see my study as complementary. Furthermore, I believe my research provides some insight as to why at times these studies are so on the mark and other times they are not. In any event, whether they or I have it backward, and whether or not my description is really as different from previous ones as I claim, is ultimately not the point of this book. The point is to describe the process as accurately as possible and then attempt to analyze its complexity.

A Preview

I have decided to "give away" the ending. This is done at some risk because I suspect at the outset the reader will either be highly skeptical

29. There are numerous examples one might cite. The first few that come to mind are Nelson W. Polsby, "The Institutionalization of the U.S. House of Representatives," *American Political Science Review*, March 1968; Richard E. Neustadt, *Presidential Power: The Politics of Leadership* (New York: John Wiley and Sons, 1976); John W. Kingdon, *Congressmen's Voting Decisions*, 2d ed. (New York: Harper and Row, 1981); and Mark Peterson, *Legislating Together: The White House and Capitol Hill from Eisenhower to Reagan* (Cambridge, Mass.: Harvard University Press, 1990).

or conclude that there is nothing new here. I simply must pray for forbearance. I choose to do this because I think it will help the reader sort out what at times seem to be contradictory statements by me and by my informants. Indeed, in the course of my research, it took me some time to figure out whether these contradictions were the result of poor interviewing or whether they could and should be resolved compatibly. To no one's surprise, I have opted for the latter. Nevertheless, I believe my conclusions are justified.

Deciding whether or not to take a case is basically a lexicographic decision process, that is, a process of decisional steps or gates through which a case must successfully pass before it will be accepted. Failure to "pass a gate" will usually mean a case will be denied. In Professor Lawrence Mohr's terms this is a "process model" as opposed to a "variance model." A variance model suggests that the decision to take a case would depend upon the combination and "weights" of certain factors in a case. In other words, rather than passing or failing to pass a series of gates, each case contains reasons to take it and not to take it. How these interact, combine, and are weighed against one another determine whether or not the case will be taken. A process model does not exclude the weighing of factors and the importance of combinations, but it holds that the combination of weights is not determinative. I argue not only that the decision process is a series of steps but that there are two very different sets of decisional steps; and, depending upon the case and the justice, a case traverses one channel or the other. I call these channels "decision modes." This is not simply the old "legal/political" dichotomy. It is justice-specific, not issue-specific. The decision process by one justice to take a case may look very different from that of another justice for the same case; and, the process used by a justice in evaluating one case will be very different from that used to evaluate a different case. All justices use both modes. I hope that this conceptualization offers a synthesis and a more helpful way of addressing the question of whether the justices act "politically" or "legally."

Though I stated that the ending was being given away by suggesting the two modes of decision making, the argument is not simply one long buildup to try to compel that conclusion. The reader may accept or find informative much of the discussion whether or not he or she accepts the idea of two decision modes. The primary purpose of this work is to elucidate the Court's agenda decision process. Most everyone is familiar with the basic processes used in Congress and the executive branch. The understanding may be oversimplified, but most would know, for example, that when a bill is proposed in Congress, it is referred to a committee, the chairman has a great deal of power in setting the agenda for the committee, and differences in bills are resolved in conference. Moreover, if one is interested in details about procedures in Congress that are not generally known, they can be found. Not so with the Court. Although some rules are published, most of the internal procedures are by consensus, are unpublished, and are frequently unknown. We on the outside find out about them only when a justice happens to mention them in a speech or an article. And the little that we think we know is often wrong. For example, as discussed in Chapter 3, our assumptions about how votes are cast in conference are just plain wrong. Because of the secrecy that surrounds the Court, we Court observers are starved for details, even those commonly known about other governmental institutions.[30]

This dearth of information was a luxury and a burden for me in writing this book. As I discussed the project with several people across fields, they urged two things: give us details, and tell us exactly what you were told. I have done just that. Much of this book, without apology, is descriptive. In the interviews I was often just trying to find out how things worked. Equally important, my descriptions, or my informants' descriptions, often directly counter or cast serious doubt upon current wisdom. I, of course, try to do more than describe, but description is important given the topic, and it accounts for a large portion of this work.

Quotations are used extensively. Interviews with justices are so rare that most everything they said deserves reporting. Unfortunately, given the scope of this work, much of what they said remains untold. As for the clerks, extensive quoting of them is desirable as well. First, much of what is interesting about the agenda-setting process is done by the clerks rather than the justices. Second, the clerks offer a different perspective, which in some situations is more valid than the justices'. Finally, these clerks are among the select group that has seen and played a part in the inside workings of the Supreme Court. They are very intelligent people, among the best and the brightest from the

30. Over the years, we have learned more and more about the internal workings of the Court thanks to studies such as: Henry Abraham, *The Judicial Process*, 5th ed. (New York: Oxford University Press, 1986); Lawrence Baum, *The Supreme Court*, 3d ed. (Washington, D.C.: Congressional Quarterly Press, 1989); Robert McCloskey, *the American Supreme Court* (Chicago: University of Chicago Press, 1960); Bruce Murphy, *The Brandeis/Frankfurter Connection* (New York: Oxford University Press, 1982); Walter Murphy, *Elements of Judicial Strategy* (Chicago: University of Chicago Press, 1964); David O'Brien, *Storm Center: The Supreme Court in American Politics*, 2d ed. (New York: W. W. Norton, 1986); Stephen Wasby, *The Supreme Court in the Federal Judicial System*, 3d ed. (Chicago: Nelson Hall Publishers, 1988). See also William Rehnquist, *The Supreme Court: How It Was, How It Is* (New York: William Morrow, 1987).

most competitive law schools. Many are currently law professors who are becoming leading scholars of the Court. They may have been "wet behind the ears" when they clerked, but now they are more mature and somewhat more detached. They are a group of people who are worth listening to and whose words are worth reporting.

An important reason for the proliferation of quotations, regardless of the source, is that the interviews do not lend themselves to summarizing. When it can be done profitably and without distortion, I do so. But given the nature of the interviews, to report that 22 percent said "x" often would be meaningless, or worse it might convey much more precision than is justifiable. I often report that *most* of my informants said something and then give several examples. In this way, I can show the reader how I came to my conclusions, even controversial ones. The interviews are my data, and I urge readers to pay close attention to them. A final explanation of the extensive use of quotations is that it is frequently necessary to give perspectives from various chambers. As Chapter 3 makes clear, the agenda-setting process is very much the product of nine different processes. At times, there is no need to quote someone from several different chambers, but at other times I feel I must. For example, the prevailing notion about the Court is that some justices are ideologues and differ greatly from the "judges' judges." A frequent theme in this work, however, is that such characterizations of the justices are far too simplistic; as such it is important to see that clerks from all chambers were often saying exactly the same thing.

At times, the reader will be frustrated by the anonymity that surrounds these interviews. There are good methodological reasons to have anonymity in elite interviewing whatever the informant's desires, but for this elite, it is virtually the only way to gain access. Justices agreed to allow me to quote them directly if I simply attributed it to "a justice of the Supreme Court." Even at that, several things were said off the record. When informants refer to a justice or his chamber, I have left the reference blank, with a few exceptions. When something is public knowledge—for example, that Justice Brennan did his own cert. petitions—there is no reason not to quote clerks from his chamber about it. Likewise, justices are referred to by name when it would be absurd not to. There is one other exception that is more problematic. There are times when the role of the chief justice is at issue. In those instances, the discussion of the office is by definition a discussion of then Chief Justice Burger. Other references to Burger, however, are treated like any other justice. This work is an effort to look at an institution, not personalities. While it may be interesting to know whether the justice being described is, say, Rehnquist or Blackmun—

indeed, at times it might be important to know in order to assess fully the import of what has been said—on balance, it is better to depersonalize.

Justices rarely grant interviews. In fact several justices told me that this was the first time that they had granted an interview to discuss internal procedures and decision criteria. Since the time of the interviews, justices have become somewhat more open, especially with regard to granting interviews with the press. Most such interviews, however, reveal little. True in-depth interviews that we have come to associate with studies of the president or congress are still exceedingly rare.[31] One who has been given this opportunity has a particular responsibility to protect access for future scholars. There is always the danger of worrying too much about protecting access. In its worst manifestation, scholars pull their punches in order to assure that they will get back into the court, the country, or the congressman's office. There are obvious trade-offs—at times it would be helpful to know who said something—but the confidentiality does not hide context or distort description, analysis, or conclusions. Ultimately, of course, all scholarship hinges on the integrity and the quality of the author.

I should warn the reader that there will be times when he or she will feel certain that a statement was made by or about a particular justice and will be dead wrong. In another effort to protect anonymity I refer to clerks randomly as either he or she without respect to their actual gender. I never refer to a justice as "she" because the reader may inevitably think of Justice O'Connor. Terms like "liberal" or "conservative" or "judge's judge" are used rather loosely. Labels are often too simplistic. Nevertheless, the words do connote something meaningful, and more important, they are words used by informants.

A few things should be said about how to read the quotations. I refer to all interviewees as informants. If the quotation is from a clerk it usually will be followed by a number, for example (C39). This indicates that it was the thirty-ninth clerk I interviewed. It also should be noted that quotations are not primarily from just a few of the same clerks. I could not number the justices 1–5 because a reader might be

---

31. The truth be known, political scientists are usually quite critical of those in the media when it comes to educating us about politicians. There are of course the great exceptions. David Broder is a better political scientist than many of us. Bill Moyers, Robert MacNeil, Jim Lehrer, Ted Koppel, and others are, of course, great interviewers. Linda Greenhouse's reporting on the Court is excellent. One person who covers the Court, however, deserves special recognition—Nina Totenberg of National Public Radio. I single her out not because I admire her work (which I do) but because she was a journalist mentioned to me frequently by my informants, most of whom had a high regard for her.

able to identify the justice by putting all the quotations together. I have used "Justice A," "Justice B," and so on, only when it is necessary for clarity. In a given context Justice A will remain Justice A, but in the next section or chapter Justice A may be an entirely different justice. I explain these details here to emphasize that Justice A is not always the same justice throughout.

Since the time of the interviews, there have been some personnel changes on the Court. I believe that does little to affect the arguments. No doubt, individuals make differences in how institutions operate, and institutions change over time, but I have tried to generalize in such a way so as to make the work, if not timeless, at least not particularly time bound.

Finally, although this book claims to be about the Court only as it relates to case selection, I believe it is much more. I believe it conveys to the reader a sense of how the Court operates generally. I was told a great deal about behavior on the Court, even though I was only systematically examining the agenda process. There certainly are differences in the agenda-setting task and the opinion-writing task, but the materials that follow are not completely task-specific. I make no claims about other decision behavior, but I have some good hunches. I hope the material is presented in such a way that the reader will know when it is and is not responsible to think beyond case selection.

Organization of the Book

Chapter 2 and the Appendix compose a discussion of jurisdiction and procedure. It is an important part of this work although honesty compels an admission that it is tedious to read. Some of the responsibility for this must rest with the writer, but the material is not the stuff of which excitement is made. Nevertheless, a thorough discussion of jurisdictional and procedural issues is required of any serious study of the agenda-setting process of the Court. Precisely because such issues do not interest political scientists, we gloss over them, and we are the worse for it. The justices care about these issues; therefore, so should we. Jurisdictional and procedural matters are often dispositive. One simply cannot understand what goes on in the case selection process without a fairly sophisticated understanding of the technical, legal issues. Trying to understand the Court's behavior absent these considerations would be like trying to understand a congressional action without understanding procedures such as dilatory amendments, or trying to understand the budget without understanding the differences between outlays and appropriations. The point, however, is not that one will become an expert in federal procedure by reading this chapter; the hope is that it will sensitize the reader to the mundane nature of much of the agenda-setting process of the Court.[32]

Chapter 3 is a detailed examination of the internal procedures in processing cert. petitions. The process is first described generically, and then the chapter examines certain aspects of the process in more detail. The chapter is primarily descriptive. It relays the workaday procedures involved in agenda setting, but it also gives insight on decision-making procedures in the Court generally. Chapter 4 continues this discussion, focusing on special situations and anomalies.

Adopting Robert Jervis's concept of indices and signals as refined by Michael Spence, Chapter 5 suggests that clerks and justices use indices and signals to help them in their decision process.

Chapters 6 and 7 examine the "political" behavior of the justices and clerks. Chapter 6 focuses on interchamber behavior, and Chapter 7 on intrachamber strategy. The chapters concentrate on agenda setting, but they also provide insight on decision making at the Court generally.

Chapter 8 examines what the justices look for in determining cert-worthiness, and Chapter 9 proffers a decision model of case selection. Finally, Chapter 10 offers some concluding thoughts.

---

32. One final apologia for the inclusion of so much detail in Chapter 2 and the Appendix is that much of this information is not easy for the nonlawyer to find. This difficulty led me to a costly sampling blunder. I hope my effort will help future scholars.

The role of procedure in the evolution and activity of political institutions has been little heeded by political scientists . . . the formalities and modes of doing business, which we characterize as procedure, though lacking in dramatic manifestations, may, like the subtle creeping in of the tide, be a powerful force in the dynamic process of government . . .

The story of . . . momentous political and economic issues lies concealed beneath the surface technicalities governing the jurisdiction of the Federal Courts.

Professor Felix Frankfurter, 1928

2 Jurisdiction and Procedure

Picture the scene. An attorney or disgruntled client emerges from some local courthouse and in front of the television cameras declares, "We will take our case all the way to the U.S. Supreme Court!" Viewers of evening newscasts have undoubtedly witnessed this scenario one time or another. Whether the declaration before the cameras is made from sincere belief, or from posturing to intimidate or save face, it is, in reality, a fairly hollow threat. In the first place, there must be a legitimate case or controversy and it must involve a federal question before the U.S. Supreme Court, or any federal court for that matter, would have jurisdiction.[1] Most cases involve state law and present no federal question. Even if a federal question exists, the threat is still most likely in vain. The Supreme Court has virtually complete discretion over which cases it chooses to hear, and proportionally it chooses very few indeed. Of all cases that seek review by the U.S. Supreme Court, fewer than 5 percent are actually taken. The notion, then, that anyone who can afford it can take his or her case "all the way to the Supreme Court" is largely a myth. Many seek, but few are chosen.[2]

1. United States Constitution, Article III, Section 2.
2. Everything is relative, of course. Though many seek review, actually only a small proportion of lower court decisions are appealed to the U.S. Supreme Court. J. Woodford Howard found that only 30 percent of the Second, Fifth, and D.C. Circuit decisions were appealed to the Supreme Court. The rate of appeals would probably be lower for other circuits. See his book *Courts of Appeals in the Federal Judicial System: A Study of the Second, Fifth, and District of Columbia Circuits* (Princeton: Princeton University Press, 1981).

Obviously some cases do make it all the way to the Supreme Court. But before one even begins to worry about the discretionary decision processes of the justices, there are important jurisdictional and procedural hurdles to overcome. A discussion of these issues is the concern of this chapter and the Appendix. Prior to entering this jurisprudential thicket, however, a preface is in order. Issues of jurisdiction and procedure can be very complex and highly technical. Treatises, law review articles, indeed entire courses in law school are devoted to these issues and the subtleties that surround them. Nuances cannot possibly be discussed here, but then such a discussion is not really necessary for our purposes. Nevertheless, during the course of my research, I was continually frustrated by the very abbreviated attention given to the most rudimentary issues of jurisdiction and procedure.[3] As Professor Frankfurter suggests in the epigraph to this chapter, we political scientists all too often ignore these "technical considerations" even though they are of great importance to the justices.[4] In short, jurisdictional and procedural issues are crucial for understanding why certain cases are accepted and why others are not.

I have tried to steer a middle course here. My intent is to answer basic questions and be thorough without rewriting Robert L. Stern and Eugene Gressman's *Supreme Court Practice*.[5] "Stern and Gressman," as it is generally called, is *the* basic reference book on practice in the Supreme Court. It contains everything from where attorneys can find the restrooms in the building to technical analyses on issues of law. It deserves attention beyond a simple footnote, because my informants, including the justices, referred to it frequently and in a way that almost seemed as if it were an official publication of the Court.[6] Stern and

3. For example, I rarely found a work listing all criteria for an appeal and was never directed with any specificity about where to look—something I should think that a scholar interested in this topic would want to know.

4. Felix Frankfurter and James M. Landis, *The Business of the Supreme Court: A Study in the Federal Judicial System* (New York: Macmillan, 1928), pp. vi–vii. His criticism of political scientists is a little unfair, particularly for 1928. Ironically, it is probably truer today. An awareness by political scientists of the importance of rules and procedures is reemerging, however, esepcially among those engaged in formal theory. See, e.g., Kenneth A. Shepsle and Barry R. Weingast, "When Do Rules of Procedure Matter?" *Journal of Politics* 46 (February 1984): 206–221.

5. Robert L. Stern and Eugene Gressman, *Supreme Court Practice*, 5th ed. (Washington, D.C.: Bureau of National Affairs, 1978).

6. It is my understanding that the Office of the Clerk of the Supreme Court, particularly Francis J. Lorson, chief deputy clerk, worked closely with the authors. Mr. Lorson was at the Court for many years and was probably as aware of its workings as anyone except the justices. Indeed, in an interview with a justice a question about how something was handled at the Court came up, and he told me I should ask Frank Lorson.

Gressman has informed much of my discussion in this chapter and the Appendix, and it has directed me to original or other sources. I borrow and quote from it liberally without always footnoting it directly.

Jurisdiction

The State Supreme Court refused to deny a lower court ruling to quash an appeal to rehear an appeal by the Circuit Court to regain jurisdiction in a previous case. In the majority opinion, Justice Memphis Crumbum wrote, "In the opinion of this Court . . . we don't know what the heck is going on here."

Jeff MacNelly, *Shoe*

There are five ways that a case can come before the U.S. Supreme Court. The number five may come as a surprise to some because one usually reads that there are three ways. There are, in fact, three principal ways: by original jurisdiction, on appeal, or by a writ of certiorari. But a case can also come by certification or by an extraordinary writ. These five paths shall be discussed in turn, although all but two—certiorari and appeal—can be disposed of rather quickly.

Original Jurisdiction

As anyone who has read *Marbury v. Madison*[7] knows, the U.S. Supreme Court has both original and appellate jurisdiction. Article III, Section 2, of the Constitution sets forth the distinction.[8] Very few cases come to the Supreme Court on original jurisdiction, however—a fact that might seem odd since, on its face, Section 2 would appear to suggest that many cases would require original jurisdiction. Granted, there may not be many cases involving "Ambassadors, other public Ministers and Consuls," but there are certainly many cases in which a "state shall be a party." Early on, however, Chief Justice John Marshall in *Cohens v. Virginia* put the quietus on the notion that the Supreme Court was required to exercise original jurisdiction in all the cases outlined in Section 2.[9] Congress may legislate that cases can be brought originally

7. 1 Cranch 137 (1803).

8. The section reads in relevant part: "In all cases affecting Ambassadors, other public Ministers and Consuls, and those in which a State shall be a Party, the Supreme Court shall have original Jurisdiction. In all the other cases before mentioned, the Supreme Court shall have appellate jurisdiction, both as to law and fact, with such exceptions, and under such regulations as the Congress shall make."

9. See Cohens v. Virginia, Wheat. 264, 392–394 (1821).

in other Courts, and it has done so.[10] Whether or not *Marbury v. Madison* can be squared with *Cohens v. Virginia,* the matter has long been settled and accepted. Today, original jurisdiction is rarely invoked.[11] As the author of one of the leading casebooks on constitutional law notes in the section "Supreme Court Jurisdiction and Practice": "The original jurisdiction need not detain us: it is rarely invoked; and it is even more rarely the source of significant constitutional interpretation."[12] Nor need original jurisdiction detain us. For the October terms 1970–1983, a total of only fifty-seven cases, or an average of four per term, came before the Court on original jurisdiction.

Appeals

The Court has *virtually* complete discretion in selecting which cases to review. There are cases where review is obligatory. Such cases are called "appeals." Since the time of my interviews, there has been a significant change in jurisdiction. In 1988, Congress removed most (but not all) categories of appeal.[13] Nevertheless, I discuss appeals here, in the Appendix, and throughout the work as they existed at the time of the interviews. I do this for two reasons. First, it is important to understand things as they were when the informants were being interviewed; moreover, the discussion of appeals frequently gave important insights into how the process worked generally. As the reader shall see, the existence of categories of appeal did not greatly affect the process. Second, though unlikely, Congress could reinstitute categories of appeals.

At the time of the interviews appeals made up about 20 to 25 percent of the cases argued before the Supreme Court. The terminology is a

10. This is provided for in Section 1251 of Title 28 U.S.C. (1982): "(a) The Supreme Court shall have original and exclusive jurisdiction of all controversies between two or more States.

"(b) The Supreme Court shall have original but not exclusive jurisdiction of:

"(1) All actions or proceedings to which ambassadors, other public ministers, consuls or vice consuls of foreign states are parties;

"(2) All controversies between the United States and a State;

"(3) All actions or proceedings by a State against the citizens of another state or against aliens."

11. Speaking for the Court in Illinois v. City of Milwaukee, 406 U.S. 91, 93 (1972), Justice Douglas said, "It has long been this Court's philosophy that 'our original jurisdiction should be invoked sparingly.'"

12. Gerald Gunther, *Cases and Materials on Constitutional Law,* 10th ed. (Mineola, N.Y.: Foundation Press, 1980), p. 61. Gunther notes that South Carolina v. Katzenbach, 383 U.S. 301 (1966), is a rare exception.

13. Public Law 100-352.

bit confusing because whenever one talks about taking a case to a higher court, one says one is appealing. Furthermore, higher courts are often referred to as appellate courts; indeed, they are named "courts of appeals" in several states just as they are at the federal level. When talking about the U.S. Supreme Court, however, saying that a case is "on appeal" means something specific that differs from the more common use of the term. Even though appeals became effectively discretionary, the distinction between appeal and certiorari is neither meaningless nor unimportant.

Certiorari

> The author of this work has been unable to find any separate treatise on the subject of Certiorari, though it is an ancient remedy; and it may be regarded as a little singular that the law writers have not deemed it proper to give us such a work . . . It is thought that a treatise giving the law of the subject, and its use in practice, will be of value to the profession. The writer has attempted, with industry and access to everything ever written upon the subject, to make the work as nearly complete as practicable . . . While it is not claimed that the work is perfect, it is submitted to the criticism of a generous profession, with great confidence in its thoroughness and value.
>
> George E. Harris, *A Treatise on the Law of Certiorari*, 1893

With a change here and there, the preface to Mr. Harris's obscure treatise might well have served as the preface to this book.[14] (I leave it to the reader's imagination which parts of his statement I would change.) Some ninety years later, certiorari is still not a particularly well understood concept even though it is the principal way cases come before the Supreme Court. To be sure, most of the "law of the subject" that concerned Mr. Harris in 1893 is now well understood and accepted, or moot. But, the *decision process* involved in granting certiorari in the U.S. Supreme Court remains somewhat of a mystery and is relatively unexplored. That is tinder for later chapters. Here I will examine the jurisdictional issues of certiorari and, briefly, the development of the Court's discretionary jurisdiction, which is primarily, though not exclusively, a discussion of certiorari.

Granting a writ of certiorari in response to a petition for a writ of certiorari, or in common parlance "granting cert.," is by far the most common way that cases come before the Supreme Court. Certiorari

---

14. George E. Harris, *A Treatise on the Law of Certiorari at Common Law and under the Statutes: Its Use in Practice* (Rochester: Lawyers' Cooperative Publishing Company, 1893), Preface.

accounts for almost all cases argued before the Court today, and about 80 percent at the time of my interviews. But what precisely is a certiorari or a "cert.?" Contrary to the television commercial, certs. are neither breath mints nor candy mints. Certiorari is a Latin term that means "to be informed of."[15] Writs of certiorari are discretionary writs, which means that they are issued at the sound discretion of a judge and are not writs of right such as an appeal or the old "writ of error." *Black's Law Dictionary* defines a writ of certiorari as: "An order by the appellate court when the court has discretion on whether or not to hear an appeal. If the writ is denied, the court refuses to hear the appeal and, in effect, the judgment below stands unchanged. If the writ is granted, then it has the effect of ordering the lower court to certify the record and send it up to the higher court which has used its discretion to hear the appeal." So, when cert. is granted, theoretically a writ of certiorari issues to the Court below and the records of a case are ordered up to the U.S. Supreme Court for review.

The Court has not always had the discretion it currently enjoys for selecting its cases. The expansion of its certiorari jurisdiction has permitted this discretion. The Appendix provides a brief history of the development of certiorari jurisdiction. The end of the story, however, is that today the Court's jurisdiction is almost completely discretionary.

Certification

A rarely used method, certification can be a way to bring a case before the Supreme Court. Section 1254 of Title 28 provides for review of cases that are in courts of appeals: "By certification at any time by a court of appeals of any question of law in any civil or criminal case as to which instructions are desired, and upon such certification the Supreme Court may give binding instructions or require the entire record to be sent up for decision of the entire matter in controversy." Certifying questions to the Supreme Court is done by the lower court, not by the litigants. This method of review, however, is virtually nonexistent. Few cases are ever certified to the Supreme Court, and the Court chooses to answer even fewer. From 1946 to 1974, only three certified questions were answered by the Court.[16]

15. *Black's Law Dictionary,* 5th ed. (St. Paul: West Publishing Co., 1979).
16. Stern and Gressman, *Supreme Court Practice,* p. 592. The cases were: United States v. Rice, 327 U.S. 742 (1946); United States v. Barnett, 376 U.S. 681 (1964); and Moody v. Albemarle Paper Co., 417 U.S. 622 (1974).

Extraordinary Writs

Title 28, Section 1651, of the *U.S. Code* states: "The Supreme Court and all courts established by Act of Congress may issue all writs necessary or appropriate in aid of their respective jurisdictions and agreeable to the usages and principles of law." The principal writs encompassed by this statement are mandamus, prohibition, habeas corpus, and certiorari.[17] Habeas corpus, however, is specifically authorized under Section 2241.[18] Mandamus and prohibition involve, respectively, ordering a lower court to do something and prohibiting a lower court from doing something. As explained in the Appendix, the version of certiorari in Section 1651 is the codification of the common law writ of certiorari, not the statutory certiorari mentioned above. "Statutory certiorari" is the one that accounts for approximately all of the Court's cases. Nevertheless, common law certiorari can, and has, brought cases before the Supreme Court, although modern occurrences have been rare.[19]

Procedure

The Supreme Court of the United States has the authority to promulgate rules of procedure for the federal courts.[20] Those it has developed for itself, "Rules of the Supreme Court of the United States" (hereafter "Rules") obviously govern procedure in the Supreme Court. The rules noted in this chapter are the published ones. The Court also has unwritten rules discussed elsewhere in this book. The published rules contain everything from the hours that the clerk's office is open, to the proper color of paper and size of type set for petitions, to jurisdictional issues. These rules govern the procedures used when

17. Stern and Gressman, *Supreme Court Practice,* p. 627.

18. 28 U.S.C. sec. 2241(a) reads in relevant part: "writs of habeas corpus may be granted by the Supreme Court, any justice thereof, the district courts and any circuit judge within their respective jurisdictions." Writs of habeas corpus seek the release of a person who claims to be unlawfully held in custody.

19. Leading cases using the common law certiorari power are: House v. Mayo, 324 U.S. 42 (1945); *Ex parte* Republic of Peru, 318 U.S. 578 (1943); and *In re* 620 Church St. Bldg. Corp., 299 U.S. 24 (1936). (See Linzer, "The Meaning of Certiorari Denials," *Columbia Law Review* 79 (November 1979): 1234, n. 50).

20. Myron J. Jacobstein and Roy M. Mersky, *Fundamentals of Legal Research* (Mineola, N.Y.: Foundation Press, 1981), p. 207.

one is seeking review in the Supreme Court.[21] Since, as with jurisdiction, the procedure involving appeals differs from that of certiorari, I will discuss them separately, again ignoring subtleties and exceptions unimportant for our purposes.

Appeals

After final judgment has been entered in the lower court or rehearing has been denied, the party wishing to appeal the case, the appellant, files a notice of appeal in the lower court. This must be done within ninety days. Within the same ninety days, appellant must also file a jurisdictional statement in the Supreme Court. This jurisdictional statement is the formal request to the Supreme Court to take the case. Contents of the jurisdictional statement are dictated in the Rules. There are many specific requirements, but basically the rule requires that the statement contain the questions presented by the appeal, a concise statement of the grounds on which the jurisdiction of the Supreme Court is invoked, and a concise statement of the case containing the facts material to consideration of the questions presented. The jurisdictional statement may not exceed thirty pages. There is an additional requirement, however, that deserves special attention, the requirement that the jurisdictional statement contain: "A statement of reasons why the questions presented are so substantial as to require plenary consideration, with briefs on the merits and oral argument, for their resolution." Remember, review of appeals is supposedly obligatory. As even the name "jurisdictional statement" implies, all that should be necessary to get into the Supreme Court is to prove that the issue invokes the appellate jurisdiction. But the requirement provides one of the major "loopholes" to avoid review. The Court can dismiss an appeal for want of a "substantial federal question." Dismissals are discussed below; I note this "loophole" here to suggest that jurisdictional statements do not really differ a great deal from petitions for

21. At this point, it should be mentioned that my study bridges some rule changes made by the Court. For the most part, however, little of substance was changed in the rules that would affect this study. The major difficulty is that the numbers for some of the rules have changed. I have chosen to discuss the rules as they exist as of this writing, using their current numbers. If and when it is necessary to point out that a change occurred, either in substance or number, I shall do so with one exception. The rule entitled "Considerations Governing Review on Certiorari," formerly Rule 19, then Rule 17, is now Rule 10. When informants mention Rule 19, I shall not always remind the reader that the rule is now number 10. These rules are printed in various places including selected volumes of the *U.S. Reports* and in the Appendix to Title 28 of the *U.S. Code*, which contains a handy table of current and past rule numbers.

certiorari. That is, appellant need not only show that jurisdiction is technically proper, but also that a particular case merits claiming some of the Court's valuable time.

On with the story. After appellant files the notice of appeal and the jurisdictional statement, the appellee may file either a motion to dismiss or a motion to affirm the lower court's ruling. Rule 16 governs this process. Paraphrasing, appellee moves to dismiss an appeal on the ground that the appeal is not within the Court's jurisdiction, or that it is not in conformity with statutes or the Rules of the Court. Motions to dismiss an appeal from a state court are made on the ground that the appeal does not present a substantial federal question; or that the federal question sought to be reviewed was not timely or properly raised and was not expressly passed on; or that the judgment rests on an adequate nonfederal basis. Appellee moves to affirm a judgment from federal court on the ground that the questions are so insubstantial as not to need further argument.[22] Finally, as a catchall, Rule 16 permits a motion to dismiss or affirm on "any other ground the appellee wishes to present as a reason why the Court should not set the case for argument." Although brevity is urged, motions to dismiss or affirm may also be a maximum of thirty pages. Appellee may choose not to respond at all, or appellee may inform the Court that she is waiving the right to respond.

Appellant then has the right to submit a reply brief of no more than ten pages opposing the motion to dismiss or affirm, but he must do so quickly because there are no time constraints at this point. If the Court disposes of the case before counsel gets around to submitting a reply brief, too bad.

Supplemental briefs of no more than ten pages may be filed at any time that a jurisdictional statement is pending by either party calling

22. According to Stern and Gressman, *Supreme Court Practice*, pp. 377–378: "When the Court feels that the decision below is correct and that no substantial question on the merits has been raised, it will affirm an appeal from a federal court, but will dismiss an appeal from a state court 'for want of a substantial federal question.' Only history would seem to justify this distinction; it would appear more sensible to affirm appeals from both state and federal courts when the reason for the summary disposition is that the decision below is correct. But if the bar fully understands that 'dismissed for want of a substantial federal question' in a state court appeal is the equivalent of affirmance on the merits insofar as the federal questions under 28 U.S.C. Section 1257(1) and (2) are concerned, and is not limited to a determination of whether there is such a federal question, the difference in nomenclature does no harm." Would that I had read this earlier. Because I was unaware of the distinction, I originally drew an improper sample. The problem was corrected, but the cost was that many decided cases had to be discarded. Yet again, another reason why political scientists simply *must* deal with issues of jurisdiction and procedure.

attention to any new cases, legislation, or intervening matter not available at the time of the party's last filing.

The Court may dispose of the appeal in various ways, but there are three principal ways: it may note probable jurisdiction; it may postpone jurisdiction; or it may treat the appeal summarily. If the Court wishes to have full briefing and oral argument on the merits, that is, the substance of the case, it will "note probable jurisdiction." Once probable jurisdiction is noted, written briefs on the merits are prepared by both sides, and a date is set for oral argument. As the word "probable" connotes, the Court may, after argument, decide that it did not properly have jurisdiction, but generally that does not happen. After argument, the Court will usually write a full opinion affirming or reversing the decision below.

Alternatively, the Court may enter an order saying that jurisdiction is postponed until after argument. This, of course, requires counsel at the argument stage to address the jurisdictional issues as well as the merits. The Court may dismiss the case after argument for lack of jurisdiction, which is more likely in this category of cases than when it has noted probable jurisdiction.

Finally, the Court may dispense with a case summarily, that is, without the benefit of the case having been briefed and argued on the merits. Sometimes, when the Court dismisses summarily, it will cite the controlling authority. In other words, there is a precedent that controls the issue so there is no need to review this case. Other times, the Court may give a short *per curiam* opinion outlining the reasons for its action. Usually, however, the Court will merely say that an appeal is affirmed, dismissed, or dismissed for want of a substantial federal question, without any further explanation.[23] There is no official list of reasons for denial that the Court must give, but reasons given for summary dismissal have included: lack of a substantial federal question, lack of a properly presented federal question, mootness, lack of jurisdiction, and a finding that the decision below rested on adequate state grounds.[24]

When the Supreme Court dismisses or affirms a case summarily, it has technically made a judgment on the merits of the case, which means the decision has precedential value, even though the merits were not fully briefed or argued. Indeed, the merits may not have been addressed at all in the jurisdictional statement. The precedential weight that should be given to an appeal decided summarily is a matter

23. Stern and Gressman, *Supreme Court Practice*, p. 377.
24. Ibid., n. 45.

of some debate among legal commentators and among the justices. Essentially, the Court has suggested that such actions should be afforded some precedential value in their own decisions but not as much as cases that are fully argued. When it comes to lower courts, however, they are to treat the summary dispositions as precedential.[25] For our purposes, the jurisprudential debate is not of particular concern except that it obviously relates to things that do concern us. The Court feels perfectly free to dismiss appeals. Nevertheless, given the fact that even a dismissed appeal carries some precedential value, whereas a denial of certiorari does not, it is not surprising that the Court is less willing to dismiss appeals as quickly as it does petitions for certiorari.

In sum, most appeals never *really* make it all the way to the Supreme Court either, but they do so in greater proportion than certs. The differences in procedure and jurisprudence between the two suggest that deciding not to decide is more troublesome for the Court for appeals than for certs.

Certiorari

Writs of certiorari are matters of grace.

Justice Murphy, speaking for the Court in *Wade v. Mayo*

Even though the jurisdictional and formal procedures for certiorari differ from appeals, the process, in reality, is not all that different. Within sixty days after a final judgment is entered in a lower court (except in those instances where certiorari is sought in a federal court of appeals prior to judgment), the party who lost, if she chooses to continue the litigation, submits a petition for certiorari. This party becomes known as petitioner. The rules specify what should be included in the petition:

> (a) The questions presented for review, expressed in the terms and circumstances of the case but without unnecessary detail. The statement of the questions should be short and concise and should not be argumentative or repetitious. They must be set forth on the first page following the cover with no other information appearing on that page. The statement of any question presented will be deemed to comprise every subsidiary question fairly included therein. Only the questions set forth in the petition, or fairly included therein, will be considered by the Court . . .

25. Ibid., pp. 327–338.

(e) A concise statement of the grounds on which the jurisdiction of this Court is invoked . . .

(f) The constitutional provisions, treaties, statutes, ordinances and regulations which the case involves . . .

(g) A *concise* statement of the case containing the facts material to the consideration of the questions presented . . .

(j) A direct and concise argument amplifying the reasons relied on for the allowance of the writ. See Rule 17.

The petition may not exceed thirty pages.

The opposing party, respondent, has thirty days after receipt of the petition to file a "brief in opposition."[26] The Court urges that this brief be just that—brief; it is not to exceed thirty pages. Respondent may choose not to file such a brief—indeed, most do not; or respondent may inform the Court that he will waive the right to respond. The Court will usually act on the basis of the petition alone, but it may ask for a response if one is not filed.

As with appeals, petitioner may answer the brief in opposition with a ten-page "reply brief," and supplemental briefs may be filed by either party calling attention to new cases, legislation, or other intervening matters not available at the time of the party's last filing.

Rule 10 is the only official information that the Court gives on what the justices consider important when evaluating a petition for certiorari. Rule 10, however, is really not much help:

.1. A review on writ of certiorari is not a matter of right, but of judicial discretion. A petition for a writ of certiorari will be granted *only when there are special and important reasons therefor. The following, while neither controlling nor fully measuring the Court's discretion, indicate the character of reasons that will be considered* [emphasis added].

(a) When a United States court of appeals has rendered a decision in conflict with the decision of another United States court of appeals on the same matter; or has decided a federal question in a way in conflict with a state court of last resort; or has so far departed from the accepted and usual course of judicial proceedings, or sanctioned such a departure by a lower court, as to call for an exercise of this Court's power of supervision.

---

26. Prior to the 1980 rule revisions, if the United States were the respondent, it was allowed fifty days to respond. Now it is treated as any other respondent.

(b) When a state court of last resort has decided a federal question in a way in conflict with the decision of another state court of last resort or of a United States court of appeals.

(c) When a state court or a United States court of appeals has decided an important question of federal law which has not been, but should be, settled by this Court, or has decided a federal question in a way in conflict with applicable decision of this Court . . .

Note that the Court says that the above conditions are not "controlling" and only "indicate the character of reasons that will be considered." With the exception of specifying certain types of conflicts, they have essentially defined certworthiness tautologically; that is, that which makes a case important enough to be certworthy is a case that we consider to be important enough to be certworthy. One can be assured that the ambiguity of Rule 10 is not some unfortunate oversight by the justices. They have intentionally enunciated murky criteria. As Stern and Gressman point out:

> Critics have complained that Rule 19 [Rule 10 currently] as interpreted and applied, provides no meaningful standards for the bar, especially in terms of the importance or unimportance of the issues involved. Suggestions have been made that the Court in all its written opinions spell out in some detail the reasons why certiorari was granted and that the Court periodically write a memorandum opinion in certain representative cases stating specifically why certiorari was being denied. Whatever the merits of these criticisms and suggestions, the fact remains that the Court has not yet seen fit to change its historic practice of refraining in most instances from detailing the reasons for denying review. And its stated reasons for granting certiorari are often little more than conclusory; sometimes they are mere afterthoughts by the opinion writer long after the conference discussion as to why certiorari should be granted. Hence the practitioner must rely as best he can upon the history of grants and denials in the various types of cases.

We might be able to accept the fact that the Court really does not want attorneys to know what it considers important and that would be that. The problem, however, is that justices are always complaining, and indeed at times scolding the bar for petitioning cases that do not belong in the Supreme Court. The problem is not a recent one. Chief Justice Hughes in a letter to Senator Wheeler on March 23, 1937, said:

"I think that it is safe to say that about 60 percent of the applications for certiorari are wholly without merit and ought never to have been made. There are probably about 20 percent or so in addition which have a fair degree of plausibility, but which fail to survive a critical examination. The remainder, falling short, I believe, of 20 percent, show substantial grounds and are granted."[27] Justice Harlan in his article "Manning the Dikes" argued:

> Of the total petitions acted on I think it must be said that more than one-half were so untenable that they never should have been filed.
> As practically all these petitions were prepared by lawyers this would seem to indicate a widespread lack of understanding at the Bar as to the factors which make for certiorari, and also, I fear, in some instances a lack of responsible forebearance in the filing of petitions which certainly should have been considered useless.[28]

Most all of the current justices have complained about this problem in one way or another. I discussed this in one of my interviews with a justice.

> *Perry:*   Several of the justices have made statements saying that lawyers are not discriminating enough when petitioning cases.
> *Justice:*   I know Justice Harlan and others tried to discourage lawyers from filing frivolous petitions, but I don't blame them for doing it. We don't give them any real incentive not to try. And sometimes we take a case that must even surprise the petitioners. So it's just going to keep going on . . . Of course lawyers are going to continue petitioning. Some of them do it simply for delaying tactics. And given the rules that we have given them, there is no reason for them not to do it.

One of the clearest statements outlining the Court's position on certiorari was made by Chief Justice Vinson, though even it is not of much help.

---

27. 81 Cong. Rec. 2814–2815 (1937).

28. John M. Harlan, "Manning the Dikes," Eighteenth Annual Benjamin N. Cardozo Lecture, delivered before the Associaton of the Bar of the City of New York, October 28, 1958; reprinted with an introduction by Ernest A. Gross (New York: Association of the Bar of the City of New York, 1958), pp. 14–15.

During the past term of Court, only about 15% of the petitions for certiorari were granted, and this figure itself is con-
siderably higher than the average in recent years. While a
great many of the 85% that were denied were far from frivolous, far too many reveal a serious misconception on the part
of counsel concerning the role of the Supreme Court in our
federal system. I should like, therefore, to turn to that subject
very briefly. The Supreme Court is not, and never has been,
primarily concerned with the correction of errors in lower
court decisions. In almost all cases within the Court's appellate
jurisdiction, the petitioner has already received one appellate
review of his case. The debates in the Constitutional Conven-
tion make clear that the purpose of the establishment of one
supreme national tribunal was, in the words of John Rutledge
of South Carolina, 'to secure the national rights & uniformity
of Judgmts.' The function of the Supreme Court is, therefore,
to resolve conflicts of opinion on federal questions that have
arisen among lower courts, to pass upon questions of wide
import under the Constitution, laws, and treaties of the
United States, and to exercise supervisory power over lower
federal courts. If we took every case in which an interesting
legal question is raised, or our *prima facie* impression is that
the decision below is erroneous, we could not fulfill the Constitutional and statutory responsibilities placed upon the
Court. To remain effective, the Supreme Court must continue
to decide only those cases which present questions whose resolution will have immediate importance far beyond the particular facts and parties involved. Those of you whose petitions
for certiorari are granted by the Supreme Court will know,
therefore, that you are, in a sense, prosecuting or defending
class actions; that you represent not only your clients, but tre-
mendously important principles, upon which are based the
plans, hopes and aspirations of a great many people throughout the country.[29]

Note the statement that the purpose of cert. is not error correction.
Time and again my informants—justices and clerks—stated that the
Supreme Court was not there to ensure justice. Even for the most
sophisticated Court observers, hearing this stated so bluntly is discon-

29. Address of Chief Justice Vinson before the American Bar Association, September
7, 1949, 69 S. Ct. v, vi.

certing, especially if the denial of justice is for a cause or a case about which they care deeply. But the Supreme Court cannot possibly serve as just one more place to take a case in hopes of getting the desired result. As shall be seen, coming to terms with the fact that the Court is not there to serve this function is something that most law clerks find difficult at first, but they soon realize that it cannot be otherwise given the resource constraint of time. Later chapters will return to this issue; for now, back to procedure.

There are several responses that the Court can give to the request for certiorari. The most obvious are cert. granted and cert. denied. If cert. is granted, except for summary judgments discussed below, the case is given plenary consideration, which means it is fully briefed on the merits and argued before the Court, and then an opinion is written. For the overwhelming number of cases (about 95 percent), however, cert. is denied.

With a few technical exceptions, if the Court refuses to take a case, the litigant has no further legal recourse.[30] That is it; it is over. The decision of the last highest court to hear the case stands. From the litigant's perspective the decision to review or not review a case is of great consequence—not to decide is to decide. Unlike appeals, however, from a jurisprudential or precedential perspective, the denial is theoretically without meaning. By refusing to take the case, the Supreme Court is *not* saying that the decision below was correct—indeed the justices may well believe that the case was incorrectly decided. The justices are saying simply that they will not review the case, that the decision below stands, and that they are making no official judgment on the correctness of the decision or the issues it raises. As Justice Frankfurter said in a frequently quoted passage from *Maryland v. Baltimore Radio Show:*

> This Court now declines to review the decision of the Maryland Court of Appeals. The sole significance of such denial for a petition for writ of certiorari need not be elucidated to those versed in the Court's procedures. It simply means that fewer than four members of the Court deemed it desirable to review a decision of the lower court as a matter of sound judicial discretion.
>
> . . . this Court has rigorously insisted that such a denial

30. For example, applications for a writ of habeas corpus may appear more than once; or, the Court might refuse to review a state court decision that upholds a criminal conviction, yet the prisoner could apply for a writ of habeas corpus in federal court. See Brown v. Allen, 344 U.S. 443.

carries with it no implication whatever regarding the Court's views on the merits of a case which it has declined to review. The Court has said this again and again; again and again the admonition has to be repeated.

The one thing that can be said with certainty about the Court's denial of Maryland's petition in this case is that it does not remotely imply approval or disapproval of what was said by the Court of Appeals of Maryland . . .

The issues considered by the Court of Appeals . . . are issues that this court has not yet adjudicated. It is not to be supposed that by implication it means to adjudicate them by refusing to adjudicate.[31]

Other justices have made the same argument time and again.[32] However, Peter Linzer in an excellent article, "The Meaning of Certiorari Denials," argues that one can in fact read more into these denials than the justices suggest. And from my study, one might well conclude that Justice Frankfurter overstates his case. Perhaps the situation is best summarized by Justice Jackson:

The Court is not quite of one mind on the subject. Some say denial means nothing, others say it means nothing much. Realistically, the first position is untenable and the second is unintelligible. How can we say that the prisoner must present his case to us and at the same time say that what we do with it means nothing to anybody . . .

. . . I agree that as *stare decisis,* denial of certiorari should be given no significance whatever. It creates no precedent and approves no statement of principle entitled to weight in any other case. But, for the case in which certiorari is denied, its minimum meaning is that this Court allows the judgment below to stand with whatever consequences it may have upon the litigants involved under the doctrine of *res judicata* as applied either by state or federal courts.[33]

31. 338 U.S. 912, 917–920.

32. See, e.g.: Justice Harlan, "Manning the Dikes"; Justice Brennan, "State Court Decisions and the Supreme Court," *Pennsylvania Bar Association Quarterly* 31 (1960): 393, 402–403; Justice Marshall in U.S. v. Kras, 409 U.S. 434, 460–461; Hughes Tool Co. v. Trans World Airlines, 409 U.S. 363, 366. See also Stern and Gressman, *Supreme Court Practice,* pp. 353–360.

33. Brown v. Allen, 344 U.S. 443, 542–543.

The Court can render a summary disposition, but the sticky prece-dential questions surrounding appeals do not plague certs. With a summary disposition, the Court grants cert. and summarily affirms, reverses, or grants vacates and remands. In these summary disposi-tions, the Court *is* technically ruling on the merits even though it is doing so without the benefit of briefing on the merits or oral argument. Thus in some ways certs. that are treated summarily resemble sum-mary appeals. The difference is that a denial of cert. is not a summary action. A textbook explanation for summary disposition is that the case below was so obviously correctly or incorrectly decided that the Court need not review the merits. As with appeals, in a summary disposition of a cert. the Court sometimes will cite an authority or give a very short *per curiam* opinion. And, as with appeals, there is criticism of the Court for using the summary technique.

Justices Marshall and Brennan have been particularly outraged at summary actions dealing with prisoners. They object to a ruling with-out the benefit of having the cases fully briefed and argued. Never-theless, the use of summary disposition is increasing. Since certiorari is discretionary and an overwhelming number of cases are simply denied, it is frequently puzzling why the Court will take a case and reverse or affirm it without the benefit of plenary review or without explanation for its action. It is a bit easier to understand a reversal. If the justices believe that the judgment below is wrong, why not reverse? Yet we know that with the cases that are simply denied, the justices frequently believe that the judgment below is wrong, indeed at times they consider it awful and still refuse to take action.

Finally, from time to time there are cases that are dismissed as improvidently granted, or as they say around the Court, "digged." The Court can dig a case at any time in the proceeding. Sometimes it happens after the briefs on the merits are received, but it also some-times happens after oral argument. When digged, it is as if the case were never granted.

Having worked through this discussion of jurisdiction and proce-dure, we can easily understand why political scientists prefer not to spend time on these considerations. After all, we are certainly aware that there are jurisdictional considerations in case selection, but those are more properly the concern of lawyers. Yet this brief and oversim-plified foray into these technical issues makes an important point. Frequently, the types of questions being adjudicated by the U.S. Su-preme Court are legalistic and technical, involving such things as whether or not an appeal properly lies under Section 1253 for certain types of cases. A large part of what goes on in the agenda setting of the Court has little to do with strategic maneuvering to further policy goals and has a lot to do with legalistic jurisprudential concerns. All too often we tend to think of the Court's work as involving mostly major issues of societal importance for which justices have strong preferences for a desired outcome. For every *Brown v. Board*,[34] however, there is a *Brown v. Allen*.[35]

The problem is not that we political scientists have focused on a minor but important part of the Court's work, for that would be defensible. Rather, the problem is that our myopia distorts our understanding of the portion that properly interests us. One cannot possibly understand how a case is chosen for review in the U.S. Supreme Court absent an understanding of legalistic concerns and an appreciation of how important these concerns are to the justices, and to any case's selection.

34. Brown v. Board of Education, 347 U.S. 483 (1954).
35. 344 U.S. 443 (1952). An important case dealing with jurisdictional issues.

Fortunately, the Clerk of the Court censors many of the petitions that have technical problems. If they exceed page limits for example, they are sent back to the litigants. But the ones that pass are tied up in a bundle of red tape. That is an unintended pun. There actually is a red tape that ties them up. They are put on the cart and it is walked around from chamber to chamber. You could hear it coming. You sit there and listen woefully as it rumbles down the hall. When we heard it coming, we would usually sit there and shoot rubber bands at the chandeliers. But the taxpayers didn't lose any money. From time to time we'd have to get up there and clean them out. (C2)

3 The Internal Process

Most clerks probably did not resort to rubber band therapy, but most did share the sense of dread expressed by this informant when recalling the cert. process. Actually, it is misleading to talk about *the* cert. process.[1] There are at least nine separate processes. Nevertheless, we begin with a generic description of the process, then proceed to examine certain aspects in more detail.

The Process: A Generic Description

Petitions for certiorari are either mailed or hand-delivered to the Clerk of the Court.[2] As described in Chapter 2, the petitioning cases must fulfill certain jurisdictional and procedural requirements. The Clerk screens the petitions for various types of technical errors such as page length and timeliness, but few are culled for such reasons.[3] From the

1. References to the cert. process by me or by informants are usually meant to include cases on appeal or original jurisdiction. Likewise, references to cert. petitions should be read to include jurisdictional statements; grant and deny include noting probable jurisdiction and dismissing. A distinction is made between cert. and appeal when it is important to do so.

2. The Clerk of the Court is an officer of the Court and should not be confused with the law clerks to the justices.

3. Seemingly obvious jurisdictional and procedural flaws, such as timing, are not always readily apparent, however, and the law clerks must search for these defects. Also, answering these seemingly objective questions sometimes requires a subjective judgment.

Clerk's office, the petitions and any accompanying papers (such as responses or appendices) are sent to each chamber on a "rumbling cart." From this point on, there are actually two different general processes.

Pool Chambers

With the number of cert. petitions increasing almost geometrically, Chief Justice Burger and several of his colleagues formed what has come to be known as the "cert. pool." Current members are Chief Justice Rehnquist and Justices White, Blackmun, O'Connor, Scalia, and Kennedy. Justice Powell was also a member. The pool was designed to reduce the workload by eliminating duplication of effort. Rather than have each chamber review every petition, the petitions are randomly assigned for evaluation among the six chambers in the pool. Each chamber then divides its one-sixth of the petitions randomly among the clerks in that chamber. A clerk will review the petitions assigned to her and then write a cert. pool memo for each of her petitions.

The pool memo follows a standard form. It lists the following basic information: whether the case is on cert. or appeal; if it is timely (in a jurisdictional sense); the court below; the name of the judges on the panel below; who wrote the opinion; and who dissented or concurred. The memo then summarizes the issues, the facts, and the opinion(s) below, followed by a cursory analysis and a recommendation to grant or deny. The pool memo runs anywhere from one to ten pages but usually is two to five. The completed memo is sent to the chief's chambers. Copies of the pool memo are then forwarded to all chambers in the pool. There, a second clerk examines the memo and "marks it up" for his justice. The markup memo may simply note that it agrees with the pool memo; or, it may analyze the case more thoroughly and disagree with the pool memo. The pool memo and the clerk's markup are then given to the justice along with the cert. petition and any accompanying papers. In most cases, the justice reads only the memo and the markup. For those cases where a decision to grant or deny is more difficult, the justice may read parts of the petition.

Nonpool Chambers

Justices Marshall and Stevens are not in the pool, nor were Justices Brennan and Stewart. Generally, each of these chambers evaluates every petition, and there is no formalized sharing of information between chambers. The process in nonpool chambers is much more informal. Petitions are divided randomly among the clerks within a chamber, and a memo is written only for one's own justice. These memos contain much of the same information that is in the pool memo, but they are usually shorter and much less formal, particularly as the term progresses. An extreme example of informality was recounted by one nonpool clerk, who recalled one memo that simply said, "this is the draft case—deny." Most cases require more than that, of course, but it indicates a type of informality that does not exist in a pool memo.

There is a good deal of variation among the nonpool chambers, however. For example, Justice Brennan did most of his own cert. work, and Justice Stevens has a different procedure altogether. The processes used in these chambers are described in more detail below.

Discuss List

After the memos have been written and the markups have been done, the chief justice prepares a list of those cases he believes to be worthy of discussion at the conference. He circulates this "discuss list" to all nine chambers. Any justice can add cases to the list simply by informing the administrative clerk in the chief's chambers. The other chambers are then informed of the additions. All cases not making the discuss list are automatically denied cert.

Conference

On Friday, conference day, the morning is spent discussing cases that have already been argued. The justices break for lunch, and they return in the afternoon to dispense with the requests for certiorari. Each justice has already developed a fairly firm idea of how he will vote prior to the conference and so goes into the conference room carrying a copy of the discuss list with each case marked as to how he plans to vote on certiorari. He also brings a cart into the room loaded with all the petitions and the memos written by his clerks with any annotations that he himself has made.

The chief justice begins discussion of the first case on the discuss list.[4] Each justice, in order of seniority, gives his comments on the case and usually announces his vote at that time.[5] If a case receives four

4. Regardless of when he is appointed, the chief justice is considered to be the most senior.

5. Information obtained from interviews. See also Stephen J. Wasby, *The Supreme Court in the Federal Judicial System* (New York: Holt, Rinehart and Winston, 1978), pp. 159–160.

votes—the "rule of four"—it is granted cert. Though formal votes are rare, if one is required, it, too, is taken in order of seniority. Traditionally, it was thought that the justices "discussed down and voted up," that is, discussion proceeded from the most senior to the most junior justice, and voting, from the most junior to the most senior. Indeed, most books on the Court report the procedure as such, and I had always assumed it to be so.[6] During an interview with a justice, however, I learned that the common wisdom is not so wise as common. We were talking about something else when he said:

> We vote by seniority, not by juniority as some textbooks say. Since Justice A is more junior than Justice B [A replaced B], I don't know how he will vote. Ninety percent of the time, I would know how Justice B would vote, but I am not sure with Justice A, although now I have more of a sense.

Later in the interview I followed up:

> *Perry:*   I noticed that you said that voting was done in order of seniority. Does that happen with votes on the merits as well as with cert.?
>
> *Justice:*   Yes. I don't know where the textbooks ever got this idea about discussing down and voting up. We have always voted down since I have been here. Perhaps this idea of voting up comes from the old docket sheets which list the most junior justice first. [He gets up and shows me a conference sheet with his name listed at the top from the time when he was the junior justice.] I asked Justice Douglas about this once and he said that they had always voted down since he had been here. Maybe Bill's memory had slipped on that. I didn't press him. Maybe at sometime they voted by juniority, but not since I have been here. I don't know where the myth came from. I guess the theory was that the chief justice's vote might influence other votes or something.

6. See, e.g., Henry J. Abraham, *The Judicial Process*, 4th ed. (New York: Oxford University Press, 1980), p. 208; David W. Rohde and Harold J. Spaeth, *Supreme Court Decision Making* (San Francisco: W. H. Freeman, 1976), p. 61; Wasby, *The Supreme Court*, p. 159.

> *Perry:* [Jokingly] Well, if nothing else, at least my research
> will clear up this issue.[7]

To confirm the voting order, I asked the remaining three justices. All
three confirmed it:

> [A former justice long since deceased] told me that years ago
> they would discuss down and vote up, and [voting up] was
> described that way in *Simple Justice*[8] so I think that the present
> procedure is new.

> We have never done that since I have been here . . . that
> would be silly. Everyone is aware of what your vote is when
> you are discussing.

> That's silly. It's silly to suggest that we vote up. What does
> happen is that sometimes on argued cases, someone might
> pass and say, "I want to hear the rest before I vote." To some
> extent Justice _____ does that.

7. The order of voting has been an issue of some controversy. Warren Weaver, Jr.,
reported in the *New York Times* in 1975 that the justices voted by seniority—senior to
junior ("The Supreme Court at Work: A Look at the Inner Sanctum," February 6, 1975,
p. 65). Shortly thereafter Rohde and Spaeth countered Weaver's assertion: "In a conversation with Harold Spaeth on May 2, 1975, Professors Beverly Blair Cook of the
University of Wisconsin at Milwaukee and Sidney Ulmer of the University of Kentucky
stated that their separate sources within the Court report that Weaver is in error and
that the order in which the justices vote (i.e., junior to senior) has not been altered"
(*Supreme Court Decision Making*, p. 68, n. 29). Also disagreeing with Weaver, Henry
Abraham states, "Weaver reports that 'this practice has been dropped' and that the
voting, like the discussion, now proceeds on the basis of seniority. My own account (i.e.,
junior to senior) was reliably reconfirmed in early 1979, however" (*The Judicial Process*,
p. 208, n. 115).
   Weaver was correct, however, and Spaeth and Abraham were apparently wrong, at
least if I am to believe what four of the justices told me. It is not a question of timing,
because some of the justices whom I interviewed had been around for many years prior
to 1975, and they explicitly said that they had always voted down as long as they had
been there. If the sources of Professors Abraham, Cook, and Ulmer were justices, then
I am at a loss to explain the discrepancy. I can only say that four justices confirmed the
seniority pattern to me, and as can be seen in the text, we discussed the issue at some
length.
   I have been reporting the correct voting order at least as far back as 1986 ("Interviewing Supreme Court Personnel," paper delivered at the Annual Meeting of the
Southern Political Science Association, Atlanta, Georgia, November 6–8, 1986; see also
Judicature, vol. 73, no. 4, where this paper was published). Nevertheless, the confusion
appears to continue.
   8. Richard Kluger, *Simple Justice* (New York: Vintage Books, 1975).

One wonders how many other "silly" notions we outsiders have. Were justices not so secretive about innocuous details, maybe scholars would not perpetuate these errors. It is easy to understand how such misinformation spreads, because rarely do justices speak out on internal procedures. And on one of those rare occasions where one did speak:

> I gave a speech one time where I said something wrong about _____ . . . and it's wrong but no one seems to believe it, and it keeps getting reprinted and rcprinted.[9]

Allowing the public to know the order of the voting procedure is innocuous. That does not mean it is unimportant. For social scientists engaged in theory building through formal modeling, for example, the ordering of decisional steps is crucial.[10] It is also important to scholars who are trying to evaluate the Court in ways other than formal modeling. If, for example, as in Congress, there is logrolling, or deference to expertise, or voting by cues, then the voting order could be key. [11]

The traditional explanation for voting up is that it was done so that the junior justices would not be influenced or intimidated by their senior brethren. Justice Goldberg, however, once characterized the notion that junior justices would be influenced or intimidated by their senior colleagues as "ridiculous."[12] The justices with whom I spoke would agree with Justice Goldberg, at least as far as cert. votes are concerned. Even so, order remains important. Recall that a justice's vote is announced at the time he discusses the case and that there is no formal vote per se. Since the discussion and vote usually occur simultaneously, the order of voting has at least one interesting consequence. As one justice pointed out:

> [The order] does raise a question in that while theoretically all we are doing is taking a tentative vote when we are discussing a case, it is rare that anyone ever changes, so sometimes as a

9. I cannot say what the "something wrong" was without revealing the justice. The error, however, is corrected in this work.

10. See, e.g., Kenneth A. Shepsle and Barry R. Weingast, "Uncovered Sets and Sophisticated Voting Outcomes with Implications for Agenda Institutions," *American Journal of Political Science*, 28 (February 1984): 49–74.

11. See, e.g., Donald R. Matthews, *U.S. Senators and Their World* (New York: Vintage Books, 1960); John W. Kingdon, *Congressmen's Voting Decisions*, 2d ed. (New York: Harper and Row, 1981). This is particularly true given the lack of interchamber communication, as discussed in Chapter 7.

12. Abraham, *The Judicial Process*, p. 208.

junior justice one doesn't have the chance to speak to convince others.

I asked all the justices in one form or another to describe what went on in conference.

> *Perry:* I would like to ask you two questions . . . What was the typical conference discussion like? Then I want to ask you what an atypical discussion would be like?
>
> *Justice:* [Of the typical conference] The chief justice is really a past master at this. He succinctly summarizes the cases he's put on, unless it's an issue that particularly troubles him. Then we discuss in order of seniority . . . I generally would say, "I don't think this is a case that we need to hear; I deny," and nothing more than that. Or, "I'd hear the case for these reasons"; or sometimes, "I would deny for these reasons." The chief begins the discussion for the cases he has listed. Now if I have listed a case, then he'll turn to me to discuss it, and I'll lay it out. I'll give my reasons and I'll say, "therefore I would grant," although there are some times I will put a case on and I will wind up suggesting to deny it because it is not ripe.
>
> *Perry:* Now can you give me an example of an atypical discussion?
>
> *Justice:* . . . if Justice _____ is all upset. For example, this Michigan Supreme Court has been kind of extreme in some of their determinations on [a criminal appeals matter]. In fact, I agree myself that some of their interpretations have been extreme . . . and so he might get all worked up about this opinion and he says, "this is so outrageously wrong I will grant and reverse summarily."

From the same justice:

> Obviously I go in with an agenda. I have the discuss list on the left, and inside the case I have my vote. I may get to conference intending to deny, yet later vote to grant because of something a colleague said on something I hadn't considered, and he might be right. But most times, though, I vote as I had planned to when I went in there. There are enough times that I change, though, to suggest that it happens.

A second justice:

> *Justice:* When we go over them, there is not a lot of time. It is up to the chief justice how much time is spent. Most all of us have our ideas and they are pretty firm when we come in there. No one has to be educated about a case.
>
> *Perry:* Can you characterize what happens . . . Do you just take a vote on the case or is there much discussion?
>
> *Justice:* We generally just vote. The vote goes from the most senior to the most junior. Of course one may make a comment along the way saying, for example, that the case on the next page is a better one for this. It isn't a process where a vote is railroaded through, although the vote is much faster than on argued cases where there is a lot of discussion.

Another justice described the process this way:

> *Justice:* There is not as much discussion as I thought there would be. The discuss list is done primarily by the chief, although a number are added by other justices . . . Those he puts on he makes some comment about. We discuss by seniority. There is a comment or a vote. Very frequently it is just a vote taken. If someone else put it on, he will initiate the discussion . . . In many cases it was only a vote. This discussion would come at the end of our Friday conference. In the morning we have discussed somewhat in depth the argued cases, and cert. has to get done in the afternoon; and of course we are a little tired by that time.
>
> *Perry:* Once people cast a vote, they rarely change?
>
> *Justice:* Right.

Finally, one justice put it this way:

> There wouldn't be much need for a conference if we were all firm in our opinions. But we generally have a tentative view. We do have some discussion, but it varies from case to case in terms of how intense or what the discussion is about.

As described by the justices, then, there is usually little discussion in conference on cert. They come to the conference with their minds made up for most cases, and they will usually vote to grant or deny on the spot.

Another vote that a justice can announce, however, is that he will "join three." Obviously, it means that if there are three others who are voting to grant, the justice will give them a fourth vote.[13] There is also a vote calling for a summary disposition. Some justices will say, "I will vote to reverse, but not to hear." This latter practice has caused controversy, some of which has been aired publicly. Justice Marshall, especially, feels that the Court should not be treating summarily many of the cases that it does. Justice Brennan tended to share that view. Other justices have criticized the Court in specific instances for disposing of a particular case in summary fashion. Nevertheless, as with the "rule of four" to grant cert., an informal operating rule of the Court has developed which says that a case may be treated summarily if six justices agree. The decision is often made at the time of the cert. vote.

Relisting

Not all cases are disposed of the first time they appear on the conference list. For various reasons, cases are sometimes relisted. One of the most common reasons to relist is to "call for a response." If the winning party below did not file a response brief in opposition to the petition for certiorari—an "opps." as they are commonly called—then the Court sometimes requests one before making a cert. decision. When that happens, the case is "put over," or "relisted," which means that it is put on the agenda for a future conference after the response has been filed. If at the original conference there are only one or two votes to grant, there is probably no reason to call for a response. However, if any justice calls for a response, or asks that a case be relisted, it is done automatically regardless of the initial vote.

One variant of calling for a response is to call for the views of the solicitor general, or the "SG" as he is commonly called. He is the person who represents the United States in the Supreme Court.[14] Until recently, the SG always filed a brief in opposition when a ruling was being appealed against the United States, but that is no longer so. The Court, then, may ask him for a response. Usually, however, calling for the views of the SG refers to a situation where the United States is not a party to the case, but where the case has a potentially significant impact upon the government. Here, the SG is asked to file an amicus brief on cert.[15]

13. "Join three" is given extended consideration in Chapter 6.
14. The role of the solicitor general is examined in greater detail in Chapter 5.
15. Many have written on the role of amicus participation in the Supreme Court.

The justices will also relist a case from time to time to "call for the record." In order to sort out issues to determine certworthiness, the justices, or their clerks, sometimes need the entire record from the courts below, most particularly the court of first instance. Poring over the record is very time consuming, however, so if certworthiness cannot be determined by the petition alone, the case is usually just denied. Finally, a justice will sometimes request that a case be put over because he is contemplating writing a dissent from denial of certiorari.[16]

A new norm has recently developed with regard to relisting. Although the rule of four means that a case is granted review if it receives at least four votes, when a case has only four votes, the chief justice may ask if the case can be relisted to see if any of the four want to reconsider. This practice has resulted from the increasing caseload; it has not been used as an attempt to undercut the rule of four. If the four granting justices want the case reviewed, it shall be. Likewise, there is no attempt to dissuade any of the granting justices. This new procedure is simply an effort to make sure that a case is really considered certworthy even though it was only able to muster four votes. After having noted that justices rarely change their votes, one justice added:

> Someone might make a very strong statement in conference and that might make someone switch; someone who has already voted to deny might then vote to relist the case. Or, when there are only four votes [to grant] the chief frequently asks if anyone would be willing to relist it. I think that is wise, because if you only have four votes and someone falls away, you will have a denial.

Two classic articles are: Lucius J. Barker, "Third Parties in Litigation: A Systemic View of the Judicial Function," *Journal of Politics* 29 (February 1967): 41–69; and Clement E. Vose, "Litigation as a Form of Pressure Group Activity," *Annals of the American Academy of Political and Social Science,* 319 (September 1958): 20–31. Karen O'Connor and Lee Epstein have written extensively on the role of interest groups in the courts, much of which occurs through amicus participation. See, e.g., their "Rise of Conservative Interest Group Litigation," *Journal of Politics* 45 (1983): 479–489. See also Lee Epstein, *Conservatives in Court* (Knoxville: University of Tennessee Press, 1985). Most of the above references focus on amicus participation on the merits. Greg Caldeira has focused on amicus participation at cert. See Gregory A. Caldeira and John R. Wright, "Organized Interests and Agenda Setting in the U.S. Supreme Court," *American Political Science Review* 82 (December 1988): 1109–1127.

16. Dissents from denial are discussed extensively in Chapter 6.

Another justice described it this way:

> If you have just four voting to grant cert. rather than five,
> often one of them will ask to have the case relisted. He usually
> wants to be sure that nothing has come up. It is kind of an
> indirect statement. This has come about largely at the chief
> justice's behest. If we just have four votes, we put it off be-
> cause once in a while a vote will fall away. But we will go
> ahead if the four votes on the case are firm.

I heard no objection from any of the justices to the practice of
relisting when there are only four votes (and they had no qualms about
telling me other things they found objectionable). The chief justice
cannot be heavy-handed in suggesting to relist cases so long as there
is a rule of four. It should be emphasized that at the time I conducted
the interviews, there was much worry about the workload, and there
was a perception by many, including the justices, that the Court was
taking too many cases.

In sum, relisting is not a favored practice unless it is to call for the
views of the SG, or when a case has only gathered four votes. One
justice put it this way:

> There is only so much time that the conference has as a body,
> and there is not much time to debate cert. on a case more
> than once. The consensus of the conference is that you vote it
> up or down on the spot.

A Closer Look at the Process

The rudiments covered, portions of the process deserve closer
examination.

The Pool

The cert. pool was designed primarily to reduce the workload. It is
questionable if it in fact achieves this aim, particularly given the
markup process. Two clerks who were members of the pool summed
up the pros and cons of the pool from a clerk's perspective pretty well.

Perry: Do you think that the pool is a good idea?

Clerk: I have mixed feelings. Given the volume of cases, it really was a way to give a more thorough review to each petition and that could be important. But there were a couple of things that were troubling. By about the fifth month, often you would just simply know that a case was not cert-worthy even though it had a very complicated fact situation. If you had to write the pool memo, you got very involved in trying to lay out the interesting distinctions in the facts, but about the only pride you could take was in the construction of it. You spent many hours but knew that the Court would not have any interest . . . I felt best about this in the early part of the year when it was a learning process and you really don't know what a lot of the issues are. You educated yourself about the issue then, and many issues recur throughout the year. But as time passed, you began seeing it as a burden to have to write these. Not only were they a burden to write, but you had to read all the stuff that the other clerks had done. In the beginning, a clerk might make a statement and I would call him up and say "what did you mean by this," and then you might say "I disagree," and it was an educative process, but by the end you didn't have much time to do that.

Perry: I've heard many people say that over the term they could reduce the amount of time that they spent on cert. Did the pool memos get shorter?

Clerk: No, I don't think they got shorter; you could just do them faster and spend less time on them. (C34)

Clerk: When writing the pool memo, you can often just look at cases and see they're frivolous. But even though the case is frivolous and you know that there is no way in hell the Court is going to grant this thing, it still might take a day to write the cert. memo. Sometimes it's a very complex fact situation and you have to work it all out so that it can easily be seen by the justice that it's a frivolous case. I've often wondered at times if, in fact, the cert. pool is counterpro-ductive. If one were just working for one justice, you could probably say, "look, this is ridiculous, there's no reason to take this case." But when you're writing a memo for all the justices, you have to lay it all out. If I were working just for Justice _____, I could have been more direct and said "this is frivolous," and not spent much time on it.

There's also somewhat of a psychological problem getting to write memos because it's a psychological drain particularly if it's long and complicated. In fact, I used to joke and say that I would love to just send around a cert. pool memo saying "this is frivolous—trust me on this one."

If everyone just wrote memos for one justice, I am not sure whether time would be saved or lost overall because though it would save time by not having to write these long memos on frivolous cases for the cert. pool, one would then have a lot more cases to do.

But really, there is an advantage to the cert. pool which I'm not sure some of my colleagues agree with. That is, you can generally look at cases more closely. I mean, justices obviously can't do it, and it means that cases do get a closer look than they would if each chamber did them all. At least, someone has read it carefully enough to prepare a formal memo for the cert. pool. I believe people get a fairer shake. Now, the fairness depends on how much a person really reads it over and gives it some thought, and I guess the cert. pool memo depends on the writer. Some are better than others.   (C8)

Another clerk said much the same thing.

We probably didn't save any time by having a cert. pool, but what we probably did do was a real thorough job of going over a case.   (C1)

Justices differ among themselves about the desirability of the pool. The general attitude of nonpool justices was that they did not care if others were members, but they made it clear that they had no desire to become members themselves. A conversation with a justice who was not a member of the pool went as follows:

Justice: You know some of our justices, five I believe, belong to a cert. pool.
Perry: Do you think the cert. pool is a good idea? I know that you are not a member.
Justice: If you came from the moon and had no preconceptions, I think that would be a pretty good system. It would be bad for all nine of us to be in it, but it is okay for some.
Perry: Why is that?

> *Justice:* Well, for one, the clerks, though they try not to bias
> something, at times may be a particular advocate for a case,
> and if we were all receiving the same memo from the cert.
> pool, that wouldn't be good.
> *Perry:* Is there some worry that there might also be some at-
> tempts to manipulate the agenda in favor of a certain jus-
> tice, or justices; or that some justices might hold sway over
> the pool?
> *Justice:* I think there is some worry of that, yes.

Having each cert. petition initially reviewed by at least four different
clerks—the pool writer, and one clerk in each nonpool chamber—
surely serves as some check on hegemony; but the independence of
nonpool clerks is perhaps not as strong as even the justices suspect.
One nonpool clerk said:

> We shared information about certain things as a time-saving
> device. In fact, on some of the real difficult cert. petitions . . .
> we would sometimes go swimming: we took a dip in the pool.
> We would ask the person doing the pool memo what they
> thought about it, and that did form some of our opinion be-
> cause they had a lot more time to research cert. petitions and
> give more thought to them. (C2)

And from another clerk from the same chambers:

> *Perry:* Did you ever look at the cert. pool memo? Another
> clerk referred to this as "going swimming."
> *Clerk:* I like that. I never heard it referred to as that but let
> me put it this way, I wore swim trunks frequently . . . I had
> friends in other chambers. (C29)

Clerks from other chambers went wading as well.

> I didn't often go to look at the pool memo, but sometimes I
> would—just to see what had been made of the fact
> situation. (C20)

Two pool clerks from different terms commented on the practice of
nonpool clerks "taking a dip" and vice versa.

> Justice _____'s clerks would come in and crib from our
> memos. (C32)

Others, in fact, would often borrow the cert. memos from us
to look over to prepare their own—Justice _____ and Justice
_____ clerks particularly. Of course they didn't tell their justice that. And there were times that we borrowed cert.
petitions. (C1)

A justice who was a member of the pool assessed it as follows:

> As you know, I am on the pool. At first, that bothered me a
> little bit. When the clerk is preparing what I call the flimsies,
> if he makes a mistake, he is making it for five, not just for
> one. But I haven't seen a disaster with the pool, and that is
> for a couple of reasons. First, all nine members are not a
> member of the pool. I would not want all nine. In fact, I was
> distressed when the chief put O'Connor on the pool. If he
> had consulted us, I would have recommended that she not be
> put on.[17]
>
> The second reason that there have been no disasters is that
> the pool memo doesn't come directly to me. My clerks review
> the pool memo and make their own recommendations, and
> they make an evaluation of what has been said. Originally
> they didn't make a recommendation, but I liked that a little
> less.

The justice then got up and showed me several copies of cert. pool
memos and how his clerks had marked them up. One simply said, "I
agree, the case should be held." Another had almost a page written
with a little bit more written in pencil about what she thought about
the case. The justice went on to say:

> Many times clerks can be very critical of other clerks' work . . .
> I like that for two reasons. One, there is a braking effect. Sec-
> ondly, it gives the clerk more of a chance to participate in the
> decision-making process. Then I would read these things and
> check them against the petition. These checks have served to
> assure me about the process, but I think it makes extra work
> for the justice, and less work for the clerk. I think the cert.
> pool memos are longer because you are writing for five or six
> people, than if they had just been written for me. My clerks

17. As an aside, the way the justice phrased his statement about O'Connor was
interesting. One would presume that the chief and the other justices would have had
nothing to say about whether or not O'Connor was in the pool.

get to know me well, and what I am not interested in. By and large, the pool has worked well. By now [November 16] the clerks know well, as do I, who the strong clerks are in the other chambers. You know that Jones is better than Smith.

The Pool Memo

The pool clerks were aware that they were writing the pool memo for five justices, and they prepared it as such. They attempted to make the memo very straightforward and formal.

> As you probably know, the cert. pool memo is very formalized. My impression is that the memos of the clerks who were not in the pool were much less formal. The cert. memo reads much like a legal product from a law firm. (C6)

> You learn to get a sense of what your justice was interested in. Although I would try to bend over backwards not to aim towards my individual justice, because when you are writing a pool memo you are writing for five and even if you know your justice is not interested in it you have got to treat it the same. I'm sure you've probably heard the _____ rule which means you have to state the facts and give a bit of detailed discussion regardless of how frivolous it is. (C62)

> In the pool memo I tried to be as impartial as possible. You were really writing for justices that had a spectrum of views. In fact, I often found it irritating if I saw another clerk trying to color the situation in line with his or her justice's ideology. You could really color facts, particularly if it were a complicated situation, though in general that was not done. (C34)

The markup, not the pool memo, was seen as the place to communicate with one's boss—particularly for more strategic considerations.

> . . . although my discussion there (in the pool memo) was not so naked as my discussion would be with Justice _____. (C60)

> We were nonstrategic in the pool memo, but in talking with Justice _____ or in the markup we would say things like "you can't get a fifth vote." (C1)

Differences among pool memos tend to be attributable to the individuals writing them rather than the fact that they were from a particular chamber. There was one exception to this that I heard often, and it was usually said with some frustration: "you could always tell a memo from Justice A's chambers."

> Frequently I would have to supplant Justice A memos; they were so truncated. They would say something to the effect that here is another one of those silly petitioners wanting such and such. (C32)

> Some of the chambers treated the cert. pool more cavalierly than others . . . particularly in Justice A's chambers. I think it was a function of the clerks' own ideological views which matched their justice. Of course you had the name of the writer at the bottom, so you could get a good judgment on their perspective when they were writing a memo. (C62)

The remarks about Justice A's clerks came from all chambers in the pool.

> *Clerk:* You quickly have a sense of the other clerks writing the memo. Effectively when someone from Justice A's chambers would write one, we would go back and check everything. And one of Justice A's clerks was just simply incompetent. It's given me a continuing bias against the law school that he came from. But I would say that in most of the cases, you have a lot of faith in the other clerks' work.
> *Perry:* Could you tell me a little bit more about what you mean with regard to the Justice A clerks?
> *Clerk:* Well, sometimes they would leave out, oh, critical facts, or they would really have a misstatement of the force of precedent, or sometimes they were even monkeying around a little with the record as far as we were concerned. So we had this kind of feeling that we were going to be super aboveboard about all this. But, then again, when I was clerking on the court, most of the clerks were a lot more liberal than their justices. (C43)

And from two more clerks:

> *Perry:*   I have heard some people say that they could tell what chambers the pool memo came from.
>
> *Clerk:*   Oh, that was not so true my year except perhaps with the exception of the Justice A chamber. They were more persistently ideological . . . They tend to be uniquely unsympathetic to i.f.p.'s.   (C48)

> [The pool memo] in essence is written to other clerks. It is blander and more restrained. I would say you could always spot a Justice A memo. Justice A is the only justice I know who tried to pick clerks who were ideologically compatible with himself. He seemed to aggressively seek that. Now the others might have been ideologically in line with their bosses but that largely has to do with the clerks wanting to work for a particular justice rather than the justice seeking clerks of that type, although Justice C's screening process might have led more to giving him certain types of clerks because his former clerks make recommendations. Clearly the Justice A cert. memos tended to be more casual.   (C47)

When I told a Justice A clerk that I had frequently heard that memos from clerks in her chambers were distinctive, she replied:

> Maybe it is easier to tell a Justice A memo. Maybe some of our biases merged. I am not sure I could tell chambers, but I learned to tell people . . . it often had to do with writing style, and one or two were particularly verbose. But I generally didn't have the sense that they were trying to promote their chamber's views. I tried to give accurate views irrespective of what my justice felt, but I would speculate that there was probably some subconscious influence. But there were times when I would make a recommendation contrary to what I knew the justice believed.   (C37)

Most of the Justice A clerks I interviewed seemed to be fairly conservative, and they were somewhat different from other clerks, including those from other conservative chambers. Indeed, I got to the point where I felt I could tell a Justice A clerk early on in an interview if I had not known it at the outset. Perhaps I could have done the same with clerks from the liberal chambers because of their generally liberal viewpoints. But there was something distinctive about Justice A's clerks: they tended to see the process somewhat more ideologically and strategically. This must be highly qualified, however. As most clerks—including Justice A clerks—pointed out, most of the cases are not ideological, and if they are, ideological differences usually emerge at the decision stage, not at cert. I did, however, interview one Justice A clerk who was quite conservative and very opinionated. During one point in the interview he had noted that Senator Lowell Weicker was a "threat to the Republic." Indeed, the clerk described himself as having "fairly doctrinaire views." In discussing the pool memo he said:

> Now obviously with Justice A I was more cordial than with the other judges. But even in the pool I would want to give my analysis of whether it was right or wrong. (C60)

All pool writers were expected to give their analysis of the correctness of the decision below, but one can well imagine that this clerk's analysis was much more ideologically oriented than the law-firm-like product from clerks in some of the other chambers.

In any event, there is little doubt that the behavior of certain Justice A clerks irritated other clerks, many of whom were ultimately sympathetic to Justice A's views. Again, the case should not be overstated. Most memos from most Justice A clerks must have fulfilled the basic requirements for the pool memo or something would have been done. But it did sound as if the Justice A clerks preferred to write pool memos that resembled the less formal memos found in the nonpool chambers. I could not determine if this behavior was encouraged by Justice A or not. In all chambers the clerks learn through an informal process, and they are rarely told explicitly what their justice wants.

The Justice A exception aside, the "bland" straightforward nature of the pool memo, necessarily so because it is being written for six justices, precludes it from being used to manipulate the agenda in any significant way. First, there are the nonpool chambers that also perform the function of first review. Second, even for a justice in the pool, there is the markup. In other words, it would be difficult to use the pool memo in a Machiavellian way and get away with it. Nevertheless, first review does provide the basis from which other decisions, most notably the markup, are made. As one clerk explained:

> A disadvantage is that you have a pyramid effect. The writer of the pool memo serves as the basis for considerations by other people. So they have given the baseline opinion. They have set out the argument. However, that is compensated for by completely independent reviews. I wouldn't want to stress

> the importance of the pool memo too much or give it too
> much deference. I didn't treat it as a predecision that I was
> supposed to necessarily go along with. Rather it was just an-
> other piece of paper to go along with the cert. petition; how-
> ever, it was important and at times you could rely pretty heav-
> ily on the memo.   (C28)

As the term progresses and there is less time for cert., authoring the
pool memo probably becomes more important. And, as with any cue
giver, some come to be trusted more than others.[18] Even the justices
become aware of the differences among clerks in other chambers.

One final aspect of memo writing for the pool should be noted: If
the opps. or reply brief came in late, it was generally the pool writer's
responsibility to write a supplemental memo if it were important. As
one clerk said, "I mean often you would say the reply brief adds
nothing, but sometimes it might. Or if the pool writer thought that it
didn't mean anything but one of us did, then we might write a memo
to our own justice" (C35).

The Markup Process

The use of the word "markup" is probably borrowed from Congress,
where committees "mark up" a bill. The markup process varies greatly
from case to case, and to some extent, from chamber to chamber.
Previous quotations suggested that at markup the clerk talks more
frankly with her justice, and strategic considerations are put forth.
That is true. But justices differ, as do clerks, in their willingness to
calculate strategies, and it is incorrect to characterize most markups as
strategy memos regardless of a justice's inclinations.

> There, at markup, one might look at the prior disposition of
> the justice, although I never felt necessarily that I was writing
> in any strategic way for the justice. I might say something
> stronger for an issue. Even on our own [cert. pool] memos, we
> might annotate them for the justice. We might refer him to
> some of his other opinions or his dissents and say that his
> views may be different in some earlier opinion or dissent,
> etc.   (C58)

18. Kingdon, *Congressmen's Voting Decisions.*

It would be misleading to think of the pool memo as this
bland sort of thing and you then said something else on your
note to the justice. On the pool memo, I didn't really pull
punches, although when you talk to your justice individually,
you might want to point out personal views, either yours or
his, more so than in a pool memo. Something like, "you seem
particularly interested in this, and I wanted to bring it to your
attention." You might point out that "this is contrary to something you have said earlier," or something like that. (C28)

Often, the purpose of the markup is simply to serve as a check on the
pool memo.

The way I saw my function in the markup was that I was to
be a screen or filter. You learn early on what the minds are of
the law clerks of the pool. Sometimes you have to screen that
for _____ [his justice] . . . there was a case where a clerk
recommended to deny cert. in an antitrust case and I knew
that the law clerk who wrote the pool memo had worked for
the judge below who had written the opinion. I agreed that it
wasn't certworthy, but for some different reasons, and I
thought that I needed to bring that to his attention. (C54)

It is when a case involves a particular area of interest to a justice that
the primary function of the markup becomes something other than a
check.

There is some truth to the fact that pool memos are written
differently as opposed to the markups. This was not so much
so in my case. But there were a few areas where he had
staked out a position, and I would couch my comments to him
in those terms. In criminal procedure my pool memo might
not look like the markup. For example, there is a certain area
where he might have thought they had made a bad decision,
and it was bringing up a whole lot of other cases. In my
markup I might say something like "this is good old x case
again, but this is really not the right case to try and set the
balance you want to set." (C48)

As the justice pointed out earlier, markup memos vary greatly. One
may simply note "I concur," and another may effectively be a new
memo. As one clerk noted, "my comments would range from one
sentence to three pages" (C1).

In addition to differences in the markup memos themselves, there is a great deal of variance in the attention given to the petition and the pool memo. There is somewhat of a systematic difference among the chambers with one justice's clerks (Justice D's) being the outliers. Virtually everyone, regardless of chambers, told me that Justice D clerks had to work the hardest generally. Specifically, they had to put much more effort in reviewing each pool memo, regardless of the situation.

> We spent a lot of time marking up in Justice D's chambers. We'd spend about as much time doing an analysis of the analysis. (C58)

> On my markup memo to the justice, it is basically the same process just boiled down a bit more. On about 90 percent of them I would read the petition *de novo* . . . In marking up I think in 50 to 60 percent of the cases I would write about a paragraph's worth. Sometimes I might point out, "I wouldn't be so concerned about this or that," or perhaps that the writer had glossed over another point. On about 5 percent of them, I would write essentially a new memo. (C47)

All Justice D clerks were not this thorough on all markups, however. As one pointed out:

> When it came to the markup stage, I think the expectation of the justice—although he never said it, it was kind of an oral tradition of the chambers—was that we were supposed to read the petitions ourselves and see if what the memo said was in line with that. But we really didn't even have time to do that. (C48)

Clerks from two of the chambers, Justice D's and Justice E's, tended to be similar in many ways, most having very "textbook" notions of proper behavior for justices, unlike, say, the clerks from Justice A's chambers (discussed above). But when it came to marking up, the behavior of D and E clerks was quite different. Justice E clerks noted:

> We didn't really do that much; certainly less than Justice D's clerks did. I would usually only write two to three sentences. The markup really wasn't all that important unless someone had really messed up, or there was something I needed to bring to his attention, because whether or not I agreed with

some other law clerk was not really important. Justice E made
up his own mind. (C57)

I would either say I agree, or disagree; there is less likelihood
that you would go ahead and read the case. If the cert. pool
memo made sense and there seemed to be a good analysis,
you wouldn't need to go read the case. If it seemed confusing
and you were bothered by something then you would go and
maybe do a little more research. If I agreed, I would note it,
if I didn't understand, I would probably discuss it with
someone. (C35)

In our chamber to do research was very infrequent. You did
learn the writer's particular biases but we didn't go over the
cert. memo all that thoroughly. Though in other chambers, I
understand, they did go over them very thoroughly, which
seems to me to do away with one of the major reasons for the
cert. pool in the first place. (C6)

Other chambers fell somewhere between the extremes of Justice E
and Justice D. Justice A markups tended to be a bit more strategic
than others. Justice F clerks spent a great deal of time trying to assess
claims of circuit conflicts. The difference in the amount of effort put
into a markup, had less to do with differences among chambers, and
more to do with the case being marked up, except for Justice D clerks.
As previously noted, when a case is in an area of particular interest to
one's justice, it receives closer attention regardless of the chamber.
Heightened scrutiny is also triggered when the pool memo recom-
mends a grant.

If it was just a decline I'd try to write a sentence to catch the
judges' attention showing that at least I had read the thing.
Now if the memo had said grant, then I had to say something
because a memo that urges a grant is almost so extraordinary
that it's presumptuous. You have to say something to address
that. (C38)

It's also interesting if one recommended a grant in a pool
memo, you had to do more work than if recommending a
deny. Often if the cert. pool memo had recommended a grant
then someone would have to go look and see if it really was
worth granting. (C24)

Most difficult, of course is overturning a recommendation in the pool memo to deny.

> If you were going to recommend a grant over a recommenda-
> tion not to grant in the pool memo, then you had to read all
> the papers and work pretty hard to show why the case should
> be granted . . . a little less so if the pool memo recommended
> a grant and you recommended deny. (C36)

This predisposition against granting will be examined in more detail in later chapters.

As has been suggested in other contexts, clerks get to know one another, and that makes a difference in the amount of time and effort put into the markup. They do not have the luxury of choosing their cue giver, but who the writer is, is a cue.

> One quickly got a sense of the other clerks who you could rely
> on, and the ones which you trusted the most, which were most
> of them. (C36)

One clerk added a slight twist.

> There are also ways to evaluate the clerk writing the memo. It
> wasn't just the person but it had to do with particular issues as
> well. For example, if the state was the losing party and a Jus-
> tice _____ clerk said it should be denied, then you know
> pretty well that there's nothing much there. It's not so much
> justice-specific as clerk-specific. Justice _____ [a conservative]
> did have a rather liberal clerk last term. You get to know what
> their positions are and so if they say there's nothing there,
> then you can probably rest assured that there isn't anything
> there. (C8)

Who the writer of the pool memo is, then, often conveys information to the clerk responsible for the markup.

The Stevens Process

Justice Stevens is not a member of the pool, and the process used in his chambers is quite different from that used in other nonpool chambers. As he has stated publicly, beginning in October Term 1977, he had his clerks write memos only on those cases that the clerks thought should be granted or discussed. If a case appeared on the discuss list for which no memo had been written, a clerk would prepare one prior to conference.

> Basically we were just preparing him for participation in the conference. There were only two of us, and he wanted to save our time and his time. There was no need to write memos on so many of the cases. Of course if anything showed up on the discuss list that we had not prepared a memo on, then we would go write one fairly quickly . . . I would often make a note why I did not write on a particular case because sometimes we would not get it right, and when we would get what we had to do for the conference, I would have to write a quick memo on it. Lots of times you can't remember. You just go through so many of these. You are getting about a hundred per week.

I asked the Stevens clerks the percentage of cases requiring memos.

> *Clerk:* Once he felt confident in his clerk's judgment, he really didn't want us to spend time on obvious denies.
> *Perry:* Can you give me some ballpark figure of how many you did not write memos on?
> *Clerk:* We wrote no memo on about 40 to 50 percent of them. We started out by writing many more, but soon you learn the standards the justices use. To get cert., a case almost has to be perfect.

> *Clerk:* I would say that we didn't write any memos on about half the unpaid [i.f.p.] list.
> *Perry:* How many memos did you write on the paid cases?
> *Clerk:* I'd say that on about 25 to 30 percent of the paid cases there were no memos written.
> *Perry:* Now am I to assume that many of the memos you did write were still cursory?
> *Clerk:* Oh yes. We'd only write about this much [he held his fingers about two inches apart]. We'd simply say, "here is another such and such case."

> *Clerk:* Incidentally, we would automatically write a memo if the SG was petitioning.

In spite of Stevens's instructions to write only on cases the clerks deemed certworthy, some clerks suggested that they often wrote cursory memos on cases that were obvious denies. I asked them why.

> *Perry:* How did you decide between whether you wrote a
> memo that was an obvious deny versus not writing a memo
> at all?
>
> *Clerk:* That's a really good question. To a certain extent, it
> was a pragmatic consideration. You were interested in pro-
> tecting yourself because if you knew that another justice was
> going to put it on the discuss list, you might as well go
> ahead and write the memo . . . Another criteria was if you
> could do a quick one, you just went ahead and did it. That
> in a sense could protect you. I don't think that was Justice
> Stevens's concept, but that's part of the way it worked . . .
> Some of the things that I thought were obvious denies and
> I knew that Justice Stevens wouldn't be interested in, I
> knew by now that other justices were interested in it . . . Of
> course you know Justice _____ got to the point where he
> wanted to hear practically every First Amendment case . . .
> Again, the process evolved. In the beginning it was real dif-
> ficult for me to tell what was an obvious deny. Everything
> looked like it deserved to be heard.

> *Clerk:* The ones that we didn't write on at all were the ones
> you'd never grant in a thousand years. For example, there
> was just a summary judgment, or there would be so many
> facts that it would take forever to explain.

The latter case is, however, precisely the type of case that Justice D's
clerks spent so much time on.

It is not clear why Justice Stevens uses this method. Perhaps it is
explained by his lack of seniority and the fact that he rarely has the
responsibility to lead a cert. discussion. More likely, it has something
to do with Justice Stevens's strong belief that the Court takes far too
many cases for review. He is probably the most vocal critic of the Court
in this regard. Perhaps he believes that allowing clerks to devote their
time to other tasks outweighs any benefit from a process that would
only serve to increase the likelihood of a case being accepted.

One practice required of Stevens's clerks was related frequently—
both by Stevens's clerks and others. Justice Stevens insisted that his
clerks dictate their cert. memos. For many of the informants, this
requirement at first seemed almost more troublesome than writing the
evaluation of the case. Having been required by my first boss to use a
Dictaphone, I could sympathize.

He insisted on our using a Dictaphone. We shared an office
and you're kind of reluctant and embarrassed to dictate while
someone is listening. I was embarrassed so that's why I did it
at home sometimes . . . Actually, I got to the point where I
could practically read the opinion (of the court below) and
dictate the memo at the same time.

The memos were then transcribed and the clerks would do a rough,
handwritten edit before giving them to Justice Stevens. Incidentally,
the office accommodations for clerks in all the chambers are quite
crowded, there is virtually no secretarial assistance, and word proces-
sors are a relatively recent addition to the Court. Clerks in other
chambers usually type their own memos.

Brennan: "The Wizard of Cert."

Justice White may be known as "Wizzer" White, but Justice Brennan
should be known as the Wizard of Cert. During the summer preceding
the first conference, Brennan clerks would function just as Stewart
and Marshall clerks and prepare cert. memos for Justice Brennan. But
once the term began, Justice Brennan read every cert. petition himself;
more precisely, he glanced at each one. Justice Brennan has said
publicly that he feels that he can make most cert. decisions based solely
on reading the "Questions Presented" section in the petition.[19] In
arguing against a National Court of Appeals, he has stated how important he thinks the case selection process is and that it is a responsibility that clearly cannot be ceded to another court.[20] Yet the reason
he did not have his clerks work on cert. cannot be that he thought it
too important to let them do it, since he had them do the cert. work
in the summer. Rather, it seems to be because he liked doing the work,
and he could do it very fast.

> Clerk: He says he has his clerks do it in the summer because
> he thinks it is important for clerks to see what goes on in
> the Court. And it's a good way of getting an overview of all
> the issues that are going on in the federal court system. It's
> total immersion. Otherwise, Justice Brennan probably would
> have done it all twelve months of the year. He liked doing
> it. He loved doing it . . . He can't wait to get his hands on it.

19. William J. Brennan, "The National Court of Appeals: Another Dissent," 40
University of Chicago Law Review (1973): 473.
   20. Ibid.

Clerk: I can give you an example. When Justice Brennan came back, there were several stacks, but we had one stack left over at the end of the summer. I took them into Justice Brennan and I told him that the four of us could get through them in about a day. I put them on his desk, and actually by the time I left his office, he had already gone through three of them.

Perry: How does he do them so quickly?

Clerk: Well, first of all he just looks and reads the questions presented. After twenty-five years, he really knows what type of issue the Supreme Court ought to be dealing with. I think it is kind of a threshold thing.

Clerk: Now the way Justice Brennan went through these is that he'd just read the question presented, and I think he decided on the basis of that a lot of times. He is one of the few people I know who has a real photographic memory. I mean, we would go in there before breakfast to talk about cases and he had a bookcase behind him that contained all the *U.S. Reports* from the time he had been on the Court. On the other wall was all the rest of them. He would say, "I think this has a relation to a certain case." He would turn around and pick up the exact book and go right to the page. He had an incredible memory, and he had a real recollection of cases and what was going on in the law. So in a lot of ways he knew when the questions were presented if they really would fit in the development of the law. He would go through a tray in about an hour. He'd write on the cert. petition itself and I think he could eliminate 90 percent of them just by looking at the questions, and probably on the other 10 percent he would read the brief. Occasionally he would read a pool memo. A lot of those pool memos were junk.

During the summer, the memos of Brennan clerks resembled others in nonpool chambers.

Up until this last summer, Justice Brennan spent his vacations in Nantucket, and we would send the memos up to him to be read up there . . . He wanted them very short . . . Sometimes they would just say, "this is a tax case involving x," and that is all it would take . . . Three pages would be an extremely long one.

Sometimes before he made a decision, Brennan would ask his clerks to do some research on a petition. I asked several Brennan clerks what this research might involve.

> *Clerk:* The easiest is when it is a technical problem. Or he might send it in and ask, "Is this really consistent with what we said earlier? What do you think?" Less frequently he would ask us questions about what's in the record. Generally, however, if there is much of a question about that, the Court doesn't want to get into such a case where it has to evaluate evidence.

> *Clerk:* Justice Brennan takes over when he gets back and we have virtually nothing to do with the cert. petitions at that point, unless he's particularly interested in a case for some more information, or unless he's going to dissent from denial. We will sometimes be involved in preparing a draft for that.

> *Perry:* [Of the number of cases Brennan asked the clerks to look at] Was this like one a week?
> *Clerk:* No. I'd say maybe fifteen or twenty the whole term.

It was unclear if Justice Brennan's particular procedure made any substantive difference. No one seemed to think he was either better or less well prepared for cert. discussions in conference. That Brennan could handle the cases as he did and that Stevens never sees many of the cases at all, suggests that the cert. decision can frequently be made on very little information.

The Clerks

As must be obvious by now, one cannot talk about the agenda-setting process without talking about the law clerks. Who are these people, and how do they learn what they are supposed to do? One need only look at the process to see that they are much more than low-level functionaries. From time to time, a justice will publicly understate the role of the clerks, but that is usually in response to some exorbitant claim that the clerks are really running things or that they are hoodwinking the justices. The clerks are not Richelieus or Rasputins, but that they play an important role in the cert. process simply cannot be denied.

Though the comparison is flawed, clerks are not completely unlike congressional staff. No staff member "controls" or "manipulates" a senator, but to deny the importance, or ignore the role staff members play in the legislative process, would be foolish.[21] Likewise, the clerks. They cannot control their justice, and the process has checks and balances, but they play a crucial role. One clerk described the clerks' influence this way:

> [On really important cases] what the clerks have to say is really less important. Justice _____ had his views . . . I would tell him my constitutional views, but that is kind of preposterous. I mean, if he has been doing his job and has been on the Court that long, he damn well better have his views about what the Constitution means . . . Now the law clerks have more influence, I would say, on the areas of law that are less socially important. Given their law review experience and usually having worked on the Court of Appeals, they may be up on some [aspect] of this law and be able to have more of an impact . . . every clerk thought he was going to get there and would help his justice change America . . . But we only had the opportunity to persuade him on an opinion here or there, because he had his own views on the major stuff.   (C29)

Obviously, the clerk was referring to more than the cert. process. Nevertheless, his assessment is a good one for the clerk's influence generally. If one sees influence only as the ability to change a justice's mind, or somehow undermine him, that rarely happens. Delegation of important tasks does happen though, particularly with regard to cert. Delegation does not mean ceding ultimate authority, but it does mean having clerks make decisions that affect and sometimes determine outcomes. Clerks are probably more influential in cert. than in opinion writing because often the justice defers to their analysis of the issues in a cert. petition, whereas in an opinion, the case is highly salient to the justice. Recall that most justices never read more than the clerk's memo if the recommendation is to deny. As one justice said:

> First I decide if I can make a decision on the basis of the memo. In fact, on most of them I can, because most of these I

21. See Robert H. Salisbury and Kenneth A. Shepsle, "Congressional Staff Turnover and the Ties-That-Bind," *American Political Science Review* 75 (June 1981): 381–395.

vote to deny. If the case is a good candidate for a grant, then I will mark the memo "read." Or I will sometimes mark a memo read even though I would vote to deny but think that others will vote to grant so I read them offensively and defensively.

Another justice suggested that he generally needed only his clerk's memo to decide most cases:

> I took home the pool memos as they were annotated by my clerks. It would usually take two to three hours. I took some home last night. I would look at their recommendations to grant or deny, and I would circle it if I agreed, or cross it out if I disagreed and then put my initials on it.

From a third justice:

> I usually could simply read their memo and tell whether or not a case deserved to be granted certiorari.

SELECTION

The justices vary in the number of clerks they hire per term, most having four, with Justices Stewart and Rehnquist, when he was not chief justice, having three, and Stevens two. Justice Stewart was known to be quite concerned that the Court was becoming too bureaucratized. One suspects that also explains Rehnquist's and Stevens's decision to have fewer clerks. Each justice selects his own clerks. Although the selection procedures vary, the primary criteria in all chambers seem to be what law school the clerk attended, how well she did, and who were her mentors. Mentors primarily consist of law professors, appeals court judges, and former clerks. Some justices have begun trying to broaden the base of law schools, but it is still very much a small network.

Some attention has already been paid to Justice A clerks—the ones who appear to be more ideological in their cert. behavior, and whose views are fairly concurrent with their justice's. According to a clerk from another chamber:

> Justice A was known to inquire about his clerks' philosophy, because I guess he assumed that there is no reason to have anyone there who would be unhappy the whole time. But he was the only one who did that, I think. Justice _____ [a liberal] had a very conservative clerk my term. (C9).

I do not know if Justice A cared about his clerks' philosophy at the time of hiring. It seems to me to be entirely appropriate if he did.[22] I did interview some clerks who were quite conservative though they clerked for a liberal justice, but most clerks for liberal justices seemed to share their justice's views.

Another clerk described his hiring experience:

> With Justice _____, I think [ideology] played almost no role at all. I'll tell you the way I got it . . . [After having clerked for Judge X on the D.C. Circuit Court of Appeals] . . . All of a sudden, Judge X called and said, "Justice _____ wants you to call him," and so I called his secretary and she said, "Why did it take you so long to call us? Are you going to clerk for us or not?" Justice _____ had never met me. (C53)

Of course, Judge X was undoubtedly aware of this clerk's ideological orientation. One clerk described her selection as follows:

> *Clerk:* Justice A hired very conservative people generally, and Justice B and Justice C clerks tended to be pretty liberal and they tended to come from the same places. Justice B's clerks were sent over from Judge X and they were sent to Judge X by some faculty member of the Harvard Law School. Justice D clerks were somewhat conservative, but not all that much. (C57)
> *Perry:* What about Justice E's [her justice's] clerks?
> *Clerk:* I don't think Justice E's clerks were chosen on ideology so much but on a certain personality. They were generally people who were nice guys . . . They were low key, kind of clean cut nice guys—kind of like the justice. I think that is at least the perception that other clerks had of us. Of course, you know it's kind of weird sometimes that you take on the justice's perceptions when you're a clerk. Like _____ who is in this firm. During his Court days he was seen as a flaming radical, and actually he now seems to be pretty conservative . . . But Justice E is generally this nice guy whom

22. Though this is "appropriate"—the primary function of personal staff is to help the boss as he sees fit—it may not be the most desirable use of staff. One might want staff who constantly challenge. But how staff can be most helpful is surely the boss's call. Many of the informants seemed to suggest that an ideology "test" was somehow inappropriate. This reflects the "ideal" notion of the dispassionate jurist.

we developed a very close personal relationship with. He
never raised his voice the whole year.

Another clerk noted the same phenomenon of mirroring his justice's
ideology.

> It would be interesting if you could come up with a term for
> something that happens. Maybe the psychologists have a term.
> You kind of take on your boss's ideology. Conservatives who
> clerk for Justice _____ [a liberal] become liberals. (C50)

A clerk from a third chamber echoed the sentiments of the above
clerks:

> *Clerk:* I never met him before I was hired. He has a commit-
> tee that interviews, and I think basically what they are look-
> ing for is someone who is easy to get along with, a pleasant
> person. Not so much their ideology. If I said really much
> more than that it would be kind of self-serving.
> *Perry:* I had heard that some justices, particularly Justice A,
> might be looking for ideologically compatible clerks.
> *Clerk:* Well, Justice A is the one that jumps out at you. But it
> is difficult to say if it is a function of the selection process or
> if you become a defender of your justice. I think that it is
> very natural that even if a particular case would not get
> your vote personally, that once your justice takes a position,
> you become a defender of it. I can remember in my term
> there was a Justice _____ [a liberal] clerk who was remark-
> ably _____-like in almost everything he did and said. Now
> he is in the government and you would think he had come
> out of Justice _____'s [conservative] chambers.

The development of symbiotic relationships between clerk and justice
was almost universal, although the intensity varied. Many whom I
interviewed would say, "I am not as conservative as Justice _____," or
"I disagreed with Justice _____ on several points," but with few exceptions, most clerks admired their justice and were almost protective
of him and his positions. The best explanation for the confluence
between clerk and justice seems to be that clerks very much want to
please their boss.[23] Whether it is a psychological phenomenon, a shared

---

23. The desire to please a boss is not, of course, unique to the Supreme Court. See
Salisbury and Shepsle, "Congressional Staff."

vision, or simply being opportunistic, the clerk begins to see the world through his justice's eyes.

I asked every informant some version of the following question:

> *Perry:* It seems to me that you might have seen your role in one of two ways—either as a surrogate for the justice, or as a devil's advocate, both of which are common forms of behavior when one works for someone else. By surrogate, I mean that you saw it as your role to evaluate a petition and make judgments you thought your justice would if only he had the time. By devil's advocate, I mean that you saw it as your responsibility to bring up every factor that you thought important regardless of whether you thought your justice would be predisposed to see it as important or would agree with it, perhaps especially bringing up issues that you knew would challenge his predisposition.

After several interviews, it became clear that the use of the phrase "devil's advocate" was unfortunate, but I continued to ask the question the same way for consistency. Many people who did not see themselves as a surrogate also refused to label themselves as a devil's advocate. What many said was that it was their responsibility to bring information to their justice that they thought was important irrespective of whether they thought the justice would find it important or persuasive. Few saw the need to be or thought that their justice wanted them to be a real devil's advocate at cert., though some thought their justice wanted them to do that at times on bench memos.[24]

If one sees the categories as extremes on a continuum, the clerks placed themselves all along it, including the extremes. Interestingly there is no significant correlation between chambers and attitude. One would have expected that clerks from certain chambers would have seen their role far differently from clerks in other chambers. Such was not the case. The primary variation was among individuals, not chambers. Of course some behavior is chamber-specific because every justice has his idiosyncrasies. But what is of concern here was how clerks saw themselves generally in the case-screening process. Reported are typical responses from along the continuum.

24. A bench memo is generally any memorandum prepared by a clerk for her justice. Usually they are done to prepare a justice for oral argument, or when he is writing an opinion.

I was definitely a surrogate. You have to be. (C45)

I was unquestionably the former [surrogate]. In our chamber
I think that was quite clear. You were to act as the eyes and
ears of the justice and supposed to winnow out cases as he
would. And you would bring to his attention a particular case
that your justice would want to push for cert. At no time did I
ever see my role as giving, for example, a prisoner some form
of advocacy so that he would get his petition heard. I never
saw Justice _____ really having the time to function as a
[judge in a] court of last resolve. Now when dealing with the
case on the merits, writing bench memos for drafting an opinion, I saw my role differently because there I could assume
that he might spend more time studying what I was saying, so
I could grind my ax a little more. (C48)

And from almost the opposite extreme:

I saw myself primarily as someone Justice _____ had hired—
an intelligent young attorney, and he wanted me to tell him
what I thought about it, knowing often that he would think I
was full of shit. But he didn't want a yes man. On the other
hand, he didn't want an obstacle either. (C36)

Another clerk also saw himself as an employee, but it led him to quite
a different conclusion:

I think I was closer to the former [surrogate] . . . I was on
track with his thinking . . . I didn't feel responsible to help
him refine his views on the law. I was an employee and I
really didn't want to make a distinction between what he
thought and what I thought the law ought to be. I was just a
twenty-five-year-old kid. (C52)

The decision to be or not to be a surrogate might depend on confidence in one's ability to know what one's justice wanted. Witness the
following different perspectives, particularly with regard to clerks'
abilities at clairvoyance.

I think most clerks thought it dangerous to try to predict how
their justice would act . . . Most clerks didn't say, "gee my
justice is a real right-winger and this is an outrageous case of
a person's Miranda rights being violated, but since he is not

interested in that kind of stuff, I won't bring it to his attention." (C19)

We had a really good sense of what the justice wanted to see. He had a clear agenda which was clear largely from his opinions; and so the surrogate role was pretty easy. [Note: this response was given before I had asked the surrogate question.] (C43)

Another clerk claimed:

More of the first [surrogate], unless I had a particular interest in the case. But I would usually ask, "would Justice _____ want to grant this case?" (C50)

Several clerks suggested that the dichotomy was too simplistic. One noted:

I think Justice _____ saw us clearly as law clerks. We were to present clear and unbiased presentations to him . . . in a law firm . . . it often works that way there too. No doubt as the term went on we learned his values, but not perfectly, even at the end . . . But it is inevitable that you want to do something which your boss will agree with. On cases that were not particularly important, I suspect my views were attempts to mirror his. On cases where I had stronger views, I was more assertive. (C6)

Most informants saw themselves as playing both roles. Even though clerks generally want to please their justice, inevitably there come times when they feel strongly one way and their justice another. Discussing this dilemma, one clerk showed what is probably a modern day sensibility.

I would flag every case that he would be interested in even though I knew that he might have a position different from mine and would do damage to that area. But you learn to resolve that in your own mind. The way I would handle most all memos is, I would begin by saying, "I think this is the approach that you would take, that you will find congenial," or "I think you are particularly interested in this." But then I would say, "but here are some concerns that I see as important, too." And that might go against what he had said. Of

> course there's a problem. You are aware of the Rehnquist
> *Brown* memo aren't you? . . . Well, evidently when Rehnquist
> was coming up for confirmation hearings, someone produced
> a memo he had written as a clerk, effectively opposing *Brown*.
> He claimed at the time that it was not his views, but that it was
> his justice's views, and that he was working in that sense. But
> as a result of that, clerks wanted to be particularly clear about
> the perspective they were taking. For example, Justice _____
> has his mind made up on capital punishment and his attitudes
> were different from mine, and so I wrote a memo one time
> recommending denial, knowing that he would disagree, but I
> said for the record, I wanted to file my own feelings about
> this, and I did that. (C43)

The clerk went on to give other examples which he asked not be
reported because he might be identified by them. Most clerks are
probably not worried about future memos coming back to haunt them,
though I did not pursue this with other clerks.

The justices seemed to prefer that their clerks act more like surrogates. It was interesting to hear certain justices say that they saw their
clerks as surrogates and then hear some of the clerks from those
chambers protest that playing such a role would be improper. The
next section helps explain this difference in perception. The pool
justices expected the pool memo to be impartial, but for markups and
for nonpool justices, they wanted their clerks to learn what they were
interested in and act accordingly. One justice gave his perception as
follows:

> It takes a little while for them to get on my curve, but basi-
> cally I see them as surrogates. That might differ for some
> justices, but as things go on, they can eventually get to the
> point of writing very short memos telling me why we should
> or should not take a case . . . I see them as surrogates once
> they get on my curve.

And from another justice, "My clerks get to know me well and what I
am not interested in." He went onto suggest that he wanted his clerks
to screen for him in light of that knowledge.

LEARNING

What is almost unbelievable about clerks is how much responsibility
these young men and women are handed despite their lack of experience and given that they are only at the Court for a year. It is for

this reason that the congressional staff analogy is largely inapposite. As noted earlier, the clerks are among the best students from the most competitive law schools. Most clerk for a federal circuit judge their first year out of law school, and then go to the Supreme Court for a one-year stint. Obviously, they are bright people, but it is really rather remarkable how little they know when they arrive at the Supreme Court and how fast they have to learn. As one clerk noted:

> Basically, when I got to the Supreme Court, I didn't know what I was doing. I was used to the Court of Appeals mode of decision making, which is where they basically resolve every-thing. It took me quite a while to figure out that cert. was not like this. It took me a while to figure out what the justice wanted. (C29)

There is little done in the way of teaching clerks what their justices want in a cert. memo.[25] Clerks are expected to plunge into the cert. process and essentially learn on their own. During the term, some justices may tell their clerks to keep their eyes open for certain types of cases, but usually clerks learn that rather than having it told to them. As the term proceeds, they get to know their justice better, what he is interested in, and what he is not. Apparently, though, no justice sits down with his clerks and tells them what he wants to see in a cert. memo when the clerks first arrive. In fact, many of the justices are not even in Washington when the clerks arrive and must begin work on the petitions.

> At the beginning, I didn't really know what the hell I was doing. I know we mailed a bunch to Justice _____'s summer home. (C29)

> I found a sizable stack of cert. petitions awaiting me . . . it was hard because we had only met Justice _____ once and that may have been by telephone. And there was no secretarial help . . . you'd pound things out on the typewriter . . . at times you would talk to your co-clerks. Previous clerks gave you certain pointers, but you didn't get that detailed of infor-mation from them, and frankly it wasn't all that consistent information. (C40)

25. Frankly, I am quite puzzled by the learning/teaching process for the law clerks. This is a topic that deserves a study all its own.

To the extent that there is any instruction, it generally comes from former clerks. In each chamber there are one or two clerks who are still there for a short time when the new clerks arrive. Also, in some chambers there are notebooks of previous cert. memos, and there are records of the pool memos. It is primarily by looking over earlier memos that new clerks learn how the process works.

> Justice _____ never said what he wanted in a cert. memo . . . I would go back and look at other pool memos to get indirect feedback . . . You were never instructed on how to write a draft opinion . . . but there was not a whole lot of formal instruction about anything . . . I hung over to instruct the new ones coming on. Generally what you do is take them around on a tour of the building, and they're asking questions and you're telling them things. You explain the types of cases he likes. The cert. process is something completely new. They had written briefs on opinions when they were on the Court of Appeals, but you're hit first and foremost with the cert. process and at this time you are not drafting any other opinions. (C24)

Aside from having to learn the esoteric cert. process, the clerk is also faced with complicated issues of law for which he has little training. One often hears the remark that when young lawyers get out of law school, they cannot find the courthouse, let alone file a motion. The Supreme Court building may be a little more august, but it is not all that different for its clerks. Law school does not give students expertise in any particular area of the law. They may gain passing familiarity with a broad range of topics, but after the exams, not many specifics are remembered. In the Supreme Court, much of the caseload deals with criminal law, often not a favorite of those who wind up clerking. As one clerk said to me rather sheepishly:

> I have to be honest. Often I used Kamisar's casebook because I didn't know a great deal about criminal law. (C43)

Having clerked for one year on the Court of Appeals is of some help, but it takes years of service before one encounters many of the complex situations faced in a federal court.

> Of course in the beginning everything is hard. You're exposed to areas you'd not even heard of. I remember I had an early pool memo on navigational water rights. It had something to

do with New Jersey, and wherever the tide affects the water it's a navigational issue. (C27)

Most new jobs are such that what seems difficult, mysterious, and time consuming at first becomes routine; one wonders why one found it so hard, confusing, and slow going at the beginning. So it is with the cert. process. What is different about this job, however, is that there is very little advice from the boss, the job is usually over after one year, and the clerk must come up to snuff very quickly. As the term proceeds, the clerk's responsibilities increase dramatically. Once oral argument starts, clerks must prepare bench memos, and then, of course, there is the drafting of opinions. Shortly into the term, the time clerks have to spend on cert. decreases dramatically. Virtually every clerk commented on how long it took to do cert. petitions at the beginning of the year, and how fast she could do them at the end of the year. The following are typical comments:

> At the beginning of the term I would do about five a day and have a six-day workweek. As the term went along, I could take what would have taken me a week, and do it in a day by the end of the term. (C29)

> Time spent on the pool memos declined over the term as the other responsibilities increased. In the beginning you would spend hours on a cert. pool memo. You would begin looking at it like you did when you were a Court of Appeals clerk, trying to determine whether the case was right or wrong and spending a lot of time looking at the merits. Gradually you realize that the Court really wasn't interested in that. And as you realize that, the time you began spending on cert. petitions decreased dramatically. You began looking for things like a real issue or a false issue. And you got to know that the justices had pet issues. (C24)

It is not only that clerks learn how to do the job faster, they soon learn how few cases the justices consider certworthy.

> Of course you do have a bit of a change of perspective from the summer when you first start and then as you get into the term. I mean at first you think most everything is interesting and certworthy . . . But then as you go on, you realize what the justices think is certworthy and what they don't. (C54)

One clerk described his socialization this way:

> I later learned that for all the time you spent on a cert. petition, they don't grant any more whether you spend all that time or not . . . One of the most instructive processes for me was putting together the cart—physically separating the petitions on the cart. Here you had something like a thousand cert. petitions on a table, and the clerks would then take the discuss list and have to sort them into piles. It was helpful, because just physically sorting these, I would see that often in a case where I saw that real issues needed to be decided, I could see that absolutely *no* justice was interested in the case— including my own . . . As time goes on you necessarily must spend less time. You have to do all the other functions expected of a clerk. Your time tends to shrink but on the other hand, your expertise increases. (C29)

Not only does a clerk's expertise increase, but so does his confidence —both in his own ability and in his relationship with his boss. A humorous example demonstrating this was relayed by one informant.

> I remember a cert. petition being circulated towards the end of the term with a memo that said, "Another fruitcake petition—deny." (C43)

Clerks also learn sooner or later that there are certain cases the justices are not going to take despite the fact that they fulfill all other criteria. One example recounted time and again was cases dealing with ineffective assistance of counsel. Several informants, clerks and justices, suggested that every term some clerk would write a very thorough and sometimes impassioned memo on an ineffective counsel case. With equal regularity, these cases would be denied. The reasons for this are discussed later. It was definitely the example most frequently used by informants to demonstrate to me that one learns rather quickly what justices are not interested in.

The best way that a clerk learns what her justice wants is simply by working with him. The justices vary in their relationships with their clerks, but the variation seems to be based more on personality and style than on differing perceptions of the clerks' role. Clerks from one chamber were fond of their justice, but his style is such that he prefers not to be quite as open with his clerks as some of the other justices. For example, with the possible exception of one other justice, all justices are quite willing to tell their clerks the cert. votes in conference.

One justice tells his clerks on a need to know basis. He does tell them votes on the merits, however, because that is necessary for opinion writing. Also his clerks told me that he would mark up their memos with "hieroglyphics," the translation of which he never explained to them. Nevertheless, several told me that they had figured them out and would pass them on to the next batch of clerks. Of course this could be a situation where no one ever asked the justice what they meant. As one of his clerk's said:

> Part of the reason Justice A clerks work so hard is because the baton is handed on by previous clerks. They pass on that you have to work until midnight every night, and we tend to believe it and pass it on to others, and you never really question it. Nobody ever said I had to wear a tie, but everyone knew we had to wear a tie. There's a funny story about Justice B's clerks. His clerks had always worn ties until finally someone asked Justice B, and he said he didn't really care, and after that they always wore jeans. (C24)

Sartorial matters aside, some justices fraternize more and some less with their clerks. Again, the difference is probably one of personality, not role expectations, but the type of relationship affects the type of feedback clerks receive.

Aside from the one or two chambers already mentioned, clerks in all other chambers could find out the cert. votes if they wished. One justice evidently made a game of it.

> Justice _____ would come in and put down his conference book and make us guess how the other justices voted. He would then leave the book for us to look at. (C1)

> He would come back after conference and bring in his book, and we'd all be dying to find out what had gone on, and he'd make us play this guessing game of how people voted. We'd hope he'd leave the cert. book, which he usually did, and we could look it up and see how people voted, although he rarely repeated conversations that had gone on. Oh, from time to time he would say, "Justice so and so said something," or "this argument this individual justice just didn't understand," particularly if he felt strongly about something . . . He didn't discuss that much what he said or what went on, but there were other ways in which you could pick up a signal. (C62)

Another justice seems to have provided his clerks with more direct feedback and learning than any other justice.

> *Clerk:* On the first batch of memos that we wrote, he wrote comments, kind of like a teacher, but then after that, he didn't really write too many. We really hardly ever discussed cert. petitions, and we really talked a lot with him too. He'd come in and plop himself down in our office, or we'd have lunch with him really quite frequently, but rarely did we talk to him about cert.
>
> *Perry:* Were you aware of how he voted in conference?
>
> *Clerk:* Oh yeah. He'd come back after conference and tell us things. He had his book with the votes marked in it, and we were permitted to go through the book. If we asked who voted a certain way, he would tell us. Sometimes he would say "someone made a nice speech about this, etc." (C45)

> *Clerk:* We talked a lot as we went along, and the preceding law clerks helped. We would get some immediate feedback by seeing what he said on our memos. He had a notebook where he kept everything, which allowed us to see what went on in conference. He'd put our memos in the notebook and go into conference, and then he'd take notes. A lot of cases we would seek out to see what happened . . . He would record the votes on our memos of how people voted. But Justice _____ was a very open justice with us, so we could see what we wanted to. (C49)

From another chamber:

> Some justices I know tried to hide the ball, at least one, and they didn't want their clerks to know what their bias was. But some were much more open with their clerks. They felt that their clerks could be used much more effectively. Justice _____ was very open with us . . . Over time, you get responses to your recommendations . . . He would talk to us about certain things. By the last six months you had a pretty good idea of what it was he was looking for and wanted. (C37)

Regarding yet another justice:

> I think the justices assume that the clerks have more knowledge than you really have. I think they assume that you know

some of their biases and interests, but the way you learn this is through conversations. The justice may come in and say, "Yes this is an interesting memo, but . . ." Then he will point out some practical aspect that you haven't thought about. Many justices take copious notes in conference. Justice _____ would allow us—in fact was eager for us—to review the notes so that we could be aware of what was going on, and we would look over them after conference. (C35)

We were very fortunate. Justice _____ treated us very openly and worked with us very closely. He would often share with us what went on in conference. At conference, he would write copious notes of what went on in notebooks. We had the job of recording things afterwards. So we saw how he voted on the issue, and we often knew how the others voted and the character of the discussion that went on. (C6)

One justice had a particularly collegial relationship with clerks. He and his clerks usually met over breakfast or coffee, and he conversed with his clerks quite frequently.

The learning process for the clerks in some ways is like that of the new prosecutor or public defender described in Milton Heumann's *Plea Bargaining*. The clerk, relatively fresh out of law school, comes to the Court with naive and textbook notions of how the Supreme Court operates. She is placed in an environment with an extraordinary case-load, unwritten rules, and important responsibilities that can have dramatic consequences on the lives of individuals. Frequently, the clerk is just trying to keep her head above the water. She often must sacrifice, or at least be willing to overlook, some of her own notions of justice and the legal system. Learning this is sometimes painful and disillusioning, but it is inevitable. The clerk, not unlike the young prosecutor, comes to believe that for good or ill, the process as it works is essentially the only way that it can work. Unlike the young public defender or prosecutor, however, the clerk does not come away disillusioned. In any event, the point is that both processes are based on adaptive behavior that comes about as a result of the environment shaping the learning rather than the teaching. Comparing clerks to those adapting to plea bargaining may or may not be particularly useful, but it does suggest that the learning process for clerks in the United States Supreme Court is not as unique as it might appear at first blush. Comparisons with others, such as congressional staff or assistant professors, might also be instructive.

Discuss List: The First Collective Agenda

The practice of using a winnowing list goes back to the time of Chief Justice Hughes. In 1950, however, the process changed somewhat.[26] Formerly, the chief justice would circulate a list known as the "dead list," which recorded all cases considered not worthy of discussion. Any case could be removed from the list by any justice. The process now is just the reverse: there is a discuss list rather than a dead list. Prior to the interviews, I assumed that having such a list was probably important, and that by authoring the list, the chief justice played a particularly significant role. Even though any justice can add cases simply for the asking, I had supposed that by drawing the list, the chief was somehow in the driver's seat for setting the agenda. But the shibboleth *primus inter pares* prevails; the chief justice is only first among equals. The discuss list is indeed important, but the role of the chief justice in authoring the list seems to be mostly administrative. As one Burger clerk said:

> *Clerk:*   Generally what you do is just put on all the cases that merit discussion. [Burger] took it as a matter of pride that he set the agenda for the conference . . . Justice _____ and Justice _____ would put cases on, maybe a couple or three. After the chief and Justice _____ were done, that took care of most everything. Any week that the discuss list was his list, he took great pride in that.
>
> *Perry:*   So he would put cases on that he wasn't interested in if he thought other justices might be?
>
> *Clerk:*   It seems so because he was so proud when the list was his.

Most of the informants agreed that Chief Justice Burger did not try to manipulate the list. The chief justice might genuinely have a different perspective on what is important and how the Court should be spending its time, but he does not try to manipulate the discuss list in any strategic sense. In this task, the chief justice acts as an agent for the other justices.[27] Since any justice can add a case simply by sending

26. Doris Marie Provine, *Case Selection in the United States Supreme Court* (Chicago: University of Chicago Press, 1980), p. 28.

27. Such behavior has been observed and discussed for other leaders. See, e.g., Kenneth Shepsle and Brian Humes, "Legislative Leadership: Organizational Entrepreneurs as Agents," paper presented at the Conference on Adaptive Institutions, Stanford University, November 8–9, 1984; and John F. Manley, "Wilbur D. Mills: A Study in Congressional Influence," *American Political Science Review* 62 (June 1969): 442–464.

a note to a clerk in the chief's chambers, there is no incentive for the chief to try to use the list for his own purposes. Several of the justices confirmed this:

> The chief does a good job of getting most of them on the list. He puts cases on the list even though they are ones that he would not personally vote to grant.

Another justice:

> I think the chief puts on a case automatically if he thinks it is something that others will be interested in.

A third justice agreed with the basic point, although he was less generous in assessing the chief's authorship of the list.

> The chief justice puts the list together, or maybe one of his clerks does. Then it comes to us. We all can suggest additions. He misses a few at times, but he always has some excuse for it [said sarcastically] . . . Some that the chief justice puts on, frankly I don't know why they are on, and sometimes he doesn't know . . . That is one of the things that makes me think his law clerks do it . . . Or there will be cases that for everyone else is a clear deny and he will have a join three.

The notion that clerks drew up the list without Burger's oversight does not jibe with the Burger clerk's statement about the pride that the chief justice took in forming the list. At the time of the interview, it sounded as if this justice were trying to make excuses for what he considered to be the chief's poor judgment. Incidentally, this justice is not one who would be considered to be one of Burger's antagonists on the Court.

If the chief puts a case on the list, he does start the discussion, whereas if another justice adds the case, that justice leads the discussion. Some have suggested that this practice gives the chief great power because it allows him to frame the case as he sees it. This may be true for certain chief justices, but it is fair to say that, rightly or wrongly, Chief Justice Burger did not command sufficient respect from his colleagues to be able to make much use of the right to lead the discussion. Yet even with a supposedly powerful and respected chief justice such as Earl Warren, the ability to formulate and lead the discussion would make little difference on cert. The process is such that it does not lend itself to deference. Except in relatively rare instances, the justices do not rely on one another's judgment at the cert. stage. There is no cue taking because their minds are usually made up prior to conference, and as detailed in Chapter 6, they communicate little prior to conference. One or more justices whom I interviewed also served during the Warren era, and thus I had the opportunity to ask questions comparing the two Courts. I did not ask a question directly about the discuss list, but from answers to other questions, the influence of the chief justice on cert. seemed much the same for Warren and Burger.

A couple of informants, however, did say a few things that might indicate that the chief's role was a little more important than I have just suggested. One clerk noted:

> Oh, there were a little politics around the discuss list, particularly if the chief didn't put a case on. I know sometimes one justice might talk to another and say he was thinking of going over [Burger's] head; or he might call to see if another justice would be putting the case on. It is clear they had some discomfort. One might subtly call the chief's chambers and ask if there were a clerical error here that such and such a case was left off the list. (C47)

Another clerk suggested that the chief was less than diligent in serving as an agent for all.

> It was always interesting to see which ones the chief would put on; he generally lists about 70 percent of the obvious ones, then he lists some of the conservative favorites, but they are supplemented with pretty much rapid fire. Justice _____ would tend to wait to see what the others sent. By nature, he did not want to bring up any cases if others did not want to discuss them. There was almost never a case that he wanted on when someone had not requested it. (C11)

Statements such as these were the exception, however, at least in terms of Burger's role.

Representative comments about the behavior of other justices regarding the discuss list follow:

> *Clerk:* Justice A all the time was putting cases on the discuss list that didn't ever get granted. I think it is a good indication though to see what he might do if he ever gets the conservative majority on the Court that he hopes for. (C62)

>*Clerk:* [Regarding the types of cases added to the discuss list] It would be hard to find more extremes in the Court than between Justice B and Justice A, but I doubt that any of those [they added to the list] were granted. (C54)

>*Perry:* How often did Justice C add cases to the discuss list?
>*Clerk:* He would put them on occasionally, but he was not one for bringing up a lot of cases. He didn't really push a lot to have cases on the list, or to get cert. granted. (C57)

>*Perry:* About how many cases do you think Justice D would add to the discuss list?
>*Clerk:* He'd add about two or three per time.

>*Clerk:* Of course Justice E is a very unpredictable justice . . . Sometimes I would be surprised by what he put on the list.
>*Perry:* Did he put many on the list?
>*Clerk:* No . . . He felt that too many cases were on there. (C49)

>*Perry:* Did Justice E add many cases to the discuss List?
>*Clerk:* He rarely put one on unless he felt very very strongly about it . . . Our year I think there was one case, maybe it was within five, he put on the list where the Court did something other than deny, like calling for a response. I don't think that any case he put on the list was granted. All the obvious cases were on the list by the time it got to him. As he moves up in seniority, he may be able to put more cases on the discuss list. (C31)

One clerk suggested that a justice's seniority might affect his discuss list behavior:

>You know, one of the things to consider is [the justice's seniority. If he is the junior justice and] he put a case on the discuss list, he had no votes. That meant that no other justice was interested in it. (C31)

In other words, if others were interested, they, having more seniority, could lead the discussion in conference; so there was no reason for the junior member to put the case on.

Several clerks said something that suggested that the discuss list was circulated hierarchically. I asked a justice about this:

> *Perry:* Is the discuss list circulated hierarchically, or do you
> all get it at once?
> *Justice:* We all get it at once.

A second justice confirmed that they receive the list simultaneously.

The discuss list serves primarily an administrative function, which is not to say that the existence of such a list is unimportant. At the very least, it tells us that there are a large number of cases considered so unworthy that there is no need for deliberation by the collective body. Moreover, any procedure used to avoid discussion in a deliberative body has implications. Different justices might think that a case does not deserve cert. for various reasons, but by not even discussing it, their reasoning need not be aired; their preferences and dispositions need not be revealed. This, at times, can be strategically useful. While such a procedure avoids unnecessary controversy, it also avoids potential enlightenment.

Leadership in Conference

As suggested earlier, while technically leading the conference, Chief Justice Burger did not seem to be particularly influential either *ex officio* or personally. Are any of the other justices seen as a leader? One clerk made an interesting comment with regard to Justice G (not his justice):

> *Clerk:* There are particular justices who have a strong role in
> conference who are not otherwise really seen as a leader on
> the Court. I think that, depending on their personalities,
> different people were much more leaders in conference.
> *Perry:* Who were the leaders in the cert. process?
> *Clerk:* Justice G takes a very strong position. He is a very oral
> justice. Perhaps he plays this role because he is in the mid-
> dle. But he seemed to take a very strong and leading role in
> cert. . . . I was surprised. I never thought that Justice G's
> opinions were that good, or led to significant doctrinal de-
> velopment. I would not have thought of him as a leader. In
> talking with older clerks, this seems always to have been the
> case with Justice G . . . I understand that Chief Justice War-
> ren was a toreador in the cert. process. He really played a
> dramatic and leading role. But I think the Court lacks that
> now.
> *Perry:* What about Justice H [his justice]?

Clerk: Justice H seemed to be fairly selective in where he asserted himself. Justice G asserted himself a lot. As you probably know, the chief justice is quite passive in this process.

A clerk from another chamber had this to say:

Clerk: Frankly the chief is just not a good chief. He doesn't
much lead.
Perry: I heard that Justice G was a real leader in the cert.
process. Would you agree with that?
Clerk: Justice G is very assertive. The rest of the Court does
look to him in some ways, but he's not a real great leader
either. There's really no one the Court can rally around.

When Justice G clerks were asked about their justice being a leader,
the responses were what one might expect.

He certainly had done his homework, sometimes a lot better
than the other justices. [In conference] I understand he is
pretty persuasive. (C62)

Definitely. I think it has to do with the fact that he is a phe-
nomenally aggressive person. He is very energetic. He gets to
work at 6:00 A.M., and he is probably more up on cases and
knows what is going on than a lot of the other justices, and
maybe they tend to defer to him on something like that. (C36)

Notwithstanding these comments about Justice G, no one justice on
this Court seems to dominate the cert. process. To the extent leadership was suggested, it usually came in self-congratulatory remarks
about one's own justice. What is unique about Justice G is that his
leadership was mentioned by a few non-G clerks. However, I think if
one or two justices did play a particularly dominant role, I would have
heard about it more than I did. This is not to say that all justices play
the same role in the cert. process. I suspect Justice G was seen by some
as domineering because he feels that many cases the Court denies
should be granted. As a result, he probably argues more in conference.
This does not make him a "leader."

The "Burger Court" was often criticized by scholars and journalists
for not having leadership—intellectual or political. Whether or not
this was true, the extent to which we see leadership in the past may
be colored by historical perspective. I suspect that Chief Justice Warren's specter influences this perception. But as with all historical fig-

ures, reputations tend to grow a bit out of proportion. No one doubts the remarkable chief justiceship of Earl Warren, but according to the justices, some of whom served on the Warren Court, if Warren were a "toreador" on cert., it was only to the extent that his brethren allowed him to be. Having good followers is, of course, often a major component in being a good leader. But I doubt that Felix Frankfurter, or Hugo Black, or William Brennan would have deferred to Warren's notion of certworthiness any more than they would to Burger or Justice G, or any other justice. Indeed, some of the most acrimonious rhetoric ever about cert. came from Frankfurter during the Warren Court. The point here is that whether or not there is political or intellectual leadership on the Court at the opinion-writing stage, given the way the cert. process works—with most decisions made in chambers, and with little discussion between chambers—there is little opportunity for leadership on cert. If I am correct, this casts doubts upon some of the political science literature on cert. and, perhaps, on broader studies of the Court as well.

There was always special treatment: whenever the cert. petitions dealt with a capital case [and were *pro se*], they had a big pink sticker on them. (C3)

4 Special Situations

The preceding chapter outlined the process for handling most cases. Certain cases, however, are treated differently. Focusing too much on these special situations or making too much of them could distort one's understanding of the case selection process. Nevertheless, these special situations are of some interest in and of themselves, and their treatment adds insight into the entire agenda-setting process and behavior on the Court more generally.

Capital Cases

I think it is common knowledge that all capital cases are discussed in conference. They were specially marked when we sent things into the justice. Even if the justices thought they were frivolous, they were at least discussed in conference. (C2)

This may be common knowledge, but I had never heard it prior to the interviews. In the thirty-eighth interview, a clerk told me:

All of the death cases are automatically discussed, I doubt if anyone's told you that. (C38)

Indeed, I had heard it several times by then. When I mentioned to a justice that I knew that all capital cases were automatically placed on the discuss list, he seemed somewhat surprised that I knew it.

> *Perry:* I understand that for some time, capital cases have automatically been put on the discuss list.
> *Justice:* [Pause] Yes, that is true.
> *Perry:* Why is that?
> *Justice:* Because of the finality of it. [Pause] That doesn't mean that they all get discussed that thoroughly though.

Regardless of the thoroughness of the discussion, the fact that all capital cases automatically make the discuss list is noteworthy. No other category of cases is guaranteed a portion of the Court's valuable conference time. Cases petitioned by the solicitor general are effectively assured a place on the list. They are different, however, because the assumption is that the SG has already screened cases.[1] Even though most individual decisions on cert. are made prior to conference, and discussion in conference is often cursory, given the dynamics that can occur in there, chances for review are substantially increased by making the discuss list. If a case is on the list, a justice at least has the chance to demonstrate certworthiness in ways that are not particularly obvious.

> Of course, death cases got special attention . . . On those we would often see if we could make the case on some grounds apart from the death issue.

> Capital cases were given a great deal of attention, although Justice _____ automatically recommended to grant vacate and remand; but still we would often look at these capital cases to see if there were other issues. We'd look for other issues that might attract other justices.

> A lot of these capital cases clearly are not certworthy and we would make distinctions. Although as a matter of principle Justice _____ did object to all the capital cases.

Justices Brennan and Marshall, of course, are on the public record opposing all capital punishment as unconstitutional.

Capital cases are advantaged not only by being automatically placed on the discuss list but also by receiving heightened scrutiny in chambers. Clerks search for any chance of review, which is quite the opposite of the normal search for any justification to deny. One would expect

---

1. The special role of the solicitor general is considered in Chapter 5.

extra attention by Brennan and Marshall, but it was surprising to learn that every chamber treats these cases with special care. From various chambers:

> *Clerk:* The only particular cases that I would outline in great detail, regardless of how frivolous they were, were the death cases . . . They all treat them seriously because of the gravity of what is involved. Everyone feels really strange about this. (C45)

> *Clerk:* [Capital cases] were starred for special treatment. (C5)

> *Clerk:* I know when I looked at the capital cases last year, I just realized how important they were, and I would go over them and look at them because you realize what it meant for the individuals. (C9)

> *Clerk:* At some point you should remind me to tell you about death cases because they are really quite different . . .
> *Perry:* . . . You suggested that I should ask you about death cases.
> *Clerk:* Yeah, I hated death cases. But Justice A had a lot of influence on death cases. Justices B, C, and D had become very important in the death case issue forming the plurality. And so in a sense they really determined what was to be the response. I mean you could count that Justice E and Justice F would generally uphold death penalties. Brennan and Marshall—you had their votes automatically and so in some ways the coalition that you really had to put together was Justices B, C, and D. You had to convince all three of them that under their criteria, the death penalty was not acceptable. But I hated working on these cases because I had to spend a disproportionate amount of time on them. (C29)

> *Clerk:* Preparation of the death cases always involved a longer memo. Justice _____ took them seriously, but I don't know to what extent that they caused him a particularly big problem. It was always our fear that we'd get a stay and have to deal with the stay for the ____th Circuit.
> *Perry:* I don't understand.
> *Clerk:* The ____th Circuit was where they kept wanting to fry people, and we had the justice who would have to make the initial response to a stay. (C57)

Clerk: Death penalty cases are treated very, very
seriously.   (C25)

Clerk: The only tricky ones with the i.f.p. cases were the
death penalty cases because . . . all death penalties are discussed at conference.   (C54)

Clerk: On the memo in death cases you would always say that
it was a death case, and you would state more specifically
where it's at. For example, you might say that you should
wait for habeas; perhaps it hadn't gone through habeas at
the federal level or only at the state level. But when it came
from review at the circuit court of appeals, then you began
saying this was it for the poor fellow.   (C38)

The close attention given to all capital cases is most certainly a
departure from standard operating procedures. No one would be-
grudge heightened scrutiny to the case of someone who is about to be
killed by the state; but to place capital cases on the discuss list automatically is an interesting decision rule. The justices continually de-
claim that they cannot be a court to ensure justice. They often let
stand what they know to be incorrectly decided cases, some of which
involve lengthy periods of incarceration, but their role, so they say, is
to clarify the law so that justice can be done in the courts below. It is
not obvious, then, why death cases should be different. If there is any
area where most lower court judges probably would be careful, for
fear of reversal if nothing else, it would be in capital cases. Despite
controversy in the public and among some justices who refuse to treat
the issue as *stare decisis*,[2] the issue of capital punishment is *res judicata*.[3]
The Court has made clear that capital punishment is allowed under
certain conditions, even if it has not made clear exactly what those
conditions are, or more precisely, how to determine when those conditions exist. Of course all capital cases are not directly challenging
capital punishment per se. Some other procedure or happenstance
may be at issue. Nevertheless, it seems that when the death penalty is
involved, the justices, except perhaps Brennan and Marshall, are simply trying to ensure justice.

Since so much is at stake for the individual, one still might not find

2. *Black's Law Dictionary:* "Policy of courts to stand by precedent and not to disturb a
settled point."
3. *Black's Law Dictionary:* "A thing or matter settled by judgment."

it surprising that capital cases are given special treatment. Yet it is arguable that a case involving life imprisonment without parole is of sufficiently high stakes that it, too, would deserve automatic inclusion on the discuss list. That does not happen. Such a case may get fairly close scrutiny in chambers, though none of the informants suggested that it would, but it clearly does not get the assurance of discussion in conference. Perhaps punishment by death constitutes a threshold rather than a matter of degree. Nevertheless, the underlying justification for a decision rule that places capital cases on the discuss list seems to be solely the severity of the punishment.

What is significant here is not that the justices have arbitrarily chosen to be extra careful when it comes to a capital case, a position most would applaud; rather it is that this decision rule has subtle implications. The rule suggests that there is really no such thing as a frivolous case per se, whereas the notion that there are unquestionably frivolous cases underlies much of the justification for the way the cert. decision process works. The concept of frivolousness is examined at length in Chapter 8, but for now we should note that justices and clerks assert that huge numbers of cases are patently and objectively frivolous because they raise no real issues of law that deserve review by the Court. That is, the petitioner simply does not like the outcome and wants one last shot at avoiding jail or paying what he owes. But it seems that even the most frivolous case, in terms of an issue of law, deserves careful consideration if the punishment is so extreme. Such a position weakens the force of the argument that cases are frivolous *prima facie*. By definition, the automatic inclusion of capital cases on the discuss list argues that the justices are saying that no case can be considered frivolous—uncertworthy perhaps but not frivolous—if the punishment involved is death. All the while, the justices are willing to accept the idea that a case can be frivolous if the punishment involves only life imprisonment. That, it seems to me, suggests that the definition of "frivolous" is tautological—a frivolous case is a case the justices consider to be frivolous. Yet when I posed this definition of frivolousness to the informants (though not in the context of capital cases), virtually every one said that such a definition was preposterous. Or, as one clerk put it:

> [The notion that] any case is potentially certworthy is a
> crock. (C31)

The treatment of capital cases belies the wholesale rejection of such a premise, however. Granted, reasonable people may agree most of the time that a case raises no particularly worthwhile issue for review in the Supreme Court, but that is always ultimately a subjective rather than objective evaluation. The special treatment of capital cases makes that point. It also lends some support to the view that the Supreme Court is in control of its agenda more than the textbook notion suggests. The Court has chosen to pay special attention to cases involving capital punishment, and in doing so, it gives less time to something else. Cases, on their face, do not compel acceptance or rejection. This might seem obvious, but it is not the underlying assumption of the cert. process.

Discussion of the special situation of capital cases provides a nice segue into the next three chapters because such cases involve some interesting strategic considerations. For example, as I discuss in Chapter 5, Justice Brennan would use dissents from denial of certiorari in capital cases, as Justice Marshall still does, to send advice to counsel below as he continues to raise habeas issues in lower courts. Also, there is a possibility that the guaranteed allotment of conference time is perhaps being used to alter capital punishment doctrine. Whether the rule always to include capital cases on the discuss list comes from general consensus, or from the knowledge that Brennan and Marshall would always put them on anyway, capital cases consume a disproportionate amount of time. Given current doctrine, the Court must review the facts and the record of a capital case very closely. The justices must review capital cases almost as lower court judges do, to see if this particular case was handled properly in light of the requirements they themselves have set forth. Therefore, even though capital cases are frequently denied review, the justices are continually forced to confront the workability of their own doctrine. This may well lead to doctrinal shifts, particularly as states execute more and more people. The most dramatic change would be a decision to reverse precedent and make capital punishment unconstitutional. Given the bitterness that has surrounded this issue on the Court, such a change seems unlikely. But what does seem possible is a shift in doctrine that would enable the Supreme Court to spend less time and angst in dealing with capital cases. One wonders if such a strategy may not be the reason why Marshall refuses, and Brennan refused, to consider the issue *res judicata*. One clerk told me that one justice who was not opposed to capital punishment was so frustrated once that he circulated something that said, "we just ought to summarily reverse all death cases" (C57). Whether or not this is a conscious strategy by Brennan and Marshall, it suggests that the discuss list procedure can have implications beyond administration.

Rule of Four Exception: The Rule of Five

An exception to the rule of four has developed that has nothing to do with relisting. There are certain issues of law (and at times, a specific case)[4] for which coalitions on the Court have rigidified into a 5–4 block. The minority block can muster the four votes to grant cert., but everyone on the Court knows that they will lose on the merits. The result is that the four do not insist that the case be heard. One area where this phenomenon of four dissenters has occurred is obscenity. One clerk noted:

> Justice _____ told me positions had rigidified on this First Amendment issue . . . some people thought that certain restrictions were always unconstitutional, and others didn't. That has the effect of overruling the rule of four. (C51)

A justice, not the one mentioned above confirmed this.

> *Perry:* I have heard that there are times that even though four vote to hear a case, they waive the right to have it argued. Is that true?
>
> *Justice:* Yes [four justices] were on the record that they thought all obscenity cases should be reversed, but they knew they wouldn't win on the merits.
>
> *Perry:* Does that happen now?
>
> *Justice:* Well it has happened, but it is very rare. Those are in the category where those who would like to grant would vote for summary reversal.

Justices sometimes make a calculation of the predictable outcome on the merits, but there are very few instances where the outcome is so well known at the cert. stage that it obviates the rule of four. As best I could determine, obscenity was the only broad area of law that had developed a "rule of five."

---

4. See, e.g., Gilmore v. Utah, 429 U.S. 1012 (1976), the Gary Gilmore case. Gilmore, of course, was the first person to be executed after Furman v. Georgia, 408 U.S. 238. Technically this was not a petition for certiorari, but it involved application for a stay of execution by Gilmore's mother. Nevertheless, four justices dissented: White, Brennan, Marshall, and Blackmun.

Summary Dispositions: The Rule of Six

It is somewhat inappropriate to discuss summary dispositions in a chapter on special situations because, in fact, they constitute a large proportion of the disposed cases (see Figure 4.1). However, summary treatment is not considered to be standard operating procedure. The legal implications of summary dispositions are discussed in Chapter 2. Recall that any properly presented appeal must be ruled upon by the Court, and as such, many appeals are technically disposed of summarily. The decision to treat a petition for certiorari (or an important

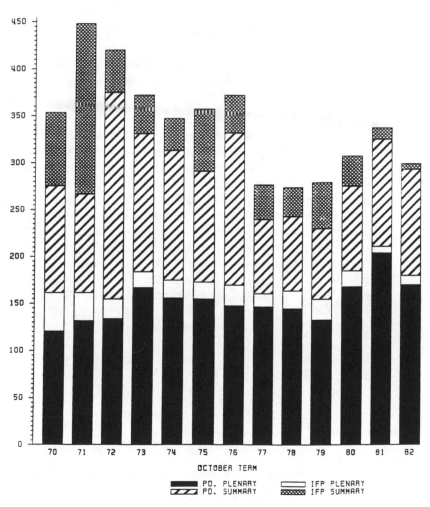

Figure 4.1 Cases granted review, by case type

appeal) in a summary manner is another matter. Also recall that the increase in summary dispositions has come under much criticism from both within and outside the Court.

The most common reason given for summary treatment implied that the increasing caseload required it.[5] If one takes seriously what the justices claim the role of the Court is—clarifying the law and not serving as a Court to ensure justice—then most summary dispositions are an enigma.[6] Summary dispositions do nothing to clarify the law. One remains puzzled as to why the Court decides cases summarily. One clerk referred to summary behavior as "the Zorro concept—where they strike like lightening to do justice." Some instances are undoubtedly explained by a result being so egregious that the justices cannot let it pass, but all summary reversals cannot fall into that category.[7] Moreover, that would not explain summary affirmances at all. One cannot draw unassailable conclusions about summary behavior from the interviews, but much of what the justices told me sheds some light on the process.

> *Justice:* The rule now, well, it is not a rule, but it is a convention, is that it takes six to do that [decide at the cert. vote to dispose of a case summarily and issue a per curiam opinion] rather than five. Often I dissent because I would have granted plenary argument. I think Justices A and B now dissent from every summary judgment. Justice C is close to that attitude, but there are times that he will join a summary opinion when a decision is so obviously wrong.
>
> A common statement . . . is that "my vote is to reverse or deny." What that means is that a justice thinks treatment is needed, but he doesn't want to hear the case on full argument. He doesn't want to spend the time hearing it. That is happening a little more frequently now.
>
> *Perry:* Does this concern you?
>
> *Justice:* I'm not too unhappy about this. I know it upsets some counsel because they want to get down here and argue. And I know it upsets lower court judges when we over-

5. Again I am reminded of plea bargaining: a heavy caseload is usually cited to justify plea bargaining, although, according to Heumann, this does not explain the need for the procedure.

6. There are instances where summary judgments are clearly appropriate. At times the Court may hold several cases pending the disposition of a similar case. The cases are then summarily affirmed, reversed, and vacated, in light of the decision.

7. The concept of "egregiousness" is discussed more thoroughly in Chapter 8.

turn summarily. You know we have stated that a summary doesn't carry as much weight as a plenary argument.[8] But most of the times it happens on procedural grounds, or something like that.

I had never heard of this "rule of six" prior to my interviews. It is an important fact about how the Court operates. Though this is not the place to go into its implications, it does cause us to rethink many things, for example, the number of justices needed to form a bloc.

Whatever the jurisprudential problems caused by summary disposition, it certainly leaves counsel unclear as to the best way to write a petition. As discussed in Chapter 2, the justices are forever chiding the bar for writing cert. petitions that argue the merits rather than concentrate on why the Court should take the case. Given the increase in summary dispositions, however, one wonders if perhaps it is not dangerous for counsel not to include a healthy discussion of the merits. I asked the justices about this.

> *Perry:* The formal rules of the Court, and guides like Stern and Gressman, urge counsel not to use the petition as a place for a discussion on the merits. But if I were a lawyer petitioning, wouldn't it be a bit dangerous not to discuss the merits in my petition?
>
> *Justice:* [Smiling] I think so. You might get it reversed summarily on you. This is one of the reasons that Justice _____ feels that we shouldn't do summary reversals. If a case is to be reversed, we should have plenary argument. There is an unfairness to summary reversals in this sense.

And from another justice of whom I asked much the same question:

> You better not risk not putting something about the merits in there because as I have suggested, sometimes the merits do make a difference. And sometimes we will just grant and vacate or affirm, and so a good lawyer probably ought to include that in there. Sometimes to talk about why the Court should hear it, you have to include a discussion of the merits. But I wouldn't leave it out of a petition. We don't help lawyers all that much with our rules. We tell them not to stress the

---

8. Precisely what a summary disposition means is actually an issue of some controversy (see Chapter 2).

merits, but as long as we are considering the merits, I am not sure I would leave it out of my petition.

One hypothesis is that summary treatment allows judgment in an area when justices agree on a result but know that if the case were argued they would never be able to agree on reasoning in the opinion, resulting in confused doctrine. Some, though not many, of the informants saw that as an explanation. Others disagreed.

I.F.P.'s

When a litigant is sufficiently impoverished so as not to have the money to carry on an appeal, he is granted leave to file *in forma pauperis*. This allows him to proceed without paying court costs such as filing fees. His petition is referred to as an i.f.p., and petitions of this kind include, but are not the same as, *pro se* petitions. A *pro se* petition is one that a litigant files himself without the help of counsel—the most famous example being Clarence Gideon. If the Court grants review, counsel is assigned. Most paupers, however, are assigned counsel in a court below, so an attorney often prepares the petition. Although a few informants said that "there were some good jailhouse lawyers down there who knew some of the right catchwords," i.f.p.'s generally are not scrawled handwritten efforts from prison libraries. Usually, they are prepared by an attorney.[9] Even so, the vast majority of i.f.p.'s are presumed to be frivolous. Most are. By and large they are criminal petitions that present no issue of law. The petitioner usually is someone dissatisfied with her verdict who wants one last shot at reversal. As with summary judgments, a discussion of i.f.p.'s in a chapter on special situations may seem inappropriate, given their prevalence. Much of the growth in the Court's caseload is attributable to the increase in i.f.p.'s. They have come to make up over half the Court's docket, yet they are granted only at a rate of 1 to 2 percent. Paid cases are granted at rates of about 7 to 10 percent. (See Figure 4.1.)

The chambers vary on the depth of review they give to i.f.p.'s. All chambers realize that most are frivolous, but three chambers pay closer attention to them than others. Even there, however, the treatment is

9. According to Stern and Gressman (*Supreme Court Practice*, 6th ed., written with Stephen M. Shapiro, Washington, D.C.: Bureau of National Affairs, 1986, p. 425), about three-fourths of all i.f.p.'s are prepared by assigned counsel or someone other than the party seeking review.

not that careful. One justice was quite upset with a change in procedure that had led to i.f.p.'s receiving even less attention.

> The solicitor general, several terms ago, adopted the practice, after talking with the chief justice about it, that they would be selective in the responses they filed to cases on the miscellaneous docket (i.f.p.'s). I objected strenuously to that, and still do. When they responded to these, I was able to rely on them because often they are filed by some poor guy down in prison who says he was treated unfairly, there was a judge who treated him unfairly, or so forth and so on. The solicitor general was able to, in his briefs, go and see what the situation was. And now I would say on about half of them they don't do that anymore. I've missed it. I've missed it terribly. That is a problem because week after week, miscellaneous petitions involve the government, and on about half of them they are not filing a response. I think it is a great disservice to the Court, and I can't possibly pay as much attention to those as I should. But then the solicitor general has the chief justice's approval, and therefore I was sounding like a voice in the wilderness. I mean I must go back to *Gideon*. It was granted on the basis of a handwritten complaint . . . But there is just no way for me to discern how important some of the issues are in these cases, and one of the things that I'm increasingly insistent upon is calling for the response of the solicitor general . . . I'm at a distinct disadvantage in evaluating these cases . . . Unless I get some help, there is really nothing I can do, and I think this is an important point that you should note.[10]

There is little doubt that the overwhelming majority of i.f.p.'s present no important issue of law. It is less certain that those that do will all be noticed. There are, of course, normative implications from the fact that less scrutiny is given i.f.p.'s. Since the Court does not see its role as ensuring justice, suggestions that "the poor" are receiving short shrift tend to fall on deaf ears. Other potential problems are more subtle. There may be cases of law which are systematically related to the types of cases that would be i.f.p.'s but which go undetected. Time

---

10. The justice's statement attests that interviewees have their agenda for an interview just as interviewers do. This is well understood when it comes to presidents. Justices could similarly use interviewers if they so chose. Undoubtedly many academics would be willing to bring things to the public's attention if the justices were willing to grant more interviews.

and again clerks and justices said that it was the lawyer's responsibility to make his case in the petition, not the clerk's to try to find it for him. Given an even stronger *a priori* presumption against certworthiness than exists for the paid case, the burden of proof gets higher, while the quality of counsel is probably lower. Ironically, those petitions that are *pro se* probably get better counsel, because if they are granted, the Supreme Court appoints a lawyer, and she is usually quite good. Whatever the implications, it is fair to say that for over half of the docket, the process is even more cursory than the standard treatment, which itself is fairly hasty.

Appeals

As stated earlier, most of the Court's appellate jurisdiction has been removed, and most cases come by certiorari. However, at the time of my interviews, appeals still constituted a significant portion of the workload. Moreover, the statements about appeals shed light on attitudes about case selection generally.

Does the Court treat appeals differently from certs.? I received varying answers. Yes:

> I think they were basically put in different categories . . . on the whole I think the court is reasonably conscientious about its statutory obligations. (C19)

No:

> They're virtually indistinguishable. There's the finest of distinctions, but they are really not approached differently. Maybe a couple of grains of sand added to the balance. (C9)

Somewhat:

> They are looked at a little bit harder; they always have to be denied with a reason, so I would say it is marginally easier to get a case heard as an appeal if you style it right. (C11)

Most informants saw little distinction between the two, although many said that certain cases were heard because they were on appeal that would not otherwise have been granted if they were on cert.[11] In terms of the process, clerks have to pay a bit more attention to appeals than certs. because they at least have to come up with a reason to deny an appeal. That is not hard to do when all that one must say is that it is "dismissed for want of a substantial federal question." Nevertheless, to some extent, the burden is shifted slightly.

The views of the justices are similar to the clerks. One said that "the Court respects, in a rough way, the appeals statutes." Two others remarked:

> *Justice:*   All of us have recommended to Congress to do away with the mandatory appeal statutes. Maybe we will get some relief on this.
> *Perry:*   Does the Court really take cases on appeal that it would not take if they came up on cert.?
> *Justice:*   Yes. We do take cases that we would not otherwise hear. Around the conference table you will hear people say, "If this were here on cert. I would deny it."

> *Perry:*   I'd like for you to clear up something else that one reads—that the Court treats appeals and certs. in virtually the same manner.
> *Justice:*   Yes. I believe that is basically true although I believe that every appeal makes it onto the discuss list. But basically we do treat them like cert. petitions under most of the same criteria we have discussed this afternoon.

As discussed in Chapter 2, although Congress has decreased substantially the mandatory jurisdiction of the Supreme Court over the last several years, it still has refused to do away with mandatory appeals completely. Ironically, justices who can get so exercised about issues of deference to legislative authority in constitutional litigation are quite willing to dismiss with a wink and a smile the appeals requirement that was put forth by Congress. This is probably because they believe that Congress has refused to remove mandatory appeals more for political reasons than for jurisprudential ones. Removing the remaining situations that would permit an appeal is probably similar to removing old

11. According to Stern and Gressman (*Surpeme Court Practice,* 6th ed., pp. 252–253), in OT's 1981 and 1982, 85 percent and 92 percent, respectively, of the appeals from state courts were disposed of summarily, whereas 55 percent and 40 percent, respectively, of the appeals from federal courts were summarily decided. During these terms, appeals from federal courts numbered 57 and 35, respectively.

laws on the books in states. They are not really enforced, but to remove them might cause an outcry. Somewhat apropos, one justice noted:

> If [workload] got to be too much of a problem, I believe that Congress would be willing to change appellate statutes, or give us changes that we would ask for. Of course, there is no steam behind it, but I believe that if the Court would get behind it, I don't think there would be any great opposition.

Why Congress did finally limit appeals when it did is unclear.

To Dig or Not to Dig

> I remember something someone told me that stuck with me at the time—although I'm not sure this is really true—but that the worst thing that could happen was to recommend a grant and then have the case digged. (C43)

From time to time, the Court will grant a case and then later dismiss it as improvidently granted. This is commonly referred to as "digging a case." A case may be digged (not dug!) at any time.

> *Perry:* Could you tell me how the process to dig a case starts?
> *Clerk:* It happens whenever the problem seems to arise, and that varies from case to case. It may come up after oral argument, or it may come up after a bench memo, or it may come up just from a discussion between the justice and his clerks. (C58)

In fact, few cases are digged.[12] The option exists but is rarely exercised, even though it would sometimes offer an easy and desirable solution. There are various reasons for digging a case, some of which are potentially interesting to the political scientist. Usually, however, the reasons are mundane, jurisprudential considerations. These issues must be examined, nevertheless, because how a decision is made to dig or not to dig may shed light on the overall decision process.

---

12. From the official statistical sheets provided to me by the Clerk of the Court, it is not possible to tell exactly how many cases have been digged. However, of those case set for oral argument in OT 1980, eight were "dismissed or remanded without argument." The figure for OT 1979 was four.

Certain problems in a case, such as jurisdictional difficulties, may emerge only upon closer scrutiny than could be given in the cert. process.

> . . . But more often what happens is that its when a record is
> a lot less clear or something was conceded in oral argument
> that wasn't in the briefs, and it made the case kind of
> silly. (C43)

Jurisprudential issues range from not having filed forms in a timely fashion, to having taken a case to resolve a constitutional principle only to realize that it cannot be reached; there is a problem of standing or mootness or a confounding issue which, when decided, disposes of the case. Sometimes a case is taken that winds up having such a messy fact situation or unclear record that the justices decide to dig it, even if there are technically no barriers to resolution. If hard cases make bad law, messy cases make worse. Therefore, if a case with any of these problems has been taken, then it makes jurisprudential sense to dig it. But as any Court observer knows, sometimes the justices go ahead and decide such cases. The concepts of mootness, ripeness, and standing are surely among the most poorly defined, imprecise, and easily ignored concepts in jurisprudence. One may know pornography when one sees it, but knowing ripeness requires far greater ratiocinative powers—indeed a skeptic might say clairvoyance. A case is ripe *ipse dixit;* that is, because the justices say it is ripe.[13] If the concept of ripeness is terribly vague, the concepts of mootness, standing, and lack of a properly presented federal question are not far behind. The point is that sometimes the Court will dig a case with jurisprudential problems and other times will go ahead and resolve it on some technical issue resulting in no real precedential or doctrinal benefit. And in still other instances, the Court will skip over jurisdictional problems quite cavalierly.

> *Clerk:* Sometimes cases are digged because they just shouldn't
> have been brought up, while on the other hand I wrote a
> case that was jurisdictionally wrong but was written nar-
> rowly enough so that I could get to the facts and just kind
> of avoid the jurisdictional issue.

13. As with frivolousness, there are certain cases most anyone would say are not ripe, but unlike frivolousness, the number of cases where there would be disagreement would be far greater.

> *Perry:* That is something that confuses me. Sometimes the
> Court will dig a case and other times they seem to go
> through this tortuous route to reach issues when obviously
> they are having jurisdictional problems.
> *Clerk:* Yes, but in this case I could write it narrowly enough
> where it really didn't make much difference; but jurisdic-
> tionally it was wrong. It's as if there is a mouse in a maze. I
> mean one will pick the easier route, but if both of them
> aren't pleasant, it is perhaps better to stay in the maze. So I
> think if the jurisdictional question were hard, and on the
> merits it was really bad, you didn't have much there, you
> would probably dig. But it you had a good argument on the
> merits and it was a good case to decide, and jurisdiction was
> bad, you would probably try to come up with a decision on
> the merits. (C40)

In asking others why some cases are digged and others carried to
decision, none of the responses were particularly enlightening or persuasive, although they were plausible. Most suggested the best way to
distinguish between those digged and those decided on narrow
grounds is by how messy the case is.

Jurisprudential issues aside, there are other potentially interesting
aspects of the ability to "ungrant" cert. as it relates to the agenda-
setting process. There are times that cases are digged for strategic
reasons. One clerk who was not disposed to seeing things strategically,
particularly his own justice's behavior on cert., said:

> I do remember one case where they really thought, four of
> them really thought, that they had the votes. Then it became
> clear after conference, or after argument, or sometime, that
> they were going to lose, and so they digged the case. (C43)

One justice also had a response that might be interpreted to allow for
the possibility of strategic behavior.

> *Perry:* Could you tell me how the decision comes about to dig
> a case?
> *Justice:* It usually occurs after argument, and we would usu-
> ally say, "how in the hell did we ever get this case?" I think
> it is a function of the depth of the study that we do on
> these cert. petitions.
> *Perry:* Is the decision to dig usually unanimous?

> *Justice:* The votes come in all shades. Some are unanimous. But the five who originally voted to deny would not be allowed to dig a case. It is usually done with six votes, unless it was granted by four and one of the four changes.

The justice's statement suggests several interesting things. Apparently it is not always obvious that a case should be digged since all digging decisions are not unanimous or nearly so. That there might be controversy over digging implies that cases might be digged for reasons other than *obvious* jurisprudential ones. However, if the ability to dig provided a real opportunity for a second chance to set the agenda, then the cert. vote might come to be seen as the penultimate decision in the agenda-setting process. Given the time constraints, or more precisely the way the justices have chosen to allocate their time, this would not be acceptable. Intriguing in theory, the ability to use digging as a strategic maneuver is, in reality, quite constrained. To use it strategically, except in a rare instance, would be easily and quickly observed, and it would completely undercut the finality of the cert. conference, which would impose significant costs on all.

The justice's comment also acknowledges how very cursory the review of cert. petitions is. Only in a few instances did any of the informants ever suggest that they were worried about how little review cert. petitions received. Glimpses of concern usually came when discussing something tangential such as digging. As one clerk noted:

> But if they are missing jurisdictional questions which are something relatively straightforward, then that may be a proxy for the idea that they are missing other things as well. (C26)

Few were willing to acknowledge, however, that the cert. process might allow an important case to be overlooked. Yet, as the opening quotation of this section suggests, clerks are worried about missing things in a case that might cause it to be digged. They acknowledge that this happens, but there is some tendency to rationalize, or lay the blame elsewhere.

> If you would look at the cases that were dismissed as improvidently granted, I'll bet all of them were worked on over the summer . . . You know we just can't check every issue at the cert. stage. For example, there was a petition that came in, and the respondent didn't raise any jurisdictional questions in opposition until the briefs came along. This was in *Webb v.*

Webb, and then it was digged. We have to rely on the lawyers. We don't have time to look at the lower court record and all of this stuff. (C9)

I think the problem is that some lawyers are not careful enough. They sometimes don't bring some of these things up until they get into oral argument. (C30)

One clerk, however, was willing to blame his fellow clerks:

> *Clerk:* . . . *The University of Texas v. Camenisch.* It was an affirmative action case dealing with the handicapped. It was a question of whether or not a person had to be provided state aid . . . The case was moot by the time they decided it. Certainly it was a waste of time . . . It was badly litigated below, and the opinion wound up as one on a civil procedure question . . . Justices usually count on their clerks to catch these things. No clerk ever really brought this issue up.
> *Perry:* Didn't the justices recognize this when they were voting for cert.?
> *Clerk:* They really count on their clerks to catch things like that. (C2)

The remarks of one informant suggested that digging might be an opportunity to bail out of a decision when it is realized that the justices cannot come together on an opinion.

> If they can't get their act together, for example, if the justice is writing an opinion and doesn't agree with anyone or none of them can agree, they might just say forget it. But most cases just wash out factually. (C36)

If digging were commonly used this way, it would be an especially interesting phenomenon to observe. Early in the interviews, I had thought that this might be the case, but later interviews revealed that this rarely happens. Digging is not seen as a way to avoid a split opinion. Either there is little concern about trying to achieve unanimity, or the initial agenda decision is seen as the appropriate time for such considerations. Over the last several years, the Court has received much criticism for its proliferation of concurring and dissenting opinions. Many have speculated why this is the case, but whatever the reason, digging offers a solution. When the justices are at loggerheads and see that an opinion is going to go eight ways, a norm might well be that jurisprudence would be better served by digging the case, which would require no explanation. Be that as it may, no such norm has developed. Frequent digging of cases would no doubt draw carping from legal scholars, but it would probably be no greater than the current criticism for having so many cases with multiple opinions, or the criticism for the increased use of per curiam opinions or summary dispositions.

Several suggested that some "bad" cases are decided rather than digged because of a feeling of sunk costs.

> I think sometimes that they have some perception of sunk cost, whether that is appropriate or not. There is some obligation to the attorney and to the public to decide cases. (C36)

> Sometimes they would dig, and other times would go ahead and decide. If the case is already here and argued, you might as well go ahead and correct it. (C01)

Contrast this with Congress. A committee may well allow certain things on its agenda, and yet doing so does not guarantee significant action or a commitment to resolution; indeed it may be put on the agenda as an attempt to stifle action. Setting aside the obvious incidences where things are put on an agenda just to relieve some constituent pressure and are not taken seriously by anyone in Congress, committees frequently will spend weeks or months on hearings about an issue, and then allow the issue to die. The reasons for this are well known, but the point is that another political institution that also has time constraints does not have a sense of sunk costs and has not developed the norm that once something is on the agenda, it is to be resolved.[14]

If the concept of sunk costs does explain the Court's reticence to dig, one wonders why this norm developed. One suspects that it has something to do with the fact that no matter how much justices proclaim they are not there to ensure justice, they are not really comfortable with that notion. When cases are not accepted, they are out of sight, and out of mind. But when a case is before them on the merits, they find it difficult to avoid ensuring that justice be done. This be-

14. See John W. Kingdon, *Agendas, Alternatives, and Public Policies* (Boston: Little, Brown, 1984). Kingdon notes that issues in many areas of government are frequently floated with no real hope of action.

havior is observed not only in cases with problems but, as seen in the next chapter, occurs other times as well.

The special situations discussed in this chapter deserve highlighting, but they must be put in perspective. As the title of the chapter suggests, they are *special* situations, and it would be wrong to try to understand the decision process absent an appreciation of their special nature. They are not aberrations, however, and are significant in and of themselves. Moreover, the fact that there is behavior that differs from the standard operating procedures, and knowing how the behavior differs, tells us something about the process generally.

Perry: So a petition from the solicitor general at least moves a petition from your frivolous pile to your non-frivolous pile?
Clerk: Yes. (C2)

I think any cert. petition that has an amicus is going to get more scrutiny. (C42)

But you know judges in the courts of appeals often try to get us to take a case, because in their opinion they would say very explicitly we are in conflict with the Seventh Circuit . . . You can be assured that grabbed our attention . . . but a lot of that was just artful on the part of the judges. (C3)

5 Indices and Signals

For all the description of discuss lists, cert. memos, markups, and so on, a rather major consideration has been touched upon yet not fully addressed. How does the Court process the huge workload involved in making certiorari decisions? In a sense, it brings us back to where we started, the handling and evaluation of cert. petitions, but we can now approach this process from a more sophisticated point of view.

In 1937, Attorney General Homer Cummings claimed that if a justice read all the paperwork filed in Court for a term, it would be like having to read *Gone with the Wind* every morning before breakfast.[1] Unlike Rhett Butler, however, those who have to sort through all the paper at the Supreme Court must "give a damn." And no dam is in sight to stop the flow of cases to the United States Supreme Court. The Court, not unlike other governmental bodies, is (one cannot resist) awash in a sea of paper. The amount of reading required for the relatively few cases that are granted each term is substantial; yet in sheer number of pages, it is minuscule compared to the workload presented by petitions for certiorari.

Review in the U.S. Supreme Court is sought for nearly five thousand cases a year. The median length of cert. petitions for non–Miscella-

---

1. U.S. Senate, Hearings before the Committee on the Judiciary, 75th Cong., 1st sess., on S. 1392, "A Bill to Reorganize the Judicial Branch of Government," March 10, 1937, p. 78; quoted in Doris Marie Provine, *Case Selection in the United States Supreme Court* (Chicago: University of Chicago Press, 1980), p. 25.

neous Docket cases is seventeen pages.[2] Court rules allow a maximum of thirty pages, but this limitation does not include materials in appendices that may number in the hundreds of pages. Material in an appendix, such as the opinion below, is frequently more important and is often examined more carefully than the actual petition.

Remarkably, the Court has not specialized. Each justice feels competent at and responsible for evaluating every cert. petition, though the evaluation will in large part be by his clerks rather than him. Nor is there specialization among the clerks. Common sense alone would tell us that there must be some shortcuts used to sift through this material. But we need not rely on common sense; we can examine the decision process. From the interviews we already know what some of the shortcuts are. For example, a clerk learns what her justice is not interested in, or a justice already knows what he believes about the exclusionary rule. It may take some time and effort to make a cert. decision on an issue once, but one need not go through the decision process every time the issue presents itself. This, of course, is not unlike the congresswoman who sees the same bill come up year after year. She need not approach the issue *de novo* every time she is confronted with it. In short, we can try to analyze the shortcut process more systematically. And because processing vast amounts of information in order to make a decision is not unique to the cert. process, there are opportunities for generalization, or at least opportunities to borrow from other decision literature. In attempting to do that, I will focus on a communication process known as signaling. The concept of signaling encompasses the idea of shortcuts, but it is more than simply that.

Cue Theory

Let us return to the initial problem—a sea of work that must be processed. Though the size of the caseload has grown substantially over the last decade, the workload issue is not a new one. Scholars for some time have noted the need for a decision procedure that reduces costs, most notably time, while conveying information so that intelligent decisions can be made. As far back as 1963, in a study examining the 1956–1958 terms, Joseph Tanenhaus and several colleagues wrote one of the earliest and most important articles by political scientists on

2. These figures are obtained from a sample of cert. petitions and jurisdictional statements for the 1976–1980 terms.

the Court's certiorari process. This study stood for some time as the major effort by political scientists to understand case selection. Even though its findings have subsequently been refuted, the basic argument, when recast, remains viable, and my notion of signaling grows out of Tanenhaus's insights. Tanenhaus argued: "We assume that certiorari petitions are so sizable and so numerous that justices saddled with many other heavy obligations (e.g., hearing argument, attending lengthy conferences, doing necessary research, and drafting and redrafting opinions) can give no more than cursory attention to a large share of the applications for certiorari."[3] Tanenhaus further assumed that a substantial portion of petitions for certiorari, "are so frivolous as to merit no serious attention at all."[4] He based this conclusion on previous statements by members of the Court, most notably Chief Justice Hughes. On the basis of those statements, he estimated that "40 to 60 percent of the appellate docket petitions have some merit, and therefore receive more or less careful attention."[5] Tanenhaus was aware that the Court created what was called a special list, or "deadlist."[6] Therefore, there was actually a two-step process—deciding cases worthy of discussion, and then deciding cases worthy of granting. These assumptions led Tanenhaus to offer what he called "Cue Theory."

> These . . . assumptions have led us to hypothesize that some method exists for separating the certiorari petitions requiring serious attention from those that are so frivolous as to be unworthy of careful study. We further hypothesized that a group of readily identifiable cues exists to serve this purpose. The presence of any one of these cues would warn a justice that a petition deserved scrutiny. If no cue were present, on the other hand, a justice could safely discard a petition without further expenditure of time and energy.[7]

In his study, Tanenhaus made no use of the certiorari documents themselves. He examined published records of the Supreme Court

---

3. Joseph Tanenhaus, Marvin Schick, Matthew Muraskin, and Daniel Rosen, "The Supreme Court's Certiorari Jurisdiction: Cue Theory," in Glendon Schubert, ed., *Judicial Decision Making* (New York: Free Press, 1963), p. 118.

4. Ibid.

5. Ibid., p. 121.

6. Recall that the modern-day counterpart is the discuss list.

7. Tanenhaus et al., "Cue Theory," p. 118.

and lower court reports for the presence of selected cues. Those cues were:

1. When the federal government seeks review.
2. When dissension has been indicated among the judges of the court immediately below, or between two or more courts and agencies in a given case.
3. When a civil liberties issue is present.
4. When an economic issue is present.

He found statistically significant results to support cues 1, 2, and 3, and he concluded that "we feel justified in considering the cue theory valid—at least until evidence is developed that casts doubt upon it".[8]

Cue Theory Reviled

The doubts have been cast. Cue theory has fallen on hard times. The papers of Justice Harold H. Burton, who sat on the Court for the 1945–1957 terms, were made public after his death in 1965. The justice kept copious notes of conference proceedings, including records of how each justice voted on petitions for certiorari. These voting records made possible more sophisticated statistical analysis. Sidney Ulmer tested the Tanenhaus theory with the Burton data.[9] His results confirmed the viability of federal government involvement as a cue, but they contradicted the other cues supported by Tanenhaus. Ulmer summarized his implications for Tanenhaus' theory as follows: "Does this development fatally undermine the provocative and imaginative theory which Tanenhaus and his associates suggested in 1963? Not necessarily. Since one of the cues—federal government as a petitioning party—has withstood all 'assaults' against it, cue theory per se may remain viable. A search for and the testing of additional cues now seems in order."[10] As a result of some of his tests, Ulmer noted in the last sentence of his article, "Further research is needed to explore this relationship and to delineate in more detail the two-stage decision 'theory' suggested here."[11] Ulmer's conclusion presages my argument.

8. Ibid., p. 130.
9. S. Sidney Ulmer, William Hintze, and Louise Kirklosky, "The Decision to Grant or Deny Certiorari: Further Consideration of Cue Theory," *Law and Society Review* (May 1972): 637–643.
10. Ibid., p. 642.
11. Ibid., pp. 642–643.

Stuart Teger and Douglas Kosinski also tested cue theory. Their first test was a more direct replication of Tanenhaus than was Ulmer's. They then proceeded to make Tanenhaus's issue cues more specific— for example, substituting race relations or search and seizure for the broad cue "civil liberties." They found strong support for the Tanenhaus cue of the federal government as petitioner, and they found some support when issue cues were made more specific. Yet they still chose to reject cue theory.

> Since the cues are, in fact, surrogates for the salient issues, they must be constantly updated. Cue theory ends up saying that the Justices tend to accept cases that they think are important. Seen in this light, cue theory is not much of a theory. The fact that Tanenhaus was able to predict fairly well what justices thought was important does not make the theory any more sound. There are no criteria for defining salience in advance of analysis (though the development of such criteria might be a topic for future research). . . Ultimately we want to predict which cases will be heard, but to do this we need much more information on the cases, the Justices, and the decision making process.[12]

An even harsher and more telling criticism of cue theory was yet to come. In her excellent book on case selection, Marie Provine devoted some time to Tanenhaus's theory because "it is cited in the literature on American politics more than any other research on case selection. The Tanenhaus research also differs from other efforts to outline review-influencing characteristics in what it undertakes to explain. This article describes factors associated with review in terms of a hypothesis about how the Court actually processes its caseload."[13] Provine's arguments, like Ulmer's, lend some support to the concept of communication by cues. She, too, used the Burton data and concluded:

> No easily identifiable case characteristics are invariably associated with special listing in the Burton period, however. This suggests that the justices do not rely on a set of cues to separate cases into those worthy of scrutiny and those to be discarded summarily. With the assistance law clerks provide in digesting cases and writing memos, there is little reason to

12. Stuart Teger and Douglas Kosinski, "The Cue Theory of Supreme Court Certiorari Jurisdiction: A Reconsideration," *Journal of Politics* 42 (August 1980): 845–846.
13. Provine, *Case Selection*, p. 77.

suppose Supreme Court justices in need of such an abbreviated preliminary screening procedure. The justices may reach a decision by engaging in a weighing process. The pattern of case selection voting in the Burton period suggests that a few case characteristics—including probably the Tanenhaus cues—may encourage the justices to vote for review, whereas others act like demerits, preventing review in the absence of strong reasons favoring review. The special-listed cases are those that contain one or more demerits and no countervailing considerations in favor of review.[14]

Empirical evidence seemed to demolish cue theory.

Cue Theory Reconsidered

On the basis of my research, I have concluded that some of the concepts in Tanenhaus are alive and well even though the empirical results of Ulmer, Teger, and Provine are devastating to his loftier claims for a cue theory of certiorari.[15] If cues are seen as a component of what I label "indices and signals," then we may save the underlying concept of his theory: that important information is conveyed in a shorthand manner. There are two basic problems with cue theory and one basic problem with its critics. First, cue theory does not "work" because there is a fundamental misperception of how the cert. decision process works. The processing of cert. petitions is complex, involving several decision makers and several points of decision. Tanenhaus seems to have assumed a much more simplistic process. The second problem is that cues, as defined by Tanenhaus and his critics, were expected to do too much; concomitantly, the problem with the critics is that they threw the baby out with the bathwater.

Let me address the latter problem first—an overly grand expectation of what a cue is and what it could do. Cues are treated as variables in a variance theory rather than facilitators of decisions in a process theory.[16] Presence or absence of a cue as a predictor of acceptance or rejection of a case is something we should not expect, given what we know about jurisprudence in the Supreme Court. We know that when

14. Ibid., p. 82.

15. Note, however, that Virginia Armstrong and Charles Johnson (in "Certiorari Decision Making by the Warren and Burger Courts: Is Cue Theory Time Bound? *Polity* 15, 1982: 141–150) do find empirical support for Tanenhaus's cues.

16. For a discussion of process theory and variance theory see Chapter 9.

the Court wishes to address an issue, that issue is usually presented in several cases, but the Court will pick only one case. So, for example, if one of our cues were the presence of some particular issue, say the exclusionary rule, given what we know about the Court, we should expect this cue to show up in many more denied cases than granted. The usual procedure is to grant one case and deny many cases that look very similar to the one selected.

As shall be discussed at greater length in Chapter 8, there is a strong predisposition to find reasons to deny any given case. The mere presence of an issue that disposes a justice favorably toward a grant is easily overwhelmed if there exists any reason to deny. Moreover, a case must pass a series of hurdles in order to be finally accepted. Chapter 9 outlines those hurdles. For now, suffice it to say that given the screening process by the clerks, and the series of hurdles a case must pass, most such cases will not only be denied, they will not make the discuss list either. Statistical significance will be very hard to achieve, not only for granting but even for making the discuss list. We should not conclude from statistical rejection that the presence of that issue did not convey important information that was somehow used in the decision process. Of course this is not to say that we would be unable to find certain things that correlate with case acceptance. For example, Ulmer has demonstrated a correlation between circuit conflict and review; but a correlation in this sense is different from a cue that would prevent a case from being seen as frivolous.[17] Underlying Tanenhaus's idea was the fact not that a case would ultimately be selected, although some critics held him to that standard, but that it would receive serious consideration in conference.[18] But even that is too much to expect. Making it onto the "discuss list" is sufficiently difficult so that the presence of a cue will probably do little to discriminate statistically.

If a cue were to be seen as something that conveyed important information but was not expected to be dispositive, then the concept would be more useful. Cue-giving and cue-seeking in the congressional context are often discussed along such lines. The concept is much more sophisticated in that literature, and it has been more productive.[19] The point is that in the cert. process, much information must

17. S. Sidney Ulmer, "The Supreme Court's Certiorari Decisions: Conflict as a Predictive Variable," *American Political Science Review* 78 (December 1984): 901–911.

18. Ulmer, however, alluded to this in the last sentence in "Further Consideration of Cue Theory" (quoted above).

19. See, e.g., John W. Kingdon, *Congressmen's Voting Decisions* (New York: Harper and Row, 1981); Donald R. Matthews and James A. Stimson, *Yeas and Nays: Normal Decision-*

be conveyed, and there exists a need to reduce time and effort in processing information, but there are many criteria that must be met in order for a case to receive serious consideration. Something like Tanenhaus's second cue, dissension on the court below, may well send a signal of the need for a closer look, but in the absence of other factors, the closer look will not last very long; that is, it will not be enough even to get the case placed on the discuss list for conference, let alone a grant. In this process, however, just getting a closer look is an important achievement.

Cues and predictive variables are not wholly unrelated. Probably the best external validation of a cue is correlation with a grant of cert. If a factor is strongly correlated with review, then the presence of that factor probably serves as a cue. Therefore, efforts to try to demonstrate factors that predict review should be applauded. Political scientists have demonstrated with varying degrees of success correlation between the presence of a characteristic and a grant of cert. It has been proven repeatedly that when the federal government seeks review, the chances are very good that the case will be taken.[20] Likewise, an association between conflict in the circuits and review has been both demonstrated empirically and reported by court observers.[21] Scholars have described the importance of amicus briefs at the cert. stage.[22] Some authors have shown the responsiveness of the Court to particular issues.[23] Still others have suggested that there is some macro life cycle to certain issues.[24]

---

making in the U.S. House of Representatives (New York: John Wiley, 1975); Cleo H. Cherryholmes and Michael J. Shapiro, *Representatives and Roll Calls* (Indianapolis: Bobbs-Merrill, 1969).

20. Tanenhaus et al., "Cue Theory"; Ulmer, Hintze and Kirklosky, "Further Consideration of Cue Theory"; Armstrong and Johnson, "Is Cue Theory Time Bound?" H. W. Perry, Jr., "Indices and Signals in the Certiorari Process," paper prepared for the Midwest Political Science Association Meeting, April 9–11, 1986.

21. Samuel Estreicher and John Sexton, *Redefining the Supreme Court's Role: A Theory of Managing the Federal Judicial Process* (New Haven: Yale University Press, 1986); Floyd Feeny, "Conflicts Involving Federal Law: A Review of Cases Presented to the Supreme Court," in Commission on Revisions of the Federal Court Appellate System, *Structure and Internal Procedures: Recommendations for Change* (Washington, D.C.: Government Printing Office, 1975); Perry, "Indices and Signals in the Certiorari Process"; S. Sidney Ulmer, "Conflict with Supreme Court Precedent and the Granting of Plenary Review," *Journal of Politics* 45 (1983): 474–477; Ulmer, Hintze, and Kirklosky, "Further Consideration of Cue Theory."

22. Gregory A. Caldeira and John R. Wright, "Organized Interests and Agenda Setting in the U.S. Supreme Court," *American Political Science Review* 82 (1988): 1109–1127; Perry, "Indices and Signals in the Certiorari Process."

23. Tanenhaus et al., "Cue Theory"; Provine, *Case Selection*; Susan Lawrence, *The Poor in Court* (Princeton: Princeton University Press, 1990).

24. Gregory A. Caldeira, "The United States Supreme Court and Criminal Cases,

Indeed, in this chapter, I shall examine a few posited cues to see if they are associated with review. But the important point is that just because something cannot statistically correlate with acceptance or with inclusion on the discuss list is not an argument against its use as a cue, or as I call it, an index or a signal.

The problem with cue theory, and much of the other literature on case selection, is that it is operates on faulty assumptions of how the decision process works. Take one example. Clearly, crucial players in this process are the law clerks. Previous studies either ignore them or see them in a role that greatly understates their importance. Chapter 3 should have put that notion to rest. Once again, saying that clerks are important is not saying that they are "powerful," or that the Court is really run by law clerks, or that clerks can hoodwink justices. The justices are very much in control. Nevertheless, one need only look at the decision process to see that clerks play a very important role in conveying information. Absent such an appreciation, any attempt at understanding case selection will be off the mark. Suffice it to say that there has developed an extraordinary system of communication with many players and many points of decision.

Signaling

The cert. petition starts a communications process. It is a process where one party is trying to send information, and another is trying to evaluate that information. For any given petition, the communication is one-way, although over time, or with repeat players, the communication may become two-way.[25] When we think of petitioning in these terms, it begins to sound like other communications processes. We of course want to be sensitive to factors that make this communication different, but this type of information exchange is not unique to the cert. process; therefore, we can make some generalizations. Indeed, a concept used to describe things as diverse as international relations and job hiring is useful in thinking about communication in the cert.

1935–1976: Alternative Models of Agenda Building," *British Journal of Political Science* 11 (1981): 449–470; William McLauchlan, "An Exploratory Analysis of the Supreme Court's Caseload from 1880 to 1976," *Judicature* 64 (1980): 32; Richard L. Pacelle, "The Supreme Court Agenda across Time: Dynamics and Determinants of Change" Ph.D. diss., Ohio State University, 1985).

25. For an exposition on repeat players, see Marc Galanter, "Why the 'Haves' Come Out Ahead: Speculations on the Limits of Legal Change," *Law and Society Review* 9 (1974): 95.

process. The notion is that information is transmitted in basically two forms—indices and signals.[26]

To my knowledge, the idea of indices and signals was first developed by Robert Jervis to explain the behavior of politicians in international relations.[27] The notion was refined and formalized by Michael Spence to examine market signaling.[28] Although Jervis's use of these terms is more complex and allows for subtler distinctions, Spence's simpler definitions are more useful for purposes here.

Spence states that market signals are, "activities or attributes of individuals in a market which, by design or accident, alter the beliefs of, or convey information to, other individuals in the market."[29] He suggests, for example, that in trying to entice the reader to read his book, the author has a signaling problem. Notice how similar his problem is to the advocate trying to get the Court to look closely at her petition.

> In short, the reader and I have a signaling problem. We are engaged in a signaling game with a reasonably complicated incentive structure. To read further is to invest in a commodity of uncertain quality . . . I may attempt to send signals to . . . create a favorable impression or, more precisely, to affect the consumer's subjective probabilistic beliefs about the quality of our products. We will do this even if the product has very little to recommend it.[30]

In a different situation—employment rather than reading a book—note the receiver's perspective:

> Although the employer (or, in another comparable context, the college admissions officer) does not know all that he would like to know at the time of making his decision, he is not totally in the dark, either. He confronts a plethora of potential signals in the form of observable attributes of the individual, ranging from personal appearance to education, employment

26. I am grateful to Evelyn Fink for introducing me to this concept. After patiently wading through much of my work, and giving me many helpful suggestions, she suggested I look at the work of Michael Spence.

27. Robert Jervis, *The Logic of Images in International Relations* (Princeton: Princeton University Press, 1970).

28. A. Michael Spence, *Market Signaling: Informational Transfer in Hiring and Related Screening Processes* (Cambridge: Harvard University Press, 1974).

29. Ibid., p. 1.

30. Ibid.

record (if any), other aspects of personal history, and race and sex. These signals will be interpreted by the employer in the light of his past experience in the market.[31]

It does not take a great deal of imagination to replace the above signals with ones in a petition for certiorari.

There are constraints, however, on the ability to manipulate the signals.

> The individual exercises some control over the image he projects to the prospective employer, and presumably he will manipulate this image to create favorable impressions. These strategic decisions may involve relatively small-scale activities, like buying and wearing a new suit, or more considerable decisions such as acquiring or extending one's education. Other aspects of the image one presents are, of course, beyond one's control. Race and sex are examples.[32]

The situation is analogous to that facing the petitioning attorney. There are certain things she can emphasize, ignore, or frame in a petition, but there are other factors of the case that may be of interest to the justices that are quite simply beyond her control. The latter are "indices," the former, "signals."

Stealing from Spence, I define these terms as follows:

1. A signal is a *manipulable* characteristic that affects a justice's assessment of certworthiness.
2. An index is a *nonmanipulable* characteristic that affects a justice's assessment of certworthiness.

Spence, Jervis, and I define these terms somewhat differently to make contextual sense, but the basic idea is the same.[33] I add to the Spence/

31. Ibid., p. 3.
32. Ibid.
33. Spence offers the following definitions (p. 10): "(1) A potential signal is an observable alterable characteristic. (2) A potential index is an observable unalterable characteristic. (3) An actual signal is a potential signal that affects an employer's conditional probability assessments of productivity. (4) An actual index is a potential index that affects an employer's conditional probability assessments of productivity."
Jervis provides these definitions (p. 18): "(1) Signals are statements or actions the meanings of that are established by tacit or explicit understandings among the actors. As all actors know, signals are issued mainly to influence the receiver's image of the sender. Both the sender and the perceiver realize that signals can be as easily issued by

Jervis concept, however, in one important way. Some signals (or indices) are universal to all chambers; others are particularistic to a certain justice or justices. Therefore, the taxonomy now is:

1. Universal Indices
2. Particularistic Indices
3. Universal Signals
4. Particularistic Signals

One final point about terminology. The verb "signaling" usually refers to the sending of both indices and signals.

By interviewing, one learns much about what justices and clerks use as indices and signals. In this chapter, I cannot begin to try to convey what all those are, but then that is not my purpose. What constitutes indices and signals are talked about throughout the book. Here, I shall simply give some examples from each of the categories to explain the concept.

It is not crucial that things fit neatly and unassailably into categories. That is, it is not so important whether or not all circuit conflicts are indices or signals. The point is that some things are manipulable and others not. Likewise, some factors affect the whole Court, and others, only certain justices. It is on these two premises that the usefulness of this whole concept depends, not the neatness with which things can be assigned to categories. It is helpful, however, to see if certain types of things usually or disproportionately fit into a category. At the least, it might generate better hypotheses to be tested empirically, but it should also raise the level of sophistication about how the cert. process works.

---

a deceiver as by an honest actor. The costs of issuing deceptive signals, if any, are deferred to the time when it is shown that the signals were misleading. Signals, then, can be thought of as promissory notes. They do not contain inherent credibility. They do not, in the absence of some sort of enforcement system, provide their own evidence that the actor will live up to them. Signals include diplomatic notes, military maneuvers, extending or breaking diplomatic relations, and choosing the shape of a negotiating table.

"(2) Indices are statements or actions that carry some inherent evidence that the image projected is correct because they are believed to be inextricably linked to the actor's capabilities or intentions. Behavior that constitutes an index is believed by the perceiver to tap dimensions and characteristics that will influence or predict an actor's later behavior and to be beyond the ability of the actor to control for the purpose of projecting a misleading image. Examples of indices include private messages the perceiver overhears or intercepts; patterns of behavior that disclose, unknown to the actor, important information (e.g., a pitcher's mannerism revealing what he will throw next); and major actions that involve high costs."

Universal Indices

Vote, Panel, and Author(s) of the Opinion(s) Below

One set of indices that all justices want their clerks to report is the vote on the decision below, who comprised the panel, and who wrote opinions. The interest is universal, and they are factors that cannot be manipulated by the petitioning attorney. These indices are ones that may or may not command heightened scrutiny of the petition, but they all convey information that all justices want to know in determining whether or not the petition bears further examination. For example, if a case had come from the D.C. Circuit at a time when the panel might have consisted of Robert Bork, Skelly Wright, and Ruth Bader Ginsburg, and the vote had been unanimous, that would have conveyed a great deal of information.[34] If those three could agree on an opinion, there is little reason to think that the Supreme Court would come out differently. There may be instances where the Court would review such a case, but it would be because something else was brought to its attention. Not all panels, of course, would convey as much information as this example, but the justices still want to know the membership of the panel, irrespective of the vote, and who authored the opinion. Justices have varying degrees of respect for circuit judges. Contrary to what I had expected, justices would rather take a case where the opinion below is from a well-respected judge, because they will start from a more informed point. They assume that Judge X, who is known for her thoroughness and careful treatment of the issues, will have written an opinion so that, if they take the case, there is less chance for surprises.

The vote on the case below is also important irrespective of who votes. When there is a dissent, all justices want to know that; and when there is a dissent, clerks and justices are much more likely to focus on the opinions below rather than the cert. petition.

Capital Cases

Another universal index would be a capital case. Recall that all justices want to know if a case involves capital punishment. It is a nonmanipulable characteristic of universal interest. Again, a justice will not automatically vote to hear any capital case, but he will give it heightened scrutiny.

---

34. These three judges were on the D.C. Circuit during the time most of my informants clerked.

Particularistic Indices
Subject Area

As noted earlier, certain justices have particular areas of concern, so that whenever a case arises in that area, they, or more precisely their clerks, look at it more closely. Some areas are universal—evidently certain First Amendment concerns are for the current Court—but most are particularistic. Take, for example, tax cases. The index may work either way. For one justice, tax cases are of particular interest, so he looks at them more closely. Another justice believes that the Supreme Court ought not to take tax cases. He (or his clerk) need only see that a petition involves a tax case, and he feels no need to read further. For other justices, seeing that a case is a tax case does not convey any particularly useful information that would call for heightened scrutiny or disdain. As an index, it is particular only to certain justices. Water rights is another example of a particularistic interest. Western justices always give them a closer look.

Particular Judge below in Dissent

This is a variation of the universal index. Interest in the makeup of the panel and the existence of a dissent is universal. When a *particular* judge is in dissent below, however, that may raise a flag for a particular justice and not for another. If cert. votes were known, one could possibly determine which judges in dissent served as indices for which justices.[35]

Particular Judge Authoring the Opinion

Authoring an opinion was not discussed as much as when a certain judge is in dissent, but it can serve as an index. As one clerk stated:

> There were certain judges in the courts below that were watched very carefully. There were certain judges who would take something and go way off; and when you saw that judge's name on an opinion, a red light would kind of go off to watch.

---

35. I have coded the individual judges below for all cases in my sample. I hope to analyze these data in the future.

Another clerk also made the point when describing his cert. memo:

> I might say Judge X wrote it and I know you particularly respect his opinion, or Judge Y wrote it and I know you think his opinions are particularly sloppy. (C21)

Counsel or Litigant

When certain clerks or justices see certain people or groups as litigants, they pay closer attention. Some are obvious. When the NAACP or the ACLU is a litigant, or if their counsel is representing someone, a justice might examine the petition more closely. A less obvious example, but one frequently mentioned in the interviews, is when the case involves a prison warden who has lost in the court below. Two justices take special note, and they instruct their clerks to bring these cases to their attention.

Sometimes who counsel is, irrespective of the cause, is important for the justices. Time and again, I was told that most state attorneys general are terrible litigators, and equally frequently I was told that there was one exception—Slade Gorton from Washington (later that state's U.S. senator)—who was highly respected by the justices. Other attorneys are known by the Court as being particularly good. When the Court has an opportunity to pick among cases to resolve an issue, the case with good counsel will usually be chosen. Unfortunately for the Court, however, the ability to choose a case based on the quality of counsel occurs only rarely. Though it would be possible to devise a coding scheme to approximate the quality of counsel, I have not done so.

Most counsel or litigants are a particularistic index because different ones would grab the attention of different justices. Having the United States as litigant (and thereby the SG as counsel in most instances) is in a different category for reasons explained below.

Universal Signals
Circuit Conflict?

Without a doubt, one of the most important things to all the justices is when there is a conflict in the circuits. All of them are disposed to resolve conflicts when they exist and want to know if a particular case poses a conflict. Of course this information is not news to attorneys familiar with the Supreme Court, so most attorneys will try to claim a conflict. Much of a clerk's time on cert. is spent trying to determine if there is indeed the conflict that the petition alleges. A conflict is a signal rather than an index, because presence of a conflict is usually manipulable. To be sure, there are instances where no one would disagree that a conflict exists; or at times even the most heroic effort by an attorney to claim a conflict would fool no one.[36] But often, conflict is in the eye of the beholder, and thus the petitioning attorney has some latitude in portraying the issue in such a way to suggest a conflict. Recall that the signal as manipulated may not ultimately be convincing, but to the extent that an attorney is successful, he will at least have his petition scrutinized very carefully by a law clerk, and quite possibly the case will get discussed in conference.

Better Case Likely?

As elaborated on in Chapter 8, one of the best ways to get a petition denied is to show that a better case is in the pipeline. A responding attorney clearly would want to so signal the Court. This is information that is important to all the justices. The petitioner, by contrast, would want to send signals showing why the present case is clearly *the* case to resolve the issue rather than one in the future. Convincing the justices that better cases are or are not in the pipeline is of universal interest but is also manipulable.

Action by the Solicitor General

One special player deserves special attention. Perhaps the best example of a characteristic to which all justices pay attention is when review is sought or encouraged by the solicitor general.[37] The SG determines which cases the government will appeal, and he represents the United States in the Supreme Court. Without exception, all informants—justices and clerks—said that they have a high regard for the SG when it comes to petitioning, and that any case he sends will receive serious consideration. His success rate for getting grants varies from about 75 to 90 percent. No other litigant or category of cases comes close to that figure.[38]

---

36. As discussed in the last section of this chapter, it is not important to have airtight categories—i.e., signal or index.

37. When I refer to the solicitor general, I usually mean the Office of the Solicitor General. I try to be explicit when I mean the solicitor general himself.

38. Susan Lawrence has done an excellent study of Legal Services and has found a remarkably high acceptance rate for petitions by legal service lawyers. See *The Poor in*

The role of the solicitor general is so important in the cert. process that it could justify a chapter on its own. I have forgone that temptation, but because of his unique role in the cert. process, an extended discussion of that office is included here. The explanation of why the SG is a signal rather than an index is deferred until the end of this section. What follows clearly demonstrates that as a cue, he is universal.

Most people in the United States probably had never heard of the solicitor general until the task of firing Watergate Special Prosecutor Archibald Cox fell to then Solicitor General Robert Bork. Yet this *eminence grise* is arguably the most important official in the Department of Justice. He is surely the most important person in the country, except the justices themselves, in determining which cases are heard in the Supreme Court.

The position of solicitor general was created at the same time as the Department of Justice, in 1870.[39] As stated in the U.S. Code: "The President shall appoint in the Department of Justice, by and with the advice and consent of the Senate, a Solicitor General, learned in the law, to assist the Attorney General in the performance of his duties."[40] The current language is virtually the same as the original language authorizing the position. From the very beginning, the primary responsibility of the solicitor general has been to handle governmental litigation, but historically he also had administrative and other responsibilities.[41] The attorney general, of course, heads the Justice Department, and the deputy attorney general and associate attorney general are under him (in that order). The solicitor general is technically fourth in command, but he is directly responsible to the attorney general.

The solicitor general today has four primary responsibilities.[42] First, he is the government's lawyer in the Supreme Court; that is, he rep-

Court: The Legal Services Program and Supreme Court Decision Making (Princeton: Princeton University Press, 1990).

39. The United States has had an attorney general since 1789, but it was not until 1870 that Congress established the Department of Justice. Prior to 1870, the attorney general had only a small staff, and he worked "in association with the United States Attorneys in the various states, but over whom he had little authority." The Department of Justice was established to save money by eliminating the cost of retaining private lawyers to litigate on behalf of the government (from remarks prepared for a speech by former Solicitor General Erwin N. Griswold).

40. 28 U.S.C.A., sec. 505.

41. In 1953, the position of deputy attorney general was created (28 U.S.C.A., sec. 504), which alleviated most of the solicitor general's administrative duties, and in 1977, the position of associate attorney general was created (28 U.S.C.A., sec. 504a).

42. Griswold speech.

resents the United States and its officers and agencies before the Court. This involves the duties of any lawyer before the Supreme Court such as preparing briefs and conducting oral arguments. Second, and most important for the purposes of this study, the SG decides which cases the government will appeal when it loses in any court—federal or state. When the appeal is sent to the U.S. Supreme Court, the decision clearly comes from the SG. Appeals at lower levels must be approved by the SG, but they receive somewhat less scrutiny by him and his staff. Third, he must give his authorization before the United States, or one of its offices or agencies, files a brief amicus curiae in any appellate court. Fourth, he must authorize any petition for an *en banc* rehearing in a United States Court of Appeals. These powers come to the solicitor general either by explicit statutory authorization or by delegation from the attorney general.[43]

When I began this study, I was aware that if the United States petitions for review in the Supreme Court, the likelihood of review being granted is far greater than for that of other petitioners. This is fairly common knowledge. I had no idea, however, that the Office of the Solicitor General plays as important a role as it does in the case selection process; nor was I aware of precisely how and why this is so.

The SG has determined that it is in his long-run interest to have his recommendation on cert. carry great weight. Working almost as a surrogate for the Court, rather than as an unrestrained advocate for the government, he has been able to assure that his judgment will usually be honored on cert. In Spence's terms, he is investing in

43. 28 U.S.C.A. Sec. 516: "Except as otherwise authorized by law, the conduct of litigation in which the United States, any agency, or officer thereof is a party, or is interested, and securing evidence therefor, is reserved to officers of the Department of Justice, under the direction of the Attorney General."

Sec. 517: "The Solicitor General, or any officer of the Department of Justice, may be sent by the Attorney General to any State or district in the United States to attend to the interests of the United States in a suit pending in a court of the United States."

Sec. 518: "(a) Except when the Attorney General in a particular case directs otherwise, the Attorney General and the Solicitor General shall conduct and argue suits and appeals in the Supreme Court and suits in the United States Claims Court or in the United States Court of Appeals for the Federal Circuit and in the Court of International Trade in which the United States is interested. (b) When the Attorney General considers it in the interests of the United States, he may personally conduct and argue any case in a court of the United States in which the United States is interested, or he may direct the Solicitor General or any officer of the Department of Justice to do so."

Sec. 519: "Except as otherwise authorized by law, the Attorney General shall supervise all litigation to which the United States, an agency, or officer thereof is a party, and shall direct all United States attorneys, assistant United States attorneys, and special attorneys under 543 of this title in the discharge of their respective duties."

signaling credibility. This raises normative questions, but there is little doubt that he has achieved his goal.

The SG screens cases very carefully. Except for those rare instances when political pressure comes from the White House, he virtually never sends up a case that would be considered frivolous. And he most certainly never tries intentionally to mislead the Court.

The following quotations are typical of most responses about the SG. I bombard the reader with quotations to demonstrate just how "universal" the phenomenon is. Quotations below come from every chamber.

> . . . but I also felt that the Court looked at the solicitor general as fulfilling part of their own screening function. They saw him as an officer of the Court doing some of the screening himself. I believe that they saw him as a bit of an extension of themselves in some ways. Let me put it this way, at least when the solicitor general submitted a brief, it passed some sort of threshold level and it got some type of serious attention. (C3)

> Generally, they are very selective, partly for the purpose of keeping up this high batting average. In fact, oftentimes a lot of government attorneys are angered because cases that they think are really important the solicitor general chooses not to petition. (C11)

> . . . he would not waste his capital on bringing up a poor case. He did a lot of prescreening. (C57)

> He in fact had screened for good cases and he was very careful not to squander his reputation with the Court by bringing bad cases. (C20)

> And in some senses he is going through his own cert. process. He has a very long tradition of not bringing up bad cases. (C28)

> But generally I, as a clerk, would think that if the SG was sitting there urging that a case be taken, I'd have to come up with some pretty good reasons not to take the case. (C25)

> The Court looks at the SG as more than just a litigant. They know he won't bamboozle them. (C6)

The SG's were generally very high quality and they were honest. I mean if they said something was in the record, it was in the record. (C53)

It is a flag. When the SG does something then it means more serious attention needs to be given to it . . . He understands a lot more about how the Court works and what it is supposed to do; and there is an internal screening process. He comes with more credibility. So that gets him past the first stage, but remember it is a two-stage process. I mean red flags come out and say it is worthy of more than three minutes' consideration. (C42)

All of the above quotations are from clerks. The justices, however, see the SG in much the same light.

He is a policeman himself. We assume that he screens out a lot of junk cases.

He does have a good batting average. This is because he culls things out. There is also a tradition of very fine work. He knows what the business of the Supreme Court should be. It is very rare that I don't read one of his cert. petitions. I don't read all of his, but it is very rare for me not to.

Every solicitor general who has been here my _____ years has taken this job very seriously; . . . not to get us to take things that don't require our attention relative to other things that do. They are very careful in their screening and they exercise veto over what can be brought to the board.

Although the screening function seemed to explain why the SG's petitions were treated so seriously, several of the informants also suggested that the lawyers were of extremely high quality. Another reason had to do with the fact that when the United States was involved in a case that it was petitioning, the issue was likely to be fairly important. The SG, however, also knew some of the tricks of signaling.

But the solicitor general also knows all the catchwords, and they just know how to write them in a brief; they know how to put things. (C11)

We jokingly referred to the SG's petition as the answer sheet. (C51)

Finally, a perspective from the sender, an attorney in the SG's office:

> The truth is that there is a real screening process. I'm on kind of a roll. I've recommended [to the SG] against cert. in eight straight cases. We're very careful here about what we recommend for cert. Maybe even more careful than we should be. I mean, I've never had a petition denied cert. . . . Now 100 percent of the cases we write on at least go to conference and they make the discuss list. (S6)

Tanenhaus, Ulmer, and Teger all confirmed statistically the importance of the presence of the United States government in case selection. It indeed acts as a cue in the strictest sense. Having interviewed the decision makers, however, we have a better understanding of how the communication works. Reading Tanenhaus, or at least how his critics read him, one might conclude that the propensity to review cases where the United States is a litigant suggests that the Court is somehow deferential to the government. Although this deference is a factor, my informants seemed to suggest that the high acceptance rate has much more to do with screening. Many cases that the government (or some portion of it) would like to petition are simply screened out by the SG.

Classifying the SG as a signal rather than an index, as other litigants are, is a bit problematic. The SG is a repeat player who clearly invests in signaling credibility. His decision to take a particular case is manipulable. Of course, as an amicus, he is naturally a signal. As petitioner, he chooses whether or not to press an issue, and frequently he has a choice of cases in which to take the issue before the Court. As respondent, he chooses either actively to oppose cert. with an opps. or not. In short, whenever, and how, he chooses to weigh in sends a signal.

Particularistic Signals
What Is at Issue?

The issue of law to be resolved is different from the subject area. How the issue of law is framed may make all the difference. In praising the solicitor general's petitions, one justice noted:

> They also boil down the questions on a million different issues to a central question that is easy to decide whether or not it is

an issue for the Supreme Court. And they may drop a footnote and say, "other questions were raised, but we're not raising this right now."

And from a clerk:

> One of the ways to tell a bad cert. petition is if it raises lots of
> questions. There are very few cases ever granted cert. in the
> Supreme Court, so it is very doubtful whether one case would
> raise several different types of questions.   (C2)

The preceding quotations allude to tactics, but underlying them is the
notion that what is at issue in a case is manipulable to some degree by
counsel. The best of attorneys may not be able to frame a very interesting issue out of most cases, but there are some cases where the
creativity of counsel clearly makes a difference. Recall that the "Questions Presented" section is one of the first things in a petition, and
Justice Brennan often makes a decision to deny based solely on this
section. Even if the case is not ultimately selected, a clever petition will
get closer scrutiny. In short, what is at issue is manipulable. As with
subject areas, the justices have different issues that command their
attention, but area is an index, and issue is a signal, because the latter
is manipulable, and the former is not.

Egregiousness

From time to time observers are befuddled as to why the Court will
take a particular case. For all the admonitions from the justices about
not being there to ensure justice and right every wrong, at times the
only explanation of why they take a case is that they are so offended
by the result. All the justices admitted that they do this, and the clerks
talked about it as well. The term used over and over was "egregious."
Different cases strike different justices as being egregious. Counsel
might be able to play to a justice's sense of moral outrage. Certain
"Supreme Court lawyers," or former clerks have an advantage. Only
a very close observer of the Court might have an inkling as to what
sort of case would strike a particular justice as egregious. Of course to
get a case granted, the attorney would have to appeal to four justices,
but at times, it seems to work. To do this, however, is somewhat risky
because it calls for a fairly detailed discussion of the merits in a cert.
petition, and justices frequently complain that cert. petitions contain
too much discussion of the merits. Nevertheless, portrayed in the right

way, a case might at least get a summary reversal on the basis of the petition.

Amicus Briefs

Filing an amicus brief at cert. is a sufficiently rare occurrence that it usually draws attention. The demonstration of interest outside the parties to the case may signal importance. As such, the filing of any amicus may be a universal signal. But as with the litigant index, particular justices may be interested in the presence of particular amici. Though there are some restrictions on when such briefs may be filed, they are relatively loose. Counsel may well want to stimulate amicus briefs at the cert. stage, as is frequently done at the merits stage.

Indices and Signals as Predictors of Review

Once again, factors that predict review probably serve as cues, but cues need not be correlated with review.

A random sample of cert. petitions were coded for this project. These data, of course, cannot "confirm" what I was told in the interviews—for example, that "vote below" is an index. Moreover, despite the presence of a signal in a petition, other information might encourage a justice *not* to accept a case, or wish not to have it appear on the discuss list. And, signals can be negative as well as positive. The signals discussed here, however, are ones that the informants suggested have the effect of conveying information such that the justice (or clerk) gives the petition a closer look, which increases its chances of appearing on the discuss list, which in turn, increases the chance of a grant. Originally I intended to try to predict acceptance, as is done in previous research. For the reasons I have suggested, such an enterprise would be very difficult, and in any event my primary goal is to explain rather than predict. Still, interesting suggestions come out of coded data even though little can be said in a conclusive way. The analysis I have done is only exploratory. The N's are sufficiently small so that about all that can be done is to eye percentages. Nevertheless, in the context of this chapter it might be interesting to see if the presence of an index or signal has relation to acceptance even though I would not expect much predictive capability.

Table 5.1 compares vote below with acceptance. As can be seen, cases that were unanimous below were accepted at the lowest rate. Cases that were unanimous in judgment, but where someone refused to join the opinion, had a slightly higher acceptance rate, and cases

Table 5.1   Effect of lower court agreement on grants

Court Below	Grant (%)	Deny (%)	Total (N)
Unanimous opinion	7.4	92.6	903
Unanimous judgment	12.8	87.1	101
Split	15.8	84.2	209

Table 5.2   Acceptance rates for various petitioners

Petitioner	Grant (%)	Deny (%)	Total (N)
U.S.	100.0	0.0	26
State (county, city)	12.4	87.6	226
Corporation (company)	14.3	85.7	231
Organized group	10.2	89.8	49
Individual (also individuals claiming class action)	2.9	97.1	657

where the opinion below had dissents were accepted at an even higher rate.[44] In coding petitions for litigants, it was necessary to collapse categories to: U.S.; State (or county or city); Corporation or Company; Organized Group (labor unions, Sierra Club, and so on); Individuals (including class actions). Table 5.2 shows the grant/deny rate when one of those categories is petitioner, and Table 5.3 shows when one is respondent. When petitioning, the U.S. and individuals are outliers. In my sample, the U.S. had its cases granted at the rate of 100 percent.[45] States, companies, and groups were accepted at much lower rates than the U.S., but at rates substantially higher than for individuals. Of course, this may be highly correlated with importance. Perhaps, for example, the issues that would involve the United States, or

44. Ulmer notes in "Conflict as a Predictive Variable" (p. 911): "In an earlier article I reported that the Court was sensitive to claims of conflict with Supreme Court precedent when such claims were made by dissenting judges below . . . It is possible that such a cue, as well as others, is used by clerks and justices in picking genuine intercircuit conflict cases for review. Further research on other possible cues would seem warranted."

45. In the population, cases petitioned by the U.S. are accepted at a rate of about 75–90 percent.

Table 5.3 Acceptance rates for various respondents

Respondent	Grant (%)	Deny (%)	Total (N)
U.S.	4.0	96.0	504
State (county, city)	7.7	92.3	286
Corporation (company)	8.3	91.7	120
Organized group	100.0	0.0	13
Individual (also individuals claiming class action)	17.3	82.7	266

Table 5.4 Effect of amicus on acceptance

	Grant (%)	Deny (%)	Total (N)
Amicus filed for petitioner	37.1	62.9	35
No amicus filed for petitioner	8.5	91.5	1,178

corporations to a lesser degree, are ones where it would be more likely to find issues of societal importance. Unfortunately my data cannot control for that.

When these litigants are respondents, a different pattern emerges. Not only does the government have signaling credibility as petitioner, but it is rarely brought to Court against its will. Organized groups, by contrast, suffer a remarkably different fate, though obviously the high rate is some artifact of my sample. The consequences for states and individuals is relatively nondescript.

One can see from Table 5.4 that an amicus brief filed on behalf of petitioner increases the acceptance rate from 8.5 to 37.1 percent.[46] In this instance the effect of the SG could be controlled. Table 5.5 shows that in those cases where an amicus is filed, the SG gets his cases accepted at a rate of 100 percent, obviously inflating the overall importance of an amicus, but when the amicus is someone other than the SG, it dramatically increases acceptance as well.

46. Since this was originally written, Caldeira and Wright have demonstrated empirically that the presence of an amicus increases the likelihood of cert.; Caldeira and Wright, "Organized Interests and Agenda Setting in the U.S. Supreme Court," pp. 1109–1127.

Table 5.5 Success rate of SG compared to other amici

	Grant (%)	Deny (%)	Total (N)
Amicus filed for petitioner by SG	100.0	0.0	5
Amicus filed for petitioner by others	26.7	73.3	30

Cert. decisions at the Court are usually the sum of nine individual decisions, but some things about the justices' decision processes are very similar, and other things differ greatly. Confusion exists about the cert. process because observers have either treated the justices as too much alike or as too idiosyncratic. Some concerns are universal. Others are particularistic.

I borrowed the idea of communication through indices and signals from a different context, and yet it seems applicable to the cert. process. Legal scholars often see the Court as so unique that they fail to draw upon other social science. This is particularly true when the focus is something as esoteric as cert. decisions. Yet portions of the cert. process resemble other decision processes and are generalizable. Building intellectual bridges is always useful if one is careful to note when comparisons become inappropriate.

For example, let us return to Spence. His analysis deals with people who are on the market only once, or sufficiently infrequently, so that they do not invest in establishing signaling credibility. The employer, knowing that, will rightly discount the signals rather heavily.[47] The situation is analogous to the typical cert. petition. Frequently the attorney (or litigant) is someone who will never again have a case before the Supreme Court. Therefore, advocacy may border on the disingenuous.[48] The solicitor general, however, is a repeat player.[49] Spence posits: "General Electric and I expect to be in our respective markets for some time to come, and hence there may be some merit in considering the long-run benefits of investing now in our future abilities to

47. Spence, *Market Signaling*, pp. 1–2.

48. There is some constraint, however. Unlike the person seeking a job, the petitioner for a grant is really after a penultimate goal. If he gets his case accepted, he still must argue that case, and to have overly distorted signals could ultimately be counterproductive at the merits stage.

49. See Galanter, "Why the 'Haves' Come Out Ahead," p. 95, for the classic formulation of the role of repeat players in the litigation process. The notion of iterative games is also prominent in game theory literature. See Robert Axelrod, *Evolution of Cooperation* (New York: Basic Books, 1984).

communicate via the establishment of our signaling credibility. To do so would not be to act without precedent. Ski resorts have long engaged in reporting ski conditions to the public."[50]

Spence has been able to formalize and generalize the concept of indices and signals when discussing hiring. There is no reason, in principle, that that cannot be done for case selection, although it would be difficult. I must leave that task for another day, or to someone more competent in modeling than I. Even so, the concept of indices and signals is a good heuristic device because it captures the decision *process* better than the concept of "cues" or what we learn from variance models. It highlights the complexity of the communications that transpire and, at the same time, renders them analyzable.

The communications are even infinitely more complex than can be discussed here. For example, when the litigant is petitioning the Court he is faced with an index—the vote below. However, if the communication we are concerned with is between judge and justice, then the decision by a judge below to dissent is a signal. There is signaling going on between judges and justices, clerks and justices, and among the justices themselves. Much of the discussion in this chapter has been about the communication process between the litigant and the justices, but there is other communication going on. Lower court judges are also sending signals to the Supreme Court. Many of the D.C. Circuit judges whom I interviewed said that often they do not think about the Supreme Court when they are writing their opinions; at other times they definitely do. Several told me that they would often write a dissent to attract the attention of a particular justice. Some judges attempt to "certproof" a case by writing a very complicated opinion that blurs the issues. Indeed, the cert. process as seen through the eyes of the circuit judges is quite interesting. I was amazed at how little they knew about the cert. process, but telling that story must await another forum. In any event, the indices and signals between the circuit courts and the Supreme Court are identifiable and analyzable as they are between the litigants and the Court.

Good theory should help explain as well as predict, and I believe the notion of communication through indices and signals does that.

50. Spence, *Market Signaling*, p. 2.

What's in a name? That which we call a rose
By any other name would smell as sweet.

Shakespeare, Romeo and Juliet

We don't negotiate, we accommodate.

U.S. Supreme Court Justice

6 Bargaining, Negotiation, and Accommodation

Do justices of the U.S. Supreme Court bargain and act strategically to achieve certain ends? Of course they do. Less easily answered, but more interesting, are the what, when, and how questions: What does one mean by "bargaining" (or "negotiation") and "strategy?" When and how do justices bargain and act strategically? These questions are dealt with throughout the book, but this chapter and the next are devoted to them specifically. They examine interchamber and intrachamber processes, respectively. In addition to answering these questions, we should try to understand the answers theoretically. Before tackling either the interrogatives or the theory, however, the discussion needs to be placed in the context of prevailing assumptions.

Context

Political scientists probably consider an effort to answer the question that opened this chapter—mine, not Juliet's—as tilting with a straw man. But to add a cliché to a mixed metaphor, some rumors die hard. Legal realism has been around since the 1920s, yet the public and the legal profession still have a somewhat idealized and distorted notion of the role of law and the Supreme Court.[1] Ideally, so the notion goes,

---

1. The classic work advancing the concept of legal realism is Jerome Frank, *Law and the Modern Mind* (New York: Brentano's, 1930). See also Karl Llewellyn, *The Bramble Bush* (New York: Oceana Publications, 1951).

the law should be found deductively, by brilliant dispassionate jurists. Truth and justice should emerge from an analytical process in which bargaining and strategy hold no sway. The public, of course, believes not that this is the way it *does* happen, but only that this is the way it *should*.[2] Those more familiar with the law and courts, and here I mean primarily lawyers and judges, are not so naive. Legal realism has taught them that the law is not "found." Still, their *ideal* Supreme Court justice looks much the same as the public's. Reality may force admission that the ideal is unattainable, either because justices are not of the intellectual caliber to persuade others by their brilliance and the sheer force of their arguments, or because they are forced to act in more basely political ways given the shenanigans of other justices. Nevertheless, when one wants to be complimentary about a justice, even among the cognoscenti, the perceived way to be so is to make him sound more like the ideal; and anything that hints of other behavior is said apologetically or defensively.

It is difficult for the political scientist to imagine how many alarms go off in heads, particularly of former clerks, when one starts talking about bargaining or strategy by justices. Words such as "political," "bargaining," and "strategy" need not connote smoke-filled back rooms and shady deals. Politics, after all, only means that values are being authoritatively allocated.[3] Acting strategically can mean many different things; it need not carry a taint nor contradict notions of fairness and justice. Nevertheless, the words were not welcome. Interestingly, I found the justices to be far less sensitive on this subject than their clerks. Even when couched in tepid or more qualified terms, there is still reluctance to admit something at variance with a textbook model of jurisprudence. Of course, those in the legal community are not the only ones enamored with textbook notions—just ask a congressman what the proper role of a representative should be. Yet when congressmen, scholars, or voters argue about whether or not a legislator should be a trustee or an instructed delegate, both sides can claim the high ground. The normative high ground for a justice seems to be only on the side of the nonbargaining, rational, dispassionate, Weberian jurist. That does not mean he has no ideology or philosophy. But bringing others to his conclusion is supposed to be achieved solely by

2. For an overview of literature on public opinion and courts, see Gregory A. Caldeira, "Courts and Public Opinion," in John B. Gates and Charles A. Johnson, eds., *The American Courts: A Critical Assessment* (Washington, D.C.: Congressional Quarterly Press, 1991).

3. The reference, of course, is to David Easton's famous definition of politics as the authoritative allocation of values.

the force of reason, which should render his conclusion inescapable. Again, most observers of the Court realize that this is a naive assumption, but as an ideal, it is firmly entrenched.

One book launched a broadside at the myth. Regardless of what one thinks of it, the publication of *The Brethren* was not inconsequential. It requires discussion here for a couple of reasons. First, it had methodological implications for my research. Second, much of what my informants said and much of what I argue are contrary to many of its descriptions; and, for good or ill, the book affects many people's perceptions about the operation of the Court.

Any political scientist who read *The Brethren* surely came away with the notion that there was nothing really new here except some juicy gossip. Most of what Woodward and Armstrong "revealed" about how the Court operates had been said by Walter Murphy some fifteen years before in *Elements of Judicial Strategy*, or by other political scientists, historians, and lawyers.[4] Prior to *The Brethren*, students of the Court knew that justices are not angels; that justices sometimes use indelicate language; that there is no love lost between some of them; that at times justices act strategically; that notions of the dispassionate jurist are a myth; and, that as with any political institution, its members behave politically. My biggest criticism of the book is not that it "unveils" these things, or even that some of the incidents it describes may not have happened, but that it takes them out of context, out of perspective. After reading the book, one gets a sense that behavior at the Court differs little from that in Congress, or the Chicago city government for that matter. The chambers sound like cloakrooms. In short, *The Brethren* creates a misleading notion of how the Supreme Court operates.

My informants were no more favorable toward the book. Many of the justices have either publicly or privately criticized it.[5] One clerk's evaluation was typical of the comments I heard:

> . . . You know one of the things that is so wrong with *The Brethren* is that they assume that there is much more discus-

4. Walter F. Murphy, *Elements of Judicial Strategy* (Chicago: University of Chicago Press, 1964). David M. O'Brien, *Storm Center: The Supreme Court in American Politics*, 2d ed. (New York: W. W. Norton, 1990). See also Alexander M. Bickel, *The Unpublished Opinions of Mr. Justice Brandeis* (Cambridge: Belknap Press of Harvard University Press, 1957).

5. One clerk told me: "Justice _____ had us all read *The Brethren* very closely because he wanted to make sure that we knew what some of the potential problems could be. I think it had something to do with the problems of confidentiality. He said he didn't want to have to read it but he wanted us to read it closely" (C62).

sion that goes on among chambers. To read that you would think that people are constantly running down the hall talking to one another. Actually, justices don't think that much about what the other justices are doing. They spend little time with them and they rarely see each other. They often come in and sit by themselves day after day without really talking to any of the other justices. (C2)

Even those informants most critical or cynical about the Court felt that the book was way off the mark. One clerk who might otherwise agree with some of the book's harsh evaluations said:

Although part of what I must admit about the Court is that some justices are really not up to it, . . . *The Brethren* seemed to have a bizarre tone to it; it had people running around changing their minds. (C11)

Compare Walter Murphy's *Elements of Judicial Strategy.* Not only does Murphy have well-reasoned, persuasive, theoretically grounded arguments, but he has wonderful anecdotes about the attempts of a justice like Frankfurter to convince or cajole his colleagues. Murphy illustrates the *potential* for strategic behavior, but he maintains perspective by making important qualifications and by showing the constraints on justices. Murphy clearly lives up to Pritchett's admonition that political scientists must remember it is "still jurisprudence."[6] *Elements of Judicial Strategy,* in my opinion, is one of the most important books written on the U.S. Supreme Court, and I suspect it is among the top sellers for political science courses, but I doubt that many in the general public have read it. Such is the fate of the academic writer.[7] Yet I never cease to be amazed at the number of law professors who also are unfamiliar with Murphy's work.[8]

Murphy demonstrates opportunities for justices to bargain or be strategic. In other words, much of his book is on how justices might act if they so chose, though the book is replete with examples of actual behavior. My book focuses more on their choice. The argument does not contradict Murphy, but it does leave a different impression. Walter Murphy and many other political scientists have demonstrated to us

6. See Chapter 1.

7. Maybe that is why he wrote *The Vicar of Christ* (New York: Ballantine Books, 1980), which also does its fair share of educating.

8. See the discussion in Chapter 1 noting the general lack of familiarity with political science literature.

unequivocally that the classical jurisprudential understanding of behavior on the Court was incomplete. As a result of their efforts, we
do not even blink at the suggestion that the Court is a political institution and that judges exhibit political behavior. Indeed we expect
them to. Now, it is those times that justices act in ways that are different
from others involved in similar political tasks that the social scientist
should find interesting and remarkable.

Should this contextual discussion seem overwrought, there is a reason for it. In much of this work, I am arguing that the Court acts
much less strategically than we political scientists might expect. The
overwhelming impression I received from my research is that there is
little bargaining and strategy on the Court with regard to the cert.
process. There is some, however, and it is more than most of the
clerks, and perhaps some of the justices, acknowledge. Still, it is only
minimal when compared to the potential for its use as demonstrated
by Murphy, and there is certainly less than described in *The Brethren*.
There is also probably less bargaining and strategy at the opinion
writing stage than we commonly imagine, although there is clearly
more than at cert.[9] If I am correct, it poses some problems for some
of the underpinnings of our empirical work, much of which presumes
highly strategic behavior. Lest lawyers take heart that a political scientist has finally seen the light, I suspect that many of my evaluations
and conclusions will not sit well with them either. Political behavior is
occurring more frequently and in ways different from those lawyers
usually take into account when trying to understand the Court. I often
saw political behavior in the very situations my informants thought
they were describing as apolitical.

Bargaining

Perry: You have said that often you would send around
          many drafts of an opinion to negotiate—
Justice: [Interrupting and smiling, with sarcasm in his voice]
          We don't negotiate, we accommodate. And this is a perfectly
          appropriate and good procedure because this is a court of
          nine people and it is our responsibility to have an opinion
          of the Court—a unanimous opinion if possible when the

9. I did not systematically examine opinion-writing behavior during my interviews,
but naturally I heard many interesting things about it.

>   Court can come up with one. And so it is good to have this
>   accommodation, and attempts to accommodate.
> *Perry:*   I understand, and I am wondering if anything like
>   that goes on to facilitate accommodation when making deci-
>   sions on cert.?

The justice's response to this question is given later, but he saw very
little. Discussion with a second justice went as follows:

> *Perry:*   When you are writing an opinion, you send around
>   drafts and another justice says, drop this section or drop
>   that section—
> *Justice:*   [Interrupting] Clearly, and that's something we ought
>   to do. In fact in _____ v. _____,[10] which I wrote, I was
>   checking once and I noticed that there were over twenty
>   circulations, and for many cases there are a half dozen or
>   more circulations. Sometimes when I am looking at [the
>   case] I am utterly amazed at how many I did. But with cert.,
>   that never happens.

The question, of course, is why. If justices believe that it is construc-
tive and appropriate at the opinion writing stage to try to persuade,
to discuss, to bargain (or accommodate) on dropping a line from an
opinion, then conceivably an attempt to persuade at the cert. stage
might also be helpful and appropriate. Moreover, when working with
a group of nine people, sometimes the best strategy would be to try
to persuade one or two colleagues in private. We know that when
justices draft an opinion, they do not always send copies of all drafts
to all justices. There are certainly times when they communicate one-
on-one. In fact, I had just gone into one justice's chambers when a
phone call from another justice was put through to him. He said:

> _____, thank you for making the changes, and I would be
> delighted to join now. You have done a real nice job with this
> one.

---

10. This was a truly landmark case. I regret that I cannot reveal the case without
identifying the justice, but I am somewhat surprised that there were twenty circulations.
I am sure that this is a case where there was a strong desire to have a unanimous
opinion, but given the dissents that were eventually published, it is difficult for me to
imagine that there was ever any hope that unanimity could be achieved.

Surely the accommodation going on between these two justices is appropriate, indeed desirable—"an open covenant openly arrived at."[11] Why, then, should not a justice try to call and convince another justice to vote a particular way on cert.? Why would it not be wise and perfectly appropriate for a justice to make the following hypothetical phone call:

> Sandra, there is a case coming up this Friday, *Montague v. Capulet,* which I think raises the issue that concerned you in your dissent in *Lear.* Although it wasn't obvious to me at first, I believe *Montague* is a particularly good case to allow us to get to your concern without bringing in the complications we faced in *Lear.* I am sure in this case that Byron would join us on the merits. But I am worried that it may be difficult to get four on this one for cert., because Harry and John don't want the evidence issue raised again, which could come up in this case. But if we can get this case reviewed, I think we can meet your concerns without raising the problems that bother Thurgood, and frankly, I think Harry and John are wrong.

There seems to me to be nothing improper here. In principle it does not seem to differ from trying to persuade another justice for a vote on the merits, or for the inclusion or exclusion of a phrase in an opinion. The fact of the matter is, however, that such a discussion rarely transpires. And for some reason, many of my informants recoiled, or at least cringed, at the suggestion that it might. A few thought it would be a good idea but said it just did not happen. Others, while steadfastly maintaining that no bargaining or maneuvering goes on, would proceed to describe situations that by any other name would still smell like bargaining. It would not, however, resemble the above hypothetical scenario.

One question asked of every informant was whether or not there was any bargaining, or phone calling, or attempts to persuade other justices on cert. I soon learned that this question had to be phrased very carefully. It became necessary to reassure most of the informants that "admitting" the justices act politically at times is not admitting any

11. Witnessing this telephone conversation reminded me of the statement by Senator Alben W. Barkley after an explicit deal had been made on the floor of the U.S. Senate: "The colloquy just had confirms and justifies the Woodrow Wilsonian doctrine of open covenants openly arrived at (Laughter)." *Congressional Record* (Daily Edition), February 16, 1956, pp. 2300–2301, as quoted in Donald R. Matthews, *U.S. Senators and Their World* (New York: Vintage Books, 1960), p. 100.

impropriety. I, of course, would not say this per se. I tried to do it by the way I phrased the question. After my first interview with a justice, who happened to be the one quoted above about "accommodation," I usually prefaced the question by saying something like:

> We are aware from historical papers and common knowledge that justices bargain and negotiate over certain passages in opinions, trying to persuade one another. Perhaps they agree to drop a phrase to try to bring a justice on board; or they may call or talk to one another to persuade on a certain issue. And we of course have all those wonderful anecdotes about Frankfurter and his attempts at persuasion. In my interview with a justice, he smiled and said, "we don't negotiate, we accommodate." So we know that accommodation and strategy take place at the opinion writing stage. I want to ask if anything like this goes on at cert.

Over the next several pages, one can see how many of the informants answered this question, and what they said about interchamber bargaining and negotiating generally. First I report what the justices have to say about their own behavior; then what the clerks have to say about the justices; and finally, what clerks say about their fellow clerks.

Justices on Justices

Perry: Are there any calls chamber to chamber, or discussion between chambers on cert.?

Justice: Well, not with me. It does not occur, to my knowledge, prior to conference. Never have I had anyone call me or suggest how I ought to vote.

Perry: What about after a case has been relisted? Is that somewhat of an invitation to another justice saying "convince me?"

Justice: No, I try to convince myself. Now there are times that there may be written memos and further thoughts. There are second looks. That may be on three or four cases per conference. But the arguments are there in the papers so I don't really think it would make much difference.

One can see that this justice seems to think that his time is better spent studying "the papers" (the actual documents, not memos from another justice) rather than engaging in collegial discussion. Witness what he said in another context.

> Chief Justice Warren was credited a lot for having a unanimous Court in *Brown*. The cost was having "all deliberate speed" come in. I think it would have been better to have the dissent spelled out . . . have the dissenters tell their problems, and then have a strong opinion to answer the dissent rather than coming down with a weak opinion so that everyone would sign. I think it is better to acknowledge what argument there is on a controversial issue like that.

I found this statement quite surprising. I had always assumed, and I think the literature does, that the desire for unanimity among the justices is stronger than this justice implies. He, however, is probably an outlier in this regard.

The other justices seemed to suggest that some interchamber communication takes place, but they emphasized that it was rare.[12] Incidentally, it was not because they were giving textbook descriptions— one only need look at what they told me about other strategies to see that they were willing to acknowledge their political nature. But for reasons elaborated by the clerks, reported below, the justices rarely bargain or try to persuade on cert.

A second justice gave what appears to be a very different response from the first.

> *Perry:* Is there ever any talking between justices before you go in [to conference] to plan strategy?
> *Justice:* That depends on the justice and the case, but that does go on sometime, yes.

This response is somewhat out of context, however, because he suggests later in the interview that such occurrences are rare. The perspective of another justice:

12. Several justices have disclosed that little interchamber communication exists and Justice Powell, in particular, has referred to the Court as nine separate law firms. In a speech to the American Bar Association in the summer of 1976 (quoted in Richard L. Williams, "Supreme Court of the United States," *Smithsonian*, February 1977, p. 89), Powell said: "I had thought of the Court as a collegial body in which the most characteristic activities would be consultation and cooperative deliberation, aided by a strong supporting staff. I was in for more than a little surprise . . . The Court is perhaps one of the last citadels of jealously preserved individualism . . . Indeed, a Justice may go through an entire term without being once in the chambers of all the eight other members of the Court."

Justice: At the opinion writing stage we don't have enough of
that in my opinion. We are writing too much; too many
concurrences and too many dissents. I am as great a violator
as anyone. At the cert. stage, the talking is even less, but I
don't want to say none . . . There really isn't much inter-
course among chambers about picking up a fourth vote.
Now there is a good deal of institutional discussion [in con-
ference] over which case to choose to resolve an issue, and
many times we don't agree about that.

Perry: Some have suggested that circulating dissents from denials facilitates a discussion process between chambers.

Justice: Writing does this somewhat, but you don't have the
types of visits that one associates with Felix Frankfurter or
Justice Stone.

A third justice offered some explanation of why interchamber discussion is rare.

Maybe if we had time to circulate something, you might get
better decisions on cert., but there is really not the time. We've
got to hear oral arguments, write opinions, and do all these
other things. If you go back to [earlier] times where they
spent all Saturday in conference and sometimes Monday or
Tuesday . . . we just wouldn't have time for that. Now there
are plenty of strategic considerations, but I think those are
really made in the individual chambers.

Notice three things: the concern with time and concomitantly the idea
that the proper way to communicate among justices is through writing.
These are flagged here because they are discussed later at some length.
Also note the separation of "inter-" from "intra-" chamber strategy.
The justice went on to say:

I suppose that for people who debate this in the abstract, they
might be more interested in the dynamics. Lawyers break
things down into such minute little parts that we may not see
the importance of the dynamics as well as a political scientist.

The justice was making one of two points: either, that political scientists
can navel gaze and can suggest that interchamber negotiation might
be profitable, while the day-to-day reality justices face precludes them
from the luxury of engaging in such tactics; or, as lawyers, his brethren
are not looking at the bigger picture as perhaps they should.

Clerks on Justices

A litany of responses by clerks to my initial question on bargaining
and strategy follows. I point out that this was an initial question; often
when I probed on specifics in a different context, I would hear things
that to me sounded like negotiation or strategy—the informant all the
while maintaining that the cert. process was devoid of such activity.

The first quotation is obviously from someone who is not naive
politically and has some basis for a comparative evaluation.

> Now if you're talking about bargaining in the Machiavellian
> sense, I saw it occur in other branches of government, for
> example when I worked in [the executive branch]. It was
> really amazingly absent from the Court, and I didn't under-
> stand quite how free the Court was of it until I did work in
> other areas of government. There is an integrity about the
> process almost beyond belief. Now that is not to say that there
> are not people with strong views and they might try to lure in
> a compatriot by a certain analysis . . . But, that's how the
> Court probably should work. There was never to my knowl-
> edge a deal such as I'll trade a vote on Case A for a vote on
> Case B. That goes on in the Congress and the White House
> all the time. It is routine there. You don't support something,
> or you threaten not to support something. It doesn't happen
> that way in the Court. For someone who is standing looking at
> it, I would think that they would be amazed. It's incredible
> how it doesn't go on. I think cases are each decided on their
> merits. Justices vote on Case A and they vote on Case B.
> When I went to [the executive branch] people would disbe-
> lieve me when I would say that. They insisted that political
> processes work differently. But that just doesn't happen in the
> cert. process. (C19)

They may not believe it in the executive branch, and political scientists
might be skeptical, but most clerks gave initial answers along the same
lines. Two clerks from different chambers offer another comparative
perspective:

> I saw a lot more bargaining and stuff going on when I was on
> the Circuit Court than on the Supreme Court. (C14)

> Very little of that went on in the Supreme Court compared to
> the ____th Circuit where I clerked. The justices didn't do

enough of it in my opinion . . . I can only remember one or two times where anyone ever even went down to another chamber. (C45)

One clerk described the situation as only a young lawyer could: "I'm not really aware of any *ex parte* contacts" (C49). Another clerk, who would not object to such contacts, said:

I think there is nothing wrong with that. I think informal communication should occur. But they seem to make up their minds on cert. independently . . . There is a real press of cases, so this kind of discussion tends not to happen even if it would be helpful. (C63)

One clerk suggested that his justice, though a collegial person, made his decisions absent collegial discussion.

He had a lot of contact and was friendly with the justices, some to a greater extent than others, but he really wasn't willing to accommodate very much, and a lot of his separate opinions really hinge on some rather minor distinctions. I would be surprised if the justice never called on an issue, but I don't think there was much of that that went on. He wrote on the memo "deny," "grant," or "question mark." I don't really ever remember him changing his vote after conference. At some time he may have said, "Justice _____ had a persuasive speech," and he might have changed a vote, but I don't really remember it. (C52)

One clerk indicated that there was some interchamber phone calling between justices, but it did not seem to be frequent or to be an attempt at persuasion.

There was some phone calling. Someone would call Justice _____ and ask if he had seen a certain case and what do you think; that is, is there really an issue here, should we do something? Or when they had lunch together, he might come back and say Justice _____ wants me to take a look at this. (C53)

The remaining responses to the general bargaining question are grouped under common reasons that emerged to explain the lack of bargaining. An evaluation of these reasons follows.

TIME

The prominent explanation for such little preconference contact had to do with time.

> One might well expect that of a group and I don't think that it would be inappropriate; it would make sense. But the truth of it is there is so little time that I think most of what goes on, goes on in conference. (C21)

> There really isn't that much time, but I wouldn't be surprised if they communicated some, maybe at lunch. But there is not real politics. (C28)

> Time pressures militate against using the cert. process [to bargain]. (C58)

> I rarely saw that . . . Before conference, there was very little. For one reason, justices got ready at different times for going into conference . . . but basically there's not the time and there is really not that much of an opportunity. (C8)

NOTHING TO NEGOTIATE

Several felt that on cert., unlike an opinion, there is nothing really to negotiate. They presume that negotiation would never involve more than one case at a time.[13]

> There is no real way to bargain on cert. as there is with opinions, because the cert. vote is up or down, so there is no real room to bargain. (C11)

Two informants qualified this notion, but their comments deal with discussion in conference, not between chambers before conference.

> There's not really much to bargain with. Your options are pretty limited. It's basically to grant or not. Not like the writing of an opinion. There were times there would be a series of cases which all raised the same issue and there was some discussion over which one of the cases they should take. So, there's that type of give-and-take. (C8)

13. This presumption is explored in greater detail later in this chapter.

There is nothing really to bargain with. Well, with the exception that two think the case should be granted and summarily reversed, and two others think that there should be argument on the merits. There may be some bargaining on that. (C6)

CASE FUNGIBILITY

A third frequently heard explanation for the lack of bargaining is that no individual case is seen as that important, so there is no need to waste time negotiating for a particular case. If the issue is important, it will come up again in another case, and the latter case may well have attributes that will cause recalcitrant justices to vote to grant. This sentiment that a given case is not particularly important was heard frequently in many different contexts. I have dubbed it the "fungibility of cases" and will return to it later.

Frankly, they don't care enough about any individual case to spend a lot of time politicking . . . Another case may come up with the issue. (C2)

I think one of the reasons you don't have more lobbying is that it just isn't that important to anybody. Almost any important issue will come up again. I would be very astonished if the justice would call and try to convince someone on a cert. (C31)

No, I don't think they see any one case as being that important. Oh, maybe Justice _____ or Justice _____ did, but I don't think [his justice] ever did. (C36)

There is no bargaining before the cert. process to my knowledge. They certainly didn't have any horse trading of votes. It is hard to imagine that. Largely because it is hard to imagine that an important issue they are interested in wouldn't come up again. There is really even very little interplay among the clerks on the cert. process. (C48)

It is very rare that taking one case would be particularly important . . . Cases are not that important in and of themselves, and if they did do any bargaining, it would have to be a pretty rare case. I once heard that Justice Harlan made a great plea to take *Cohen v. California.* (C46)

NORMS

Another set of responses seemed to suggest that preconference discussion was somehow "against the rules."

> *Clerk:* They do play by the rules. Look, judges have more business-like attitudes than one might think are possible with such great issues. I mean they treat it in a business way, they don't get all that emotionally involved in most of these . . . I want to emphasize that Justice E and Justice F and Justice G still think of themselves as lawyers deciding issues. They just don't spend much time in collegiate little discussion. They just vote. I think there is very little politicking before a conference.
>
> *Perry:* What about Justices H and J?
>
> *Clerk:* I think there was probably surprisingly little politicking there too. (C2)

> *Clerk:* I think when I was there, agenda setting went pretty much according to the rules. This is the way I think that the Court ought to be—following the rules. Maybe it was quite different on the Warren Court. (C55)

Of course, there are no such rules, yet many seem to believe there is an unwritten rule prohibiting bargaining and attempts at persuasion.

AVOIDANCE

Finally, several clerks suggested that some justices did not like to deal with other justices in face-to-face situations.

> In some ways, this working like nine separate law firms is one of the things I think is a problem with this Court. They don't talk to each other when a controversial issue comes up. It seems like you would want to get together and talk because new approaches would develop, but instead when controversy arises they seem to all go into their own different little worlds, and I think the reason for that is that there are no real politicians . . . They find it somewhat uncomfortable to talk to one another. (C63)

> I'd say there's little to none [interchamber discussion]. The only time there may be some of that is when occasionally Justice _____ put a case on the discuss list. There may be some at that stage, but the justices don't talk that much to each

other. It was a big event whenever anyone from the other chambers came by. And some almost never came by. They really worked by memo. In fact, there was not as much bargaining on an opinion as one might think. I think they have kind of a respect for each other's individual egos, and they don't enjoy treading on it too much. (C51)

They have to live with each other too long and at too close quarters to go about lobbying. (C34)

The Supreme Court is really not a very collegial body in a lot of ways. I can only remember Justice _____ talking to about half the other justices when they weren't in conference. (C26)

Phone calls exist to some extent, although they're very worried about talking to each other too much. In a sense it's really difficult to live with each other. They've got to be congenial and be with each other for a long time, and they're facing very tough issues and it's kind of difficult to live with each other in some ways. And so rather than confront each other face to face, they often put it in writing . . . It's like being in a fraternity or a sorority, or any group. You get to the point that when they leave their socks out it really starts driving you crazy. You've got to learn to live with it. They feel very strongly about the organization. In an organizational sense, by writing and not doing this type of stuff it gives rules to abide by, and if you bend the rules too much and go around discussing things ad hoc, you'll have real problems with an organization. (C27)

Tempting as it is, I shall resist cheap metaphorical comparisons between the Court and fraternities. I will suggest that the last informant has a rather simplified understanding of organizational dynamics. But if his view is widely shared, then that may be all that is important.

The vast majority of responses showed little or no interchamber communication prior to conference. This assessment was not universal, however, so I report some of the contradictions. The exceptions were heard rarely, and they even more rarely dealt with cert. considerations. Moreover, they usually did not imply that the justices tried one-on-one persuasion, but simply indicated that some justices were more gregarious than others. The most dramatic description to counter the picture I have painted was from a clerk about his own justice.

> Sometimes you would look out and see Justice A in the hall,
> and he'd have one arm around the shoulder of Justice B and
> his other hand holding his elbow. You may have heard other
> people refer to him as a . . . ward boss. He acted that way
> sometimes. He was probably effective in a lot of
> instances. (C59)

This was the only clerk who even came close to suggesting such overt
political behavior between justices, and therefore I am skeptical of his
interpretation of the behavior he observed. Even so, all this clerk is
suggesting is that the justice tried to persuade people outside conference. Undoubtedly some justices may think more politically than others, and some may have a personal style that is more like a politician.
Some people are just more outgoing than others.

Most observers would assume that if "politicking" did go on, its
instigation would most probably come from the ideological wings of
the Court. Some justices do tend to be more strategic than others, as
I shall discuss in the next chapter, but when it comes to attempts at
persuasion, the more ideological justices did not sound much different
from the "judges' judges."

Of the few clerks who did see some justice as a wheeler dealer, it
was usually never their own. One clerk's musings were amusing:

> Justice _____ did very little of that; though we often won-
> dered if justices in the middle bloc plotted and tried to decide
> where people were going to come out and were planning cert.
> decisions with a sense of the strategy. (C21)

And of course, there were some contradictory assessments.

> Justice A of course was all over the court lobbying as were his
> clerks and to a large extent so were B and C and their clerks.
> Justice D [his justice] really didn't do that much. I never really
> remember him going around lobbying to grant a case. I never
> really remember us going around lobbying to grant a case. Of
> course when you write a pool memo you have some stake in it
> hoping that the Court will accept your recommendation. (C24)

> To my knowledge, Justice A never lobbied for a particular
> cert. decision with other justices. I'm not so sure that that was
> the case with all of the justices. What he did do is, sometimes
> he'd write something and circulate it but there was little of
> this telephoning and little Machiavellian maneuvering from

Justice A. *The Brethren* was very misleading, all this talking and discussion going back and forth. It just really didn't happen that way. (C9)

Justice C didn't really form alliances. I suspect A and B did, and E and some of the others. I suspect they talk a lot because sometimes it's a lot of trouble to have to write something, but Justice C was a fast writer and wrote a lot. When I had to draft an opinion, he always gave me something to write from, and as you know he writes a lot of separate opinions. He writes very fast. (C41)

But most clerks saw none of the justices as bargaining types, especially not their own. The following quotation is typical of responses I received about every justice.

Justice _____ . . . never really played politics. I don't think he knew how; he wasn't particularly good at counting noses and this type of thing.

No doubt from time to time one justice will try to persuade another on some issue outside conference. And, of course, such behavior is entirely appropriate. But most attempts at persuading and strategy take some form other than a one-on-one lobbying effort.

Clerks on Clerks

Though most informants agreed that there was little discussion among justices on cert., there was a wider range of opinion over the extent to which clerks engaged in interchamber conversations. Indeed, the preceding set of quotations demonstrate an inexorable tendency to imagine palace intrigue. Some of what follows has already been said in the previous chapters, but it bears additional examination in the present context. Clerks vary as to how they see their role generally, and as one might expect, that affects their behavior at cert.

Clerk: There's a fair amount of talk at lunch, like "I read your cert. memo and I can't possibly believe you came out with that decision"; or "your boss really let us down on this one." But I don't ever remember anyone saying, "could you try and talk your boss into voting to grant cert. on that." There's just not a lot of time to focus on cert. petitions, even for the clerks. And you are just less likely to get

worked up about any particular case on cert. because there
are so many of them and there's so little time. (C25)

Clerk: I think there is a significant discrepancy among clerks
to the extent that they involved themselves in politics. There
was variance within Justice _____'s chambers and across
chambers . . . Some saw themselves as real involved in all
kinds of political machinations . . . Some of my own co-
clerks thought bargaining and trading were appropriate.
They were more fond of authority. But really they had
nothing to offer in exchange. Although you might have a
discussion, I don't think there was much sallying forth to try
and recruit [other clerks] although that was done more in
written opinions. (C40)

Clerk: Part of the job of clerks is to get a feel for what is
going on in the other chambers and have a feel for what
would be acceptable as a bare minimum in any chamber,
and that helps you to know how you are going to have to
write and deal with them. (C60)

Perry: If the justices didn't talk and plan strategy, did the
clerks?
Clerk: There was an exchange of ideas among the clerks on
cert., but it often had to do with technical problems—trying
to get another opinion on it and talking about the difficulty
of the question and whether it was important for the Court
to take it now, etc., as well as somewhat of an exchange of
ideas on the merits. But, clearly the exchanges among the
clerks were more frequent once the case was being decided
on the merits. (C23)

Clerk: There is a great deal of discussion among the clerks,
although it is often informal—on the basketball court or in
the cafeteria. But most of it is in defense of what the boss
has already decided.
Perry: That sounds like after a decision on cert., but do you
get much of this before?
Clerk: There just isn't the time to do it. Although at times
some clerk will come down and ask someone else's opinion
on a particular case. (C5)

Clerk: Sure I talked to other clerks. I can remember one case in particular . . . but I still didn't get a grant. (C37)

Clerk: . . . the clerks talk about cert. petitions over lunch. (C7)

Clerk: Now among clerks [bargaining] probably did go on somewhat. Certainly some would get excited and try to point out some aspect of a case and urge other clerks to perhaps lobby their justices, but I doubt that much of this type of discussion went on among justices. (C26)

Clerk: There is always talk among clerks, but even then there was fragmentation because not all clerks within a chamber feel the same way. (C58)

One informant gave an explanation for the much greater activity on the part of the clerks in contrast to the justices.

Among the clerks there is a lot of hysteria in the cert. process, but this pans out because the justices are much more experienced. It is difficult to be a clerk at first because you see a lot of courts and judges in the nation screwing up terribly and the horrible injustice that is occurring, and it takes awhile to learn that the Supreme Court is not there to right all wrongs in cases. It is not infrequent for clerks to talk and get phone calls, "did you see that cert. petition?" and "how do you think your justice will vote on this? Will he vote to grant cert.?" That type of stuff. (C11)

The next several quotations suggest that some of this clerk activity is at the behest of a justice, although these responses deal with behavior generally and not just with cert. The first two quotations were from an interview where both informants were present (the only such interview).

There are three ways you can talk about strategies: among the justices, a justice through his clerk, and clerks freelancing on their own. I saw some using of a clerk by a justice, somewhat more among the justices themselves, and I saw it among the clerks a lot. (C33)

I did not sense that it went on a lot among the justices. I never was used by [his justice] because I just didn't work that way. I didn't do that with Judge _____ on the Court of Appeals. I do know, however, that Justice _____ did do that with some clerks at times. (C32)

Along these same lines, a clerk from another chamber said:

Clerk: Some of the justices would use their clerks as emissaries.

Perry: Do you mean to try to convince other clerks to try to convince their justice?

Clerk: Well, less that, although they did that, but also to find out what other people were thinking.

Perry: What about [your justice]?

Clerk: Justice _____ was not inclined to use his clerks. He is a very direct person and usually to find out what he wanted to know, he would do it himself. (C56)

Finally, from a clerk from yet another chamber:

Clerk: Some clerks do talk. Occasionally a justice will speak through a clerk.

Perry: Do you mean to try to convince another justice to vote on cert.?

Clerk: No, usually minor issues, for example wording on an opinion or something. Sometimes it is known that the clerk is speaking on the authority and in behalf of his justice.

Perry: Why do they do that?

Clerk: I think to kind of save face and not confront one another. (C27)

The preceding torrent of quotations about the behavior of clerks must be kept in perspective. While clerks seem to talk among themselves more about cert. than do the justices, there still is relatively little discussion, particularly when compared to discussion on the merits. Of course, clerks have some different incentives given that they are on the Court for only one year, but by and large, the clerks face the same constraints that the justices do.[14]

14. Nelson Polsby pointed out to me that the incentives are quite different because every clerk wants to write his or her *Carolene Products* footnote, and they only have one year to do it. I think he is right, however the ambition tends to manifest itself at the

Evaluation

Many commentators, from law professors to some of the justices themselves, have suggested that there is not enough discussion among the justices; but that is usually said in reference to opinion writing. If it is true there, it is even truer at the agenda-setting stage. What little discussion goes on goes on in conference, and as seen in Chapter 3, that is very little indeed. Outside conference, attempts at persuasion are rare. I feel confident of that. I am less confident as to why. Now I do not want to overstate the case. Obviously there are times when two or three justices will have a conversation about a case, be it over lunch or by telephone, but it certainly does not appear to be the standard operating procedure; and among some justices, it virtually never occurs. I suspect that most all of the reasons mentioned by the informants are indeed partial factors in explaining the lack of interchamber communication. But the reasons given do not compel such behavior and are neither inherent in nor unique to this institution. Nevertheless, let us examine those reasons in more detail.

Time pressure probably is a major factor, but the justices, if they so chose, could allocate their time differently. They might well decide that extra time spent on cert. would be time saved in other ways. Or even if it did not save time, they still might choose to place a higher priority on cert. considerations. This may or may not be a wise use of time, but it is incorrect to assert, as most of my informants did, that it is something beyond the justices' control.

The notion that cases are fungible is also probably a factor. Justices do believe that important issues will come up again, but for reasons described in the next chapter, cases are not quite as fungible as suggested in this context.

If the justices perceive that attempting to persuade one another orally rather than in writing is inappropriate, that it is "against the rules" and would somehow impair the functioning of the institution, then it makes some sense that they would engage in such behavior infrequently. It is a strange notion, though. Justices obviously do not feel constrained from engaging in bitter confrontation in written opin-

---

opinion-writing stage. Most of the clerks disliked the cert. process and preferred to spend their time talking about decisions on the merits—both at the Court and with me. They considered opinion writing to be much more interesting and important than the cert. process. This is ironic because their role in cert. is arguably their most influential role, precisely because cert. *is* seen as less important. I suspect it is rare for a clerk to alter significantly a justice's thinking on an issue that is being given plenary consideration, whereas a creative cert. memo just might.

ions, which might also hurt the institution. But for some reason, fighting in writing is considered acceptable behavior whereas face-to-face confrontation is not. Certainly, it is often easier to confront someone in writing than in person. Yet consider the United States Senate. That institution is known for its norms to ensure collegiality, and yet the *modus operandi* there is face-to-face attempts at persuasion.[15] Granted, senators do not have life tenure, but the Senate is an organization where the most powerful senators have careers as long as many justices, and they have extraordinary institutional loyalty. On the other hand, Bauer, Pool, and Dexter tell us that lobbyists rarely confront their opponents in attempts to persuade them.[16] They, too, avoid the opposition and prefer indirect persuasion. It seems to me, however, that justices would be more like senators than lobbyists. Reluctance to engage one another verbally seems even stranger given that justices are lawyers. One would think that if there were any group that could take heated discussions in a way that would be understood not to be personal, it would be they. However, one justice made a comment to me that suggests that when there is a topic of concern, talking it over is not how things get resolved. The comment was made with regard to a speech Justice Stevens had made recently at New York University, where he discussed the rule of four.[17]

> [Another justice], I think, was hurt by that speech. Nothing has been said around the table about it at all.

This is an isolated example, but one gets the feeling that this Court is not a particularly open, collegial body. Of course, bringing up thorny issues with any group of colleagues is never a bed of roses; indeed, it is not always wise. But if a norm of noncommunication exists, then even when it might be helpful to try to hammer out a problem, people are not in practice and are unlikely to attempt it. Vocally contentious bodies, be they Congress or a college department, work out norms to sustain the institution even though there are sometimes rather nasty

15. I do not mean to suggest open, personal confrontation on the floor. Indeed, that rarely occurs. My point is that informal, private attempts at persuasion are used. See Ralph Huitt, "Democratic Party Leadership in the Senate," *American Political Science Review* 55 (1961): 331–344, and Matthews, *U.S. Senators and Their World*.

16. Raymond A. Bauer, Ithiel De Sola Pool, and Louis Anthony Dexter, *American Business and Public Policy* (Chicago: Aldine, 1974).

17. John Paul Stevens, "The Life Span of a Judge-Made Rule," James Madison Lecture, New York University School of Law, October 27, 1982.

personal confrontations and rebuffs. The Court has done this, but the norm need not have been one of personal avoidance.

Rose Is a Rose Is a Rose?

According to the picture painted thus far, the cert. process is relatively atomistic with decisions being made within chambers and the outcome on cert. being primarily the sum of nine individual decision processes. As a general description, that is correct. But there are subtleties, and there are exceptions. The concept of bargaining can be broken down and examined more precisely. Bargaining can take several forms and by any other name still be bargaining. The premise of "no bargaining" is now reconsidered with an eye toward more subtle distinctions.

Horse Trading

The most straightforward form of bargaining is, "I'll give you a vote here, if you'll give me one there." It is interesting how frequently one hears the same terminology from informants. The expression of the hour was "horse trading"—a term I never used. Many of the quotations already cited have indicated that horse trading did not occur. It is an important point to elaborate though. Not a single informant mentioned anything resembling horse trading, and many said explicitly that it never occurred. This is really rather remarkable given that the Court is a political institution where democratic procedures, such as voting, are used.[18] But witness their remarks, some of which presage later arguments:

> There really wasn't any bargaining in the cert. process. There certainly isn't any horse trading—I'll keep this off if you'll keep that off. (C28)

> I'm not aware of people ever trading votes. I'll vote for this if you'll vote for that. Now there was an attempt to take it up next week if someone thought they may be able to convince

18. It is not a case of informants simply giving the party line. As discussed in Chapter 3, the interviewer learns ways around that; and some of my informants—both clerks and justices—were quite willing to tell me stories, or give their opinions, or say some very uncomplimentary things that would prove embarrassing to certain justices or the Court. Even the most cynical, however, denied any vote trading.

someone to vote to grant. . . But I was unaware of the justices ever trading. I cannot really imagine that happening. (C20)

From a clerk who had quoted Laswell to me earlier:

> I can say that I never saw any vote trading per se, either at the opinion stage or at the cert. stage, but there definitely are situations where a justice is at the crossroads. There is never any logrolling or vote trading, but there may be a tendency to vote with your brethren if you think you're at a crossroads and don't really know how you want to go on this issue. (C21)

Comments from others:

> There is none in the cert. process if you mean by that horse trading. (C34)

> I was never aware of out and out vote trading—we've got three votes on this one and you've got three on that one we'll trade one for one. But, I do recall instances where there were three votes for cert. and the decision was put off for a week, so I assumed that was done in hopes that a justice would be persuaded, and there may have been some attempt to try and persuade a justice. But it was certainly nothing like what went on with opinions. (C25)

There was one justice I had assumed to be most likely to bargain. But I heard the following statement about him, and something close to it from several of his clerks and from many others as well, including justices.

> I would be very surprised if bargaining occurred from one case to another. I know how offended Justice _____ was at the suggestion in *The Brethren* that [justices] would allow consideration of one case to affect another. Given the depth of his indignation, I really believe he just didn't allow that to happen. (C26)

Unlike answers on some issues, the responses of the justices and the clerks on trading votes are virtually indistinguishable. One justice put it bluntly:

I think one of the greatest disservices to this Court was done
by really a great friend of the Court, Anthony Lewis, when he
wrote his book on *Gideon*.[19] I think that's one of the best descriptions of what had gone on in this Court that I have ever
seen; however, when he suggested that someone swaps this
vote for that vote, why it was just wrong. We were speaking
together once and I gave him hell for it. I mean, the very
notion that cases are fungible is just untrue. We'd never do
something like that. It would just be horrible, and in the next
edition that portion was deleted. I hope that's something you
will tell in your work that that kind of swapping doesn't go
on.

Okay, I have told it in my work, but let us examine more closely
that *bête noire*—horse trading. Recall that my informants argued that
there is an inability to accommodate at cert. because, unlike an opinion,
the vote is up or down—there is nothing to negotiate. That is not true.
Accommodation could occur if the justices were willing to "horse-
trade." I begin by saying that I am convinced that *quid pro quo*'s do not
occur at cert. I am less persuaded that it would be such a bad thing if
they did. The reasoning for no vote trading on the merits is more
understandable. In resolving a case or controversy, no justice would
uphold what he considered to be an erroneous result in order to twist
the arm of another justice. That strikes too close to the heart of our
norm of "justice." Actually, one might argue that vote trading would
be proper on the merits in the Supreme Court given its function of
clarifying the law (though certainly not in a trial court), but there is
no need to debate that proposition here. However, a denial or grant
of cert. is something very different from a vote to affirm or reverse a
result. Justices state time and again that a denial of cert. says nothing
about the validity of a ruling below. Moreover, justices acknowledge
that they pass over many cases that they believe to be incorrectly
decided, because their primary function is not to ensure justice, but
to clarify and unify the law so that the entire judicial system can ensure
justice. Given that premise, if a justice believes that lack of action by
the Supreme Court is permitting injustice to be perpetuated in the
entire judicial system, and if all he has to do is agree to hear a case he
thinks is not important in order to get his case accepted, could it be
considered "wrong" for him not to do what he can to try to get his

19. Anthony Lewis, *Gideon's Trumpet* (New York: Vintage Books, 1966).

case granted? Why would the following hypothetical "horse trade" be so inappropriate?

> ———, I know you believe that there is a real problem over this issue in the tax code and that we are being irresponsible for not addressing it. Now you know I don't believe that tax questions belong in the U.S. Supreme Court. I don't think we handle them well, and given their complexity, they take up an inordinate amount of time. And I know you think that these water rights issues in the Western states are trivial and do not belong in the Supreme Court. But I happen to think that they are important and we are being irresponsible for not addressing them. I'll tell you what, I'll agree to take this @#%& tax case if you will agree to take the water rights case.

Granted, there is something to be said for being wary of the lawyer's version of Pandora's Box—the infamous slippery slope. Once one begins trading cert. votes at what seems to be a rather innocuous level, one might start down some lubricious scarp. But surely if anyone can deal with slippery slopes, it is justices of the U.S. Supreme Court.

I am not arguing here that the Court *should* horse-trade votes at cert. I am suggesting that contrary to what informants said, there *is* something to negotiate if one looks at more than one case; and wholesale reactions of horror and normative indignation to such a notion are probably unjustified.

Join Three

If horse trading does not occur, which we might think of as an explicit *quid pro quo,* perhaps there is a way to gain votes that is less direct. Recall the join three.[20] At first blush, this appears to be the consummate logrolling device. If three justices wish to take a case, it seems highly likely that a fourth justice, in a sense of collegiality, or strategy, would be willing to add his vote. Granted, that might not happen on the most contentious cases, but on others, why not go ahead and give a fourth vote? That is usually not the way it works, however. What join three generally means to a justice is simply that he does not feel very strongly one way or the other, but if three others do, he sees enough merit in the case to give it a fourth vote. It is not logrolling as we commonly think of it in legislatures. Not only is it not used to "buy

20. See Chapter 3.

a vote," but it is rarely used for achieving goodwill. According to my informants, there are many times a case will get three votes and not pick up a fourth. Of course, there would be a cost to doing this in terms of increasing workload, but this cost seems rarely to be weighed against the goodwill it might engender.

Again we see why understanding a decision *process* is important. If a justice is going to join three, that is a determination he has made *prior* to conference, and he has already marked "join three" on the petition. If he is a relatively senior justice, he will have cast his join three before hearing most of his colleagues' votes, so his vote cannot be a token of goodwill unless there is communication prior to conference. Any justice may change his vote after he hears discussion, but that is rare.[21] Now of course, oligopolists can price-fix without talking to one another because they know others' intentions. Political scientists refer to this in terms of anticipated reactions. Obviously that could occur with the join three, but from the interviews, that does not seem to be what it is all about. And in any event, if a justice wanted to do another justice a favor, he would just vote to grant. A join three is risky because, as described in Chapter 9, cases which receive only four votes with a join three are usually relisted.

I asked the justices about join three's.

> *Perry:*   I understand that there is something called joining three. I am not exactly sure what that means.
>
> *Justice:*   All of us use it. Some more than others. Justice _____ doesn't use it very much. He is a real black or white guy. He sees things very much one way or the other. But the way it is generally used is that it is a timid vote to grant. At times maybe there is doubt about something. What someone will say is, "if there are three to join, I'll vote to grant." It is kind of a hardy in-between vote. It is a practice I don't frown on. Sometimes you may have three or four join three's, so there aren't really three to join.
>
> *Perry:*   I've wondered about that. What happens?
>
> *Justice:*   Then it is denied. You have to have pretty much three solid votes. Generally, if a case makes it only with a join three, we will put it over because there is lukewarm interest.
>
> *Justice:*   I'll sometimes say that I join three. It is often on a case that I feel perhaps should be granted cert., but it's also

---

21. Recall the quotations from the justices in Chapter 3.

> a case where I almost feel like why waste the time. We have
> so many other important things to do. But if someone else
> feels more strongly about it, I sometimes will join three.

> *Justice:* All nine of us use the term. But I think we each have
> our own meaning. I can tell you what it means when I am
> using it. When I was voting ninth, a join three generally
> meant a grant. Obviously, when voting that late it was the
> same as a grant. When I use it, it generally means that it is
> something I would vote to grant, but that I wouldn't put it
> on the discuss list.

The last justice's response also tells us something about his attitude
about putting cases on the discuss list. It suggests that he would only
add cases that he felt should be granted, not ones that might be "iffy"
and perhaps worth some discussion. Again, he and other justices come
to the cert. conference with their minds fairly made up.

Although the first and third justices quoted above said that all nine
justices use the join three, one told me that he did not.

> *Perry:* When you were talking about the different things you
> might mark on the discuss list, for example, G, D, CFR,[22]
> one of the things you didn't mention . . .
> *Justice:* [Interrupting] Join three. That is something I never
> do. I've never done it. I don't criticize others for doing it
> . . . But I never do that because I feel more comfortable
> making my decision on my own appraisal. Some do it more
> than others. For some it is rare, and for some it is
> frequent.[23]

Once more, note the desire to have the cert. decision be the sum of
individual decisions rather than the result of a collective decision process. Were a justice trying to marshal cert. votes, a good strategy might
be to convince a colleague to "at least join three." But the fact that at
least two justices did not realize that the third justice never joins three
adds to the evidence that this vote is not used strategically. It also
affirms the notion of little interchamber communication.

One justice did see the join three mechanism in a more political way.
Again, not a *quid pro quo,* but at least he was more interested in a

22. Grant; Deny; Call for a Response. These abbreviations are common to all justices
and are what one would see written on the discuss list.
23. This was not the justice described earlier as rarely joining three.

collegial process than was the justice last quoted. The following is the
response I received after the justice said that they accommodate rather
than negotiate:

> *Perry:* . . . and I am wondering if anything like this goes on
> to facilitate accommodation when making decisions on cert.?
> *Justice:* Yes . . . and you may know this, if three justices feel
> strongly that cert. should be granted, sometimes I will give a
> fourth vote. I will say that if you all feel that strongly, I will
> vote with you on that.

Trying to determine whether or not the justices logroll with a join
three depends on what one means by the term. However one defines
"logrolling," the point to be made here is its relative absence. Even
this last justice is willing to let many cases die with three votes; it is
only on a few where feelings are particularly strong that he is willing
to accommodate. Contrast this with another collegial decision making
body, Congress. Comparing branches is always risky, but the join three
is not an example where we should necessarily expect different behavior from a congressman and a justice. No norm of "justice" comes
into play. Granting a case review is, if anything, more just. Yet, the
behavior of justices differs greatly from congressmen on the norm of
reciprocity. We believe that most members of Congress will use opportunities to do favors for their colleagues whenever they can be
done relatively costlessly; that is, by not having to sacrifice principle,
angering one's constituency, and so on. Indeed, congressmen sometimes do favors even when it is quite costly. Well documented in the
literature are the norms of reciprocity and going along with one's
fellow congressmen when not constrained to act otherwise.[24] A join
three situation seems to provide a justice with a perfect vehicle to do
the same thing. It encourages reciprocity, but it limits abuse because
there must be three solid votes to join. Yet rather than grabbing every
opportunity to do so, as we would usually expect in many collegial
decision-making bodies, the norm seems to be to resist. Of course
increasing the caseload is costly, but workload costs do not seem to
stop congressmen.

It is well to remind the reader that I am generalizing only about
one task of the Court—case selection. Nevertheless, my impression

---

24. See, e.g., John W. Kingdon, *Congressmen's Voting Decisions*, 2d ed. (New York:
Harper and Row, 1981); Matthews, *U.S. Senators and Their World*; Nelson W. Polsby,
"The Institutionalization in the U.S. House of Representatives," *American Political Science
Review* (March 1968).

based on numerous comments from the interviews, is that efforts at logrolling or accommodation are relatively absent from opinion writing as well. So, while there is no horse trading, and a device which could be used extensively for logrolling—the join three—is basically not used that way, does that mean that there is no interchamber maneuvering on cert.? No. Although my informants would not like the word "maneuvering," there is a behavior that is employed that is frequently persuasive in getting a grant when the conference is otherwise disposed to deny.

Dissents from Denial of Certiorari: Tools of Negotiation

The only sense of lobbying was if there was a circulated dissent from denial.

U. S. Supreme Court clerk

As described in Chapter 3, a few cases each conference are relisted. This is usually done to call for a response, but sometimes a justice will relist a case by saying, "I want to think about it more because I am considering writing." What he means is that he is thinking about writing a dissent from denial of certiorari. If a justice wishes to make his dissent public, he does one of two things. Either he notes a dissent, or he writes an opinion explaining why he dissents from denial. If a dissent is simply noted, the *Journal of Proceedings* usually says the following: "The petition for a writ of certiorari is denied. Justice White would grant certiorari." For an appeal: "The judgment is affirmed. Justice White would note probable jurisdiction and set the case for oral argument." Written dissents take various forms. Some are fairly brief, others quite long. Some concentrate on why the case is certworthy, and others actually go to the merits. With appeals, things are a bit different. An appeal, when disposed of summarily, is a ruling on the merits. Hence, written dissenting opinions on appeals often address the merits per se; however, even on an appeal, these written opinions are usually statements chastising the Court for summary disposition rather than for the ruling.

Dissents from denial are the one method of persuasion outside conference that is perceived to "follow the rules"; and there is reason to believe that they are used strategically. Threatening to dissent is often sufficient to achieve a grant. One phrase was uttered time and again: "Many dissents never see the light of day."

> *Perry:*   Even though you say that there is no vote trading, are there times when a justice tries to convince another justice to reconsider a cert. vote?

> *Justice:*   The way it happens is this. A case must be put on the
> discuss list first, and if it picks up one or two votes, the
> person who put it on the list may say, "let's please relist,"
> and then someone will write a dissent from denial. I have
> an unpublished stack of dissents from denials this high [he
> held his hands up showing a stack of about two feet] be-
> cause many dissents never see the light of day. But I don't
> recall any colleague, at least I don't think I remember,
> trying to get me to change my mind except by sending
> around a memo.

Another justice said, "Many times a dissent from denial will pick up a
fourth vote."

Justice Stevens has been quite vocal in opposing public dissents from
denial of certiorari. In a rare move, he wrote an opinion in response
to a dissent from denial. From the portion quoted here, it can be seen
that one of a dissent's purposes is to try to pick up votes.

> Admittedly these dissenting opinions may have some benefi-
> cial effects. Occasionally a written statement of reasons for
> granting certiorari is more persuasive than the Justice's oral
> contribution to the Conference. For that reason the written
> document sometimes persuades other Justices to change their
> votes, and a case is granted that would otherwise have been
> denied. That effect, however, merely justifies the writing and
> circulating of these memoranda within the Court; it does not
> explain why a dissent which has not accomplished its primary
> mission should be published.[25]

According to Justice Stevens, then, the *primary* mission of a dissent is
to pick up votes.

One clerk said the following about his justice and another regarding
dissents:

> *Clerk:*   [His justice] did them occasionally, but he didn't really
> do them unless he was prepared to publish them. Of
> course, Justice _____ was the big dissenter-from-denial man
> by a clear majority. He was really trying to pull votes.
> *Perry:*   Was he successful?

25. Singleton v. Commissioner of Internal Revenue, cert. denied, docket no. 78-78,
47 *Law Week* 3299.

Clerk: Oh, yeah.
Perry: Did he generally go in to the merits on these?
Clerk: Yes. This is also the time that you'd get personal comments about things, like a crime wave—ranting and raving
about crime and so forth. He may have done this in a stay
opinion. Perhaps that is what I'm thinking about. But one
time he wrote that we just ought to summarily reverse all
death cases.   (C57)

Another clerk had this to say about his justice:

He did do it. But generally his dissents were short and concise
and directed at one or two justices.   (C37)

The interesting thing about the last quotation is that the dissents were
aimed, clearly implying some strategy. Once again, one wonders why
not just phone the target justice rather than go to the trouble of writing
a dissent, particularly if time is so constrained.

One justice circulates many dissents, particularly when he perceives
a circuit split, and many of his efforts are apparently effective. Some
are not, of course, and many of his dissents that are published do in
fact deal with the need to resolve a circuit split. Use of dissents for
internal leverage is apparently not new.

Hugo Black used to write these awful dissents from denial. He
would say, "if you deny hearing this," and essentially say
something that suggested that no decent person who loved the
law could deny hearing this case. It was kind of rare, but
Black used them as a real bludgeon. I think today dissents are
used more subtly than by Black, but one gets the idea out on
the table. A dissent may or may not see the light of day.   (C60)

As a matter of principle, Brennan dissented, as Marshall does, from
denial on all capital cases using the same short statement.[26] On some
capital cases, however, they write substantially more than their
"canned" dissent. A Brennan clerk chose to classify the effort as one
of persuasion rather than a threat.

26. "Adhering to our views that the death penalty is in all circumstances cruel and
unusual punishment prohibited by the Eighth and Fourteenth Amendments, *Grigg v.
Georgia,* 428 U.S. 153, 227, 231 (1976), we would grant certiorari and vacate the death
sentences in these cases."

> *Clerk:*   Of course, we had our stock dissents from denials.
> They weren't exactly canned but you effectively knew what
> to say.
> *Perry:*   I know of the death penalty ones, but were there some
> others?
> *Clerk:*   There are some dreary little issues of _____. Brennan
> disagrees with the Court. I really didn't see threatening to
> write a dissent from denial used as a threat to try to get
> someone to go along. I think you generally wrote them to
> persuade, to record one's vote, or to pontificate.

Threat or persuasion, the intended outcome is the same.

Increased attention to a case brought about by a circulated dissent
apparently does not always yield a better decision.

> Prior to conference, there was a little communication. Occa-
> sionally I might talk to another clerk or someone might say
> that there's an interesting case that came in. But after confer-
> ence, if a case was held over there were certainly attempts at
> persuasion; maybe "persuasion" is the word, not "bargaining."
> The major vehicle for this was a dissent from denial; I mean,
> those were addressed to the Court as much as they are to the
> public. The justices get a little more vituperative if it's some-
> thing where they want to see people swayed . . . Sometimes
> because these dissents tend to be a little more impassioned the
> conference would get misled; I mean, a justice would say
> something was in there but he may not have spent a lot of
> time on it; or he really didn't know what was in the record.
> These dissents tended to be pretty powerful, and no one else
> would take a closer look and they'd wind up getting involved
> with a mess of a case.   (C57)

A justice agreed:

> Dissents from denial can be quite persuasive. In fact, some-
> times you have such advocacy that it rides roughshod over the
> facts. We would then speed over it, and grant the case and
> then have to dig it. In fact it seems to me that some [pause]
> well . . . [he refused to finish his thought].

Tactical use of dissents to pick up a vote must be put into perspective.
When asked how often circulated dissents picked up additional votes,
the numbers ranged from ten to thirty per term. Nevertheless, the

justices do use dissents as a negotiating tool within the Court. Indeed dissents from denial seem to be the primary arena for negotiation on cert. outside the conference. Surely, however, this is not a very efficient tool. The dissent might be considered a form of communication, but it is oration rather than discussion. As as one informant said:

> Maybe one or two will respond to a certain dissent, but that is rare. There is no real mechanical way to answer. A justice's silence is his answer. (C11)

Dissents from Denial That See the Light of Day

One might well ask why the justices would care if some justice goes public with a dissent from denial. Publishing dissents from denial airs disputes on certiorari, and this is generally regarded as not a good thing by the justices, although some feel more strongly than others. In an opinion, the Court sometimes will explain why a case was granted cert., but usually the reasons for granting or denying most cases are never known. As mentioned in Chapter 2, the justices do not really want the bar to know precisely why cases are granted or denied. And while justices complain that many worthless petitions are filed, there is an advantage to having some vagueness surround what makes a case certworthy.

  Published infrequently in the past, dissents from denial are becoming more commonplace, and this has led to controversy. Chapter 2 recounts Justice Frankfurter's well-known opposition to such opinions. Justice Stevens is the modern-day Frankfurter in this regard. He does not publicly dissent from the denial of cert. and is bothered by the fact that others do. Justice Stevens argues:

> One characteristic of all opinions dissenting from the denial of certiorari is manifest. They are totally unnecessary. They are examples of the purest form of dicta . . .
>   Another attribute of the opinions is that they are potentially misleading. Since the Court provides no explanation of the reasons for denying certiorari, the dissenter's arguments in favor of a grant are not answered and therefore typically appear to be more persuasive than most other opinions. Moreover since they often omit any reference to valid reasons for denying certiorari, they tend to imply that the Court has been unfaithful to its responsibilities or has implicitly reached a decision on the merits when, in fact, there is no basis for such an inference.

... But because they are so seldom answered, these opinions may also give rise to misunderstanding or incorrect impressions about how the Court actually works. Moreover the selected bits of information which they reveal tend to compromise the otherwise secret deliberations of our Conferences ...

In all events, these are the reasons why I have thus far resisted the temptation to publish opinions dissenting from denials of certiorari.[27]

Strong words, but Justice Stevens has not persuaded his brethren. For the five October terms 1976–1980, there were 818 cases where dissents were noted—716 dissents from the denial of certiorari and 102 dissents stating that they would have noted probable jurisdiction.

One justice explained the increase this way:

Perry: Publishing dissents from denial is becoming more frequent, and discussions of the cert. process generally seem to be more public these days. Can you tell me why this is happening?

Justice: I think it has something to do with personalities and differing views ... Cert. denied really doesn't mean anything.

Perry: Even though you justices continue to say that, I am wondering if you don't want it both ways—saying that it doesn't mean anything, but then coming out with all this public discussion. Might that not be misleading?

Justice: [Smiling] Well, perhaps. But it also has something to do with personalities. I think public discussion leads to confusion.

It should be pointed out that this justice has had his fair share of published dissents from denial.

One justice is interesting because his attitude about publishing dissents has changed. As another justice described him:

At times, dissents aren't recorded. Justice A won't record a dissent unless he writes. He doesn't go on the public record

27. Singleton v. Commissioner of Internal Revenue, cert. denied.

. . . Although on jurisdictional statements, Justice A will note because it is passing on the merits to some extent.[28]

Interestingly, the quoted justice is behind the times on his brother, or he was confusing the justice with Stevens because Justice A has begun dissenting publicly. One question that I asked many of the clerks was, "If I were to get an interview with your justice, what should I ask him?" One clerk suggested:

> I'd ask why he's had an increase in dissents from denials—written dissents from denials. He didn't used to do that. He joined a few, but he used to think that since a dissent from denial was not a decision on the merits, why waste the time. His practice has changed. I would ask him why he's doing it and for what effect.   (C60)

There are motives for publishing a dissent other than simply trying to pick up a fourth vote, which means that other justices must consider a threat to publish in light of these motives. A justice confirmed that there were reasons other than persuasion.

> Someone may put a case on [the discuss list] because even though he knows everyone will vote to deny it, he just wants to go on the public record.

Presumably a justice would do this either to make a statement of principle or to send out some sort of signal to future litigants.[29] Justice Marshall opposes, as Justice Brennan opposed, capital punishment as a matter of principle, and they feel so strongly about it that they always dissent. Sometimes, however, they may be doing more.

> I don't know if you understand how death cases work, but eventually what happens is that it goes back down and can come up on state habeas, and then if not there it can go back and come up on federal habeas. Brennan and Marshall's dissents from denial are not necessarily arguments to persuade the Supreme Court to take it, but they become briefs for the

28. The use of the words "to some extent" are interesting because there is a debate over the extent to which appeals should be used as precedent when decided summarily. See Chapter 2.

29. See Peter Linzer, "The Meaning of Certiorari Denials," *Columbia Law Review* 79 (November 1979).

lawyers when the lawyer is arguing in a state court or federal court on why habeas should be granted.

Several informants noted the signaling aspects of dissents.

> When an issue came up again they could point to what was said in the dissent from denial. (C62)

> More commonly you get these published dissents and in some ways it serves as an early warning system to litigants. It says these are the issues that we are interested in. It gets the message both to the litigants to go and find cases, and to the other members on the Court—effectively saying," when you publish these dissents from denials we're going to keep bitching until you take one of these cases." An example of this is this Bob Jones case. My term there was this Prince Edwards County School case. You had a dissent from denial signed by Justices _____, _____, and _____. This was kind of flagging the case. So what you've got is that Prince Edwards County Schools were not church schools but all of a sudden you have this Bob Jones University tacked on to the issue of tax deductions for private schools, and that adding of the First Amendment issue might have gotten it one more vote. . (C60)

> Of course there is an increase in dissent from denials. Some justices abuse this, I think. Denials are often attempts to persuade other justices—at least threats of denials are. Sometimes they are published as a way of communicating to future litigants. (C6)

Not only are signals sent to litigants, but another signal that might be sent is one to lower court judges saying, "we are watching you." Summary judgments were seen by many as sending such a signal, but some informants thought that dissents from denial also perform this function.

> *Clerk:* So though sometimes a case isn't important, they will take the case and say, "look, you can't ignore us." Sometimes they do that by dissents [from denial of cert.]. A justice will write to point out that the Supreme Court has taken note of this and that you can't fool anyone, and don't think you are getting away with this unnoticed.

> *Perry:* Does that mean that sometimes a dissent is published with the goodwill of the rest of the Court?
> *Clerk:* Yes, I think so. (C12)

> *Clerk:* [Dissent from denial] is often used to express revulsion to a decision below even though they don't expect the court to take it. (C9)

I asked several clerks about this idea that dissents were used to let lower courts know that they were being watched. Most said that they did not know; some thought it sounded plausible; and others said no.

> That doesn't ring true to me. I mean there are so many cases denied cert. for so many reasons. If cert. is denied, and yet there's a dissent, it really underlines that the Court really *wasn't* interested in taking the case. Because if someone's dissenting it suggests that the case at least has some merit for being considered certworthy, the Court considered it, but for whatever reason didn't take it. (C24)

Thus, responses were mixed on the use of dissents as signals to lower court judges to "behave." Many, however, did see them as communication in some form to actors below, be they judges, attorneys, or litigants.

Finally, several informants suggested that what starts out as a dissent from denial, sometimes becomes a per curiam opinion.

> Sometimes if the justice was worked up we would help write a dissent from denial of cert. And sometimes those dissents from denial became per curiam opinions. (C29)

> Sometimes summary reversals begin as dissents from denial. This is one of the bizarre things about the way the Court works because there is some kind of a bandwagon effect. (C41)

I asked the justices about dissents becoming per curiam opinions and they agreed that it happened, but they differed somewhat on the frequency.

Yes that does happen, and I think they are some of our worst per curiam opinions.

That does happen sometimes.

[Sitting back and thinking for some time] Well, that's a rarity. There has been this increase in per curiam opinions, but I'm not sure it comes out of dissents from denial.

I think that is very rare. If you have fewer than four voting for cert., the chances of picking up three votes to reverse are very unusual.[30] What is more likely is to have three who would say the case is so wrong that they would grant and reverse but not hear. Three others might say that "it seems to me that it ought to be reversed, but I am not willing to vote without hearing arguments," and the discussion would take that tone.

Whether it happens rarely or frequently, the potential for such an occurrence means that a justice must take a threat to dissent seriously. From his perspective, it may be a strategic error to let a case get decided this way. He may well prefer to vote to deny but may also figure that if the case is going to be decided, plenary consideration is clearly preferable to a summary disposition.

In sum, when a justice says he is "considering writing," there are enough potential ramifications that it might persuade another justice to vote to grant for reasons apart from the argument in the dissent.

Daylight Dissents: Data

Few scholars, particularly few political scientists, have ever concentrated on dissents from denial.[31] I do not know if this is because they have taken the justices at their word that denial of cert. means nothing, and therefore dissents from denial are generally meaningless, or because the subject has not piqued their interest. Whatever the reason, the lack of attention has probably been unwise. There is a major exception to this generalization. Peter Linzer, in his excellent article "The Meaning of Certiorari Denials," gives extended consideration to

30. Recall that an informal rule exists which says that it takes six votes to dispose of a case summarily.

31. An exception is a paper presented by Sidney Ulmer.

dissents from denial.[32] He convincingly shows the untenable nature of the justices' official position on the meaning of cert. denials. In particular, he urges attorneys to pay closer attention to dissents from denial for the signals they send to litigants and lower courts. Another exception is a section in an appendix to the Hruska Commission Report— the report which recommended a National Court of Appeals.[33] Neither of these articles, however, pays much attention to the role that the unpublished dissent plays, or to the fact that the written dissent was probably first written for internal consumption. In any event, for the reasons already stated, these dissents from denial deserve heightened scrutiny.

Unfortunately, we cannot know how many or which dissents from denial never saw the light of day. We can however, examine those dissents that did not pick up the requisite votes. I examined published dissents from denial for the terms that paralleled the terms of my informants, OT's 1976–1980. I analyzed the dissents not for content but simply to find out some basic facts such as who dissented most, who joined whom, and so on. Such summary data are easily obtainable for decisions on the merits, but not so for dissents from denial. The data were obtained by going page by page through the weekly *Journal of Proceedings* as reported in *U.S. Law Week*.

Table 6.1 gives a breakdown of agenda dissents by various categories. Included are both dissents from denial of certiorari and dissents from refusal to hear an appeal. Out of approximately 19,764 cases that sought review for the October terms 1976–1980, 18,355 of which were denied, there were 818 cases that had at least one dissent. Of the 818, only 150 contained one or more written dissents (Table 6.1.A). The large number of unwritten dissents raises an interesting question. Aside from Brennan and Marshall's standard note on capital cases (Table 6.1.E), one cannot determine whether the nonwritten dissents at one point had a draft written dissent or not. Probably they did not, but unfortunately, I did not ask about this. It is only a guess, but perhaps what happens is that a justice will threaten to write a dissent at conference, the case is relisted, but he never actually drafts a dissent.

In written opinions on the merits, dissenters (or concurrers) may join someone else, but they frequently write their own dissent. When it comes to agenda dissents, however, only four times was there more than one dissent written (Table 6.1.B). Upon reflection, this makes

32. Linzer, "Certiorari Denials," pp. 1255–1291.
33. Commission on Revision of the Federal Court Appellate System, Structure, and Internal Procedures: Recommendations for Change (Hruska Report), Washington, D.C., June 1975, Appendix B, III, pp. 112–131.

Table 6.1   Agenda dissents, October terms, 1976–1980 (total cases with
               dissent: 818)[a]

A. Noted or written		
Noted only[b]	668 (82.0%)	
Written	150 (18.0%)	
B. Number of written dissents per case		
One		146 (97.3%)
Two		4 (2.7%)
C. Number of Dissenters		
One		261 (31.9%)
Noted	239 (91.6%)	
Written	22 (8.4%)	
Two		374 (45.7%)
Noted	306 (81.8%)	
Written	68 (18.2%)	
Three		183 (22.4%)
Noted	123 (67.2%)	
Written	60 (32.8%)	
D. Appeal or cert.		
Appeal		102 (12.5%)
Noted	97 (95.1%)	
Written	5 (4.9%)	
Cert.		716 (87.6%)
Noted	571 (79.8%)	
Written	145 (20.2%)	
E. Capital cases		
Capital		119 (14.5%)
Noted[c]	106 (89.1%)	
Written	13 (10.9%)	
Noncapital		699 (85.5%)
Noted	562 (80.4%)	
Written	137 (19.6%)	
F. October term		
OT 76		130 (15.9%)
Noted	113 (86.9%)	
Written	17 (13.1%)	
OT 77		152 (18.6%)
Noted	123 (80.9%)	
Written	29 (19.1%)	
OT 78		191 (23.3%)
Noted	167 (87.4%)	
Written	24 (12.6%)	
OT 79		153 (18.7%)
Noted	128 (83.7%)	
Written	25 (16.3%)	
OT 80		192 (23.5%)
Noted	137 (71.3%)	
Written	55 (28.7%)	

a. The total number of cases with one or more dissents, not the number of dissents.

b. Cases containing both a written dissent and a noted dissent are coded as "written."

c. Includes the Brennan and Marshall standard dissent.

sense. It would be rare for two justices to feel strongly enough to write, disagree with one another on the reasons, and yet the conference still consider the case uncertworthy.

Table 6.1.C points out that most cases have two dissenters. Also note how many cases there are with three dissents, and what the data say about the norm of reciprocity. In a significant number of cases (22.4 percent) where feelings were strong—strong enough to have public dissents—a fourth vote simply could not be gotten.

The number of dissents per term varies somewhat although not dramatically (Table 6.1.F). An exception is the number of written dissents in OT 1980.

Over the long run, agenda dissents are up substantially from previous years. In the 1950s, dissents were filed for only about 30–35 cases per term.[34] Although the current totals are down from October terms of the early 1970s, the inflated numbers of that period are attributable to one justice—Douglas. In OT 1973, he alone noted 477 dissents from denial.[35] In his later years on the Court, Justice Douglas had argued that cert. votes should be made public. The other justices never accepted this idea so in his last few terms, Douglas publicly noted all his votes to deny.[36] If the Douglas anomaly is removed, one sees a rather dramatic increase in dissents since the 1950s.

One informant suggested that the number of dissents may be related to the time of the year.

> I also suspect that the time of year would be important, that you would have a correlation between the time of year and when most dissents appear. I would expect that most of them would be in the early part of the term when it's not so jammed. They have time at that point to prepare dissents and also probably more during the break; I don't know, but that's

34. Hruska Report, p. 112.
35. Ibid., p. 113.
36. In his autobiography, *Go East Young Man* (New York: Random House, 1974), p. 452, Justice Douglas wrote: "When I came on the Court Hugo Black talked to me about his idea of having every vote on every case made public. In cases taken and argued, the vote of each Justice was eventually known. But in cases where appeals were dismissed out of hand or certiorari denied, no votes were recorded publicly. I thought his idea an excellent one and backed it when he proposed to the conference that it be adopted. But the requisite votes were not available then or subsequently. As a result he and I started to note our dissents from denials of certiorari and dismissal of appeal in important cases. Gradually the practice spread to a few other Justices; and finally I ended up in the sixties noting my vote in all cases where dismissals or denials were contrary to my convictions."

just my general sense. You rarely get them in March, April,
and May because the Court is so busy. (C9)

His argument makes sense, but the data do not support his assumptions, at least as far as published dissents are concerned. Of course, he
might be right if the dissents were persuasive. Table 6.2 reports the
number of dissents, nonwritten and written, by month. October always
has the largest number, of course, because the first week of the term
includes all the petitions that accumulated over the summer. But there
is no precipitous drop off in April and May. It could be that there is
a delay in publishing a dissent that has been written earlier, but there
is no reason to believe that is the case.

The justices vary greatly in their number of public dissents. Justice
Stevens, we know, refuses to publish dissents from denial of certiorari.[37] It is difficult to know what to make of the remaining disparities

Table 6.2   Agenda dissents by month, October terms, 1976–1980

Month	OT 76		OT 77		OT 78		OT 79		OT 80	
	NW[a]	W[b]	NW	W	NW	W	NW	W	NW	W
October	24	3	32	8	35	7	25	9	38	6
November	12	4	6	0	11	2	9	1	12	7
December	7	2	2	3	12	7	10	0	9	4
January	14	1	13	1	25	3	14	1	15	5
February	12	2	14	2	12	0	13	5	10	4
March	11	2	11	1	16	0	10	1	15	5
April	10	1	10	5	13	1	12	3	6	11
May	10	1	18	5	18	2	15	2	14	6
June	10	1	17	4	23	2	18	3	17	7
July	—	—	—	—	2	—	2	—	1	—
Total	110	17	123	29	167	24	128	25	137	55

a. Nonwritten.
b. Written.

37. Justice Stevens does dissent from the dismissal of an appeal. Table 6.4, however,
shows that Stevens dissented in three cases on cert. Each case is an oddity. In Minnesota
v. Alexander (docket no. 76-1030, 45 *Law Week*, 3706), the case was brought on appeal.
As discussed in Chapter 2, when cases are considered to be improperly brought as an

and whether they say something about a justice's attitude on publicly dissenting, his willingness to threaten, or the number of times that he is a loser on cert. votes. The numbers probably reflect all these things. Tables 6.3 and 6.4 show the agenda dissenting behavior of the justices. Dissents by Justices Brennan and Marshall far outnumber those of other justices. One hundred nineteen of these dissents are capital cases, but even if they are subtracted, Brennan remains the clear leader.

Another datum is that Justices White and Rehnquist wrote more dissents than Justice Marshall, and almost as many as Justice Brennan. Brennan and Marshall joined many more written dissents, however, so that they were involved in more written dissents than White and Rehnquist. It is interesting to note who are the writers, and who are the joiners (Table 6.4). That may convey something about leadership. Authorship of opinions is assigned with some attempt to even the workload; therefore, one cannot assume any initiative on the part of a justice by looking at the number of opinions he has written, or the fact that he has written a particular opinion. Written agenda dissents are at the initiative of the author, however.

We also might want to know something about who joined whom. Tables 6.5–6.7 speak to that question. The most frequent occurrence is for Brennan to write a dissent and have Marshall join him. Somewhat

---

appeal, they are then treated as a cert. In this case, Stevens insisted that the case was an appeal. Technically, however, since the Court treated it as a cert., his dissent showed up.

In Huffman v. Florida (docket no. 77-6025, 46 *Law Week*, 3678), a case involving a black who was convicted by an all-white jury, Justice Marshall wrote an impassioned dissent from denial wherein he addressed many procedural questions. Justice Stevens responded: "I write only to identify this as one of the many cases in which a persuasive dissent may create the unwarranted impression that the Court has acted arbitrarily in denying a petition for cert."

Finally, in Illinois v. Gray (docket no. 77-943, 46 *Law Week*, 3678), rather than simply saying cert. denied, the Court said: "The petition for certiorari is denied, it appearing that the judgment of the Illinois Supreme Court rests on an adequate state ground." This caused Justice Stevens to respond: "The Court's occasional practice of explaining its denials of certiorari, cf. Michigan v. Allensworth, 77-333 (Mar. 20, 1978); Illinois v. Pendleton, 77-1175 (April 3, 1978); Illinois v. Garlick, 77-311 (Dec. 5, 1977), is, I believe, inconsistent with the rule that such denials have no precedential value. Since I regard that rule as an important aspect of our practice, I do not join the Court's explanation in this case." The journal also reported that "Mr. Justice Stewart and Mr. Justice Marshall would deny the petition for certiorari without explanation." One wonders why Stewart and Marshall refused to join Stevens's statement. These three cases, then, are not really dissents from denial of cert. The decision to code them as such is arbitrary and debatable. It really does not matter, but given my discussion of dissents as tools of negotiation, they are interesting. I suspect that Stevens threatened to respond if these dissents were published. When they were, he had to make good on this threat.

Table 6.3 Agenda dissents by justice, October terms, 1976–1980

Justice	N	%
Burger	44	2.8
Brennan	426	27.4
Stewart	179	11.5
White	188	12.1
Marshall	341	22.0
Blackmun	158	10.2
Powell	117	7.5
Rehnquist	61	3.9
Stevens	39	2.5
Total	1,553[a]	99.9

a. The total number of dissents, not the number of cases with a dissent. Since many of the 818 cases with a dissent had more than one dissent, the number of dissents does not equal the number of cases.

less frequently, Brennan joins Marshall. More intriguing, however, are the next several pairings. The third most popular pair is Brennan joining White, followed closely by Stewart joining Brennan. Indeed, Brennan joins White three times more than does any other justice, and Stewart joins Brennan far more often than he joins any other justice. These totals are affected by the total number of times that given justices dissent, but still these are probably not the pairings that one would expect *a priori*. It is also interesting to observe that Justice Rehnquist writes alone over twice as many times as anyone else even though he is frequently joined by other justices.

Table 6.6 shows the pairings for justices for all dissent votes, noted and written, irrespective of who wrote. Some odd pairings emerge. Again, the Marshall-Brennan relationship stands out as by far the most frequent, but the next most frequent pairings are somewhat of a surprise—Brennan-Stewart; Brennan-White; Stewart-Marshall; White-Marshall; Blackmun-Powell; White-Blackmun. This table and Table 6.7, like Table 6.5, are affected by the sheer number of dissents by Marshall and Brennan, but that does not solely account for the pairings. Just because Brennan dissents a lot does not mean that when Stewart chooses to dissent, it would be on the same cases as Brennan. I have suggested that these pairings are not what one would expect. Such a statement is largely intuitive. Table 6.7 provides a slight im-

Table 6.4   Agenda dissents by justice and by type, October terms,
             1976–1980

A. Burger
Total dissents   44
  Appeal   2
  Certiorari   42
    Voted only   21
    Wrote dissent   3
    Joined written dissent   10

B. Brennan
Total dissents   426
  Appeal   53
  Certiorari   373
    Voted only   351
    Wrote dissent   37
    Joined written dissent   38

C. Stewart
Total dissents   179
  Appeal   15
  Certiorari   164
    Voted only   151
    Wrote dissent   6
    Joined written dissent   22

D. White
Total dissents   188
  Appeal   28
  Certiorari   160
    Voted only   155
    Wrote dissent   30
    Joined written dissent   3

E. Marshall
Total dissents   341
  Appeal   24
  Certiorari   317
    Voted only   271
    Wrote dissent   25
    Joined written dissent   45

F. Blackmun
Total dissents   158
  Appeal   19
  Certiorari   139
    Voted only   138
    Wrote dissent   11
    Joined written dissent   9

Table 6.4   (continued)

G. Powell		
Total dissents		117
Appeal	17	
Certiorari	100	
Voted only	91	
Wrote dissent	7	
Joined written dissent	19	
H. Rehnquist		
Total dissents		61
Appeal	9	
Certiorari	52	
Voted only	16	
Wrote dissent	33	
Joined written dissent	12	
I. Stevens		
Total dissents		39
Appeal	36	
Certiorari	3	
Voted only	37	
Wrote dissent	2	
Joined written dissent	0	

provement over intuition. It compares agenda dissenting behavior to voting behavior on the merits. The number to the left of the slash indicates the ranking of pairings on agenda dissents; that is, it reflects the information in Table 6.6 so that the most frequent pair to vote together in dissent, Brennan and Marshall, is ranked 1, and the least frequent pair, Burger and Stevens is ranked 36. The number to the right of the slash is the ranking of pairings for voting behavior on the merits for the same five terms. Using numbers or percentages rather than rank ordering in this table would make no sense given that, for the most part, every justice participates in every decision on the merits, whereas agenda dissents always involve only one to three justices. Rank ordering, then, seems to be the best method of comparison, even though rankings are related to propensity to dissent. In many instances, the rankings are fairly close, in others, surprisingly different. This table demonstrates that there are some differences between agenda behavior and behavior on the merits, particularly for certain justices.[38] That point supports arguments made later.

38. The more apt comparison would be all cert. votes to votes on the merits. Those

Table 6.5 Agenda dissent writers and joiners

Writer	Dissent alone	Joiner								
		Burger	Brennan	Stewart	White	Marshall	Blackmun	Powell	Rehnquist	Stevens
Burger	0	—	0	0	0	0	3 2% 50% 33%	0	3 2% 50% 25%	0
Brennan	3 2% 6% 9%	0	—	13 7% 26% 59%	1 .5% 2% 33%	33 17% 66% 73%	0	0	0	0
Stewart	3 2% 60% 9%	0	0	—	0	2 1% 40% 4%	0	0	0	0
White	6 3% 16% 18%	0	15 8% 41% 41%	3 2% 8% 14%	—	5 3% 14% 11%	2 1% 5% 22%	2 1% 5% 10%	4 2% 11% 33%	0
Marshall	5 3% 19% 15%	0	18 9% 69% 48%	0	0	—	0	3 2% 12% 15%	0	0

	(alone)									
Blackmun	3 2% 20% 9%	0	4 2% 27% 11%	0	1 =% 2=% 9%	1 .5% 7% 33%	—	2 1% 13% 10%	1 .5% 7% 8%	0
Powell	2 1% 25% 6%	1 .5% 13% 10%	0	1 .5% 13% 5%	0 ●	0 ●	1 .5% 13% 11%	—	3 2% 37% 25%	0
Rehnquist	12 6% 28% 35%	9 5% 21% 90%	0	5 3% 12% 23%	1 .5% 2% 33%	●	3 2% 7% 33%	13 7% 30% 65%	—	0
Stevens	0	0	0	0 .5% 50% 2%	0 .5% 50% 2%		0	0 .5% 50% 8%	1	—
Total	34 18%	10 5%	37 19%	22 11%	3 2%	45 25%	9 5%	20 10%	12 6%	0

Note: The first number in each cell is the number of dissents written by the justice at left, either alone (in the first column) or with another justice (in the remaining columns). The percentages below are cell, row, and column percents (in that order).

Table 6.6 Agenda dissent pairs, October terms, 1976–1980

	Burger	Brennan	Stewart	White	Marshall	Blackmun	Powell	Rehnquist	Stevens
Burger	—								
Brennan	2 0.2%	—							
Stewart	3 0.3%	90 9.8%	—						
White	6 0.7%	73 7.9%	15 1.6%	—					
Marshall	1 0.1%	290 31.6%	70 7.6%	36 3.9%	—				
Blackmun	20 2.2%	26 2.8%	9 1.0%	27 2.9%	17 1.8%	—			
Powell	14 1.5%	14 1.5%	26 2.8%	21 2.3%	6 0.7%	28 3.0%	—		
Rehnquist	21 2.3%	1 0.1%	8 0.8%	13 1.4%	2 0.2%	12 1.3%	20 2.2%	—	
Stevens	0 0%	18 2.0%	5 0.5%	6 0.6%	9 0.9%	5 0.5%	3 0.3%	2 0.2%	—

Note: The first number in each cell is the number of times the pair voted together in agenda dissents. The percentage below (cell percent) is the percentage of all dissent votes.

Table 6.7 Comparison of agenda dissent pairs to merits pairs, October terms, 1976–1980

	Burger	Brennan	Stewart	White	Marshall	Blackmun	Powell	Rehnquist	Stevens
Burger	—								
Brennan	31/32	—							
Stewart	30/7	2/27	—						
White	25/9	3/16	16/13	—					
Marshall	35/33	1/1	4/30	5/20	—				
Blackmun	12/11	8/21	21/22	7/6	15/28	—			
Powell	18/3	17/31	9/4	21/8	24/31	6/12	—		
Rehnquist	11/2	34/34	23/10	19/14	32/35	20/19	13/5	—	
Stevens	36/25	14/18	27/15	26/17	22/24	28/26	29/23	33/29	—

Note: The number to the left of the slash is the rank of the pair on agenda dissents; the number to the right is the rank of the pair on votes on the merits. See text for details.

Justices and clerks would gladly admit that justices try to persuade one another. Normatively, persuasion enjoys general approval. To the extent that one persuades someone else, it could be seen as influence. Use of that term, however, begins to make the hair rise on the backs of necks. As one justice said, he likes to come to his own decisions from "the papers." Bargaining, in its purest sense, implies influence through exchange. A suggestion that that occurs generates resounding denial and disapprobation. A broader understanding of "bargaining" might be "if you'll vote for cert., I won't publish the dissent from denial," or vice versa. The point here, however, is not to define "bargaining," "influence," "persuasion," or "politics." Rather it is to demonstrate what behavior occurs.[39] The interesting thing is that in the cert. process, there is little attempt to do any of these things. Interpersonal influence is rare and generally not acceptable except by argument in conference (very little of which occurs because most decisions are made prior to conference) or by drafting dissents from denial. This is decision-making behavior that one may not expect *a priori* in a political institution. Moreover, it is behavior that one would not expect *a priori* of the Supreme Court.

The next chapter continues this discussion by examining intrachamber strategy, but for now, let us examine the decision behavior in a different light.

Decision Theory

At first blush, the decision-making behavior of the justices at cert. seems rather strange. In a collegial decision process where one might expect a great amount of bargaining or negotiation, little is found. To the extent that it exists, it happens in a formal meeting just prior to a decision, or it is done in writing (or by threatening to write), which seems to be a highly inefficient use of time in an institution where time is supposedly such a scarce resource. While those who have worked at the Court give plausible explanations of why the behavior takes the form that it does, these explanations (time, the perception

---

data are not available. Using dissent data is probably a fairly decent surrogate, although it is undoubtedly affected by the differences in justices' willingness to dissent publicly. In addition to being a surrogate measure however, public dissents indicate those cases for which justices had particularly strong feelings, so observing this subset is somewhat like observing nonunanimous cases on the merits.

39. I am grateful to Larry Baum for his thoughts about what these terms mean and for forcing me to think more about how I use them.

of nothing to negotiate, and so on) do not fully explain the choice of the instrumental behavior. Decision theory can aid in this endeavor. Social science has fairly well developed theories of decision making ranging from rational choice to organization theory. This knowledge is not thoroughly exploited here, partly because of space and partly because of inability. Other scholars more talented in this regard can consider the data in more theoretical ways. Nevertheless, a cursory look can help explain the "strange" choice not to negotiate in the cert. process.

In his article, "Organizations, Decisions, and Courts," Professor Lawrence Mohr synthesized some decision theories and applied them to local courts. In the article, he developed a theory of choice of decision submodels. The submodels are based largely upon the works of other scholars, but he added the crucial component of showing why and when different submodels would be chosen.[40] To simplify, I use Mohr's understanding of the decision literature rather than the original works. It is a fair rendering. As shown in Table 6.8, Mohr posits that there are four decision submodels, each of which has a choice mechanism and typical instrumental behavior. Mohr defines a choice mechanism as "a criterion for selecting the levels at which the various goals relevant

Table 6.8   Decision submodels

	Firm	Rational	Garbage can	Political
Choice mechanism	Satisficing	Maximizing	Strategic agglomeration	Domination
Typical instrumental behavior	Bargaining	Analysis, persuasion	Going, coming, waiting	Contention, struggle, force

Source: This table reproduces the top portion of Lawrence B. Mohr, "Organizations, Decisions, and Courts," *Law and Society Review* 10 (1976): 634; reprinted by permission of the Law and Society Association.

40. Lawrence B. Mohr, "Organizations, Decisions, and Courts," *Law and Society Review* 10 (1976): 621–642. The most important part of Mohr's article deals with the relationship between certain contextual variables and the choice of instrumental behavior. I do not deal with that here. I have written a paper using Mohr's basic idea to examine Supreme Court behavior for opinion writing. I hope eventually to examine his theory in light of cert., but that task is left for another day.

to a collective decision will be satisfied."[41] Each choice mechanism is associated with, "instrumental decision behavior that is typical of that mechanism."

The garbage can submodel, which has been so effective in explaining decision making in other contexts, is probably of little use here. Oversimplifying, this submodel explains choices that are made when they are attached to another "central choice." Case selection behavior is very purposive, and the selection of a case *is* the central choice. Interestingly, the garbage can may help explain doctrinal development. Sometimes in making a decision on one matter, justices may inadvertently make choices that have attached themselves to the central issue being decided. But the decision to take a case would not fit that description.

The political submodel brings about an attempt to dominate so that the "goals most satisfied are those favored by the conqueror." Because justices are equally powerful and are in a collegial body with relatively stable membership, there is little attempt to vanquish one's foes, especially in the cert. process. Indeed, the rule of four is in some sense a procedure to prevent a majority from being able to dominate the agenda. Attempts at domination may occur on the merits in a few highly contentious cases, but at cert., such attempts are probably nonexistent. If such behavior began, the entire process would come unraveled.[42]

Thanks primarily to Richard Cyert, James March, and Herbert Simon, one decision submodel, the firm, is well known to social scientists. The choice mechanism for the firm is satisficing. Satisficing occurs when "all goals in the active demand set are satisfied at least at minimally acceptable levels (this is opposed, for example to satisfying some goals maximally and others not at all)." The method by which "the final and true levels of aspiration in the active demand set are made known" is bargaining.

Mohr suggests that the firm submodel is probably "the most prevalent mode of group decision making in Western societies." Indeed, it can be observed everywhere from department store pricing decisions

41. When explaining Mohr's concepts for the next several paragraphs, I quote him or his ideas without complete citation. His discussion is found on pp. 629–634 of the article cited in the previous note.

42. For example, surely a "vanquished" justice would have no incentive to allow things such as the discuss list to facilitate decisions. He would have every incentive to extract costs in any way possible so that he could force bargaining. Moreover, if domination became a viable strategy, the justices would have to become much more involved in the case selection process than they currently are or have any desire to be.

to the Cuban Missile Crisis. Yet clearly, satisficing is not what takes place in cert. decisions. Justices are not willing to bargain by trading votes or cases in order to satisfice. Why is this choice mechanism, so prevalent elsewhere, absent in cert. decisions? After all, justices have many goals. They may include the criteria for case selection, but they may also involve allocation of resources, normative understandings of how judges should behave, and many other things. Nevertheless, generally, we do not associate satisficing with "justice" or "the law," and justices do not either. The whole notion is counter to the ideal of "legal reasoning." Though justices may have to satisfice on the merits, they need not on cert. Socialization partially explains the lack of willingness to bargain even though, as pointed out in my hypothetical examples, bargaining might well make sense and be "more just."

Bargaining does happen in the legal arena of course. Plea bargaining is probably the best example.[43] And, justices satisfice when it comes to the reasoning in an opinion, if not the judgment. We know that bargaining (or accommodation) takes place at that stage. A justice tries to extract concessions for his signature, but frequently he will decide that it is better to join an opinion than to write a concurring opinion. The desire for unanimity and clarity in the law becomes an important goal that supersedes, or at least must be balanced by, some other goal. But for whatever reason, satisficing does not seem to be an acceptable goal when it comes to cert. decisions, and as a result there is little bargaining or negotiation.[44]

Case selection exhibits the rational submodel. The accompanying choice mechanism, maximization, is described by Mohr as one such that "logic and facts are adduced to discover and select the alternative that best attains a particular goal or weighted goal set." Maximization, of course, parallels the concept of "legal reasoning." As stated early in this chapter, this is the ideal to which justices and most all lawyers are socialized. Maximization requires the instrumental behavior that lawyers are most comfortable with—analysis and persuasion. Maximizing assumes that the relevant goal set is shared by all of the group; and, indeed, when it comes to case selection, most relevant goals are probably widely shared. The goal set undoubtedly involves some notion of

43. See, e.g., Milton Heumann, *Plea Bargaining: The Experience of Prosecutors, Judges, and Defense Attorneys* (Chicago: University of Chicago Press, 1977).

44. It may be true that an individual judge satisfices in some sense with his own decision. That is, he has a limited amount of time and therefore cannot spend inordinate amounts of time examining the cert. petition. As I describe the decision, however, I am referring to the decision of the Court. Given that individual justices have come to a decision about disposition, there is little in the way of satisficing that occurs.

what type of cases are certworthy, how the Court should spend its time, the role of the Supreme Court in the federal judicial system, *stare decisis,* and so on. Later chapters elaborate on what this shared goal set might contain. For now as an example, one shared goal is the perception that an important role of the Supreme Court is to resolve legitimate nontrivial splits among the federal circuits. Likewise, the Court does not want to review a case for the purpose of resolving a split if a split does not exist, or if the case can be distinguished on the facts. Determining if a case presents such a split is often difficult. The Court wants to maximize, not satisfice. It wants to be sure that, in fact, a split in the circuits exists. Given enough time for analysis and persuasion, the Court can try to achieve and maximize this shared goal. To the extent that relevant goals are shared, maximization makes much more sense than using some other decision strategy.

The decision to maximize helps explain certain "unexpected" behavior. For example, "joining three" to build goodwill would not be maximizing behavior. By contrast, if one justice thought that a case possibly achieved a goal, he might be willing to join three others who had determined that it did. He would defer to their analyses. This is maximizing behavior. Thus, it makes sense that sometimes a justice will join three, and other times he will let a case die with three votes.

Given time constraints faced by the justices, they can only afford to spend so much time at analysis and persuasion, the instrumental behavior for maximization. What they have done is to assume that their collective wisdom as reflected in the sum of their predetermined cert. votes is a surrogate for collegial analysis and persuasion. This is not completely satisfactory, of course, else there would be no need for discussion at conference. Yet, if after conference one justice is dissatisfied with a denial of cert., others are not willing to join him just because they do not strongly oppose hearing the case. That would be satisficing—balancing a goal of collegiality with a minimally acceptable case. Rather, a justice must engage in an extraordinary attempt at analysis and persuasion—writing a dissent or threatening to write a dissent. If he succeeds because of persuasion, then they have maximized.

Threatening to publish a dissent, however, may lead to satisficing. A justice may go ahead and give a vote to grant rather than have a dissent published. If one of his colleagues feels so strongly about the case that he is willing to put the time and effort into the extraordinary procedure of writing a dissent, collegiality may begin to weigh in a little more heavily. Or, the resisting justice may feel that the negatives of publishing a dissent—among them signal sending, airing a dispute, and turning into a per curiam—would cause him to vote to grant so as to avoid this happening. This is not maximizing. Subtle though it may be, negotiation is taking place and the justice is willing to satisfice. Nonshared goals have entered the active demand set. Acknowledging that this happens does not counter all that was said above. The fact that written dissents are published indicates that justices are willing to resist pressures to satisfice. Nevertheless, threats to publish dissents from denial are used as a negotiation tool, and they sometimes "persuade" in ways that do not connote persuasion of the maximizing kind.

Most agenda-setting studies of the Court rest on the concept of strategic behavior through coalition building. Indeed, that is true of much of all behavioral literature on the Court.[45] Agenda studies rarely discuss interchamber behavior per se, but a fair inference from them would be that interchamber communication must be fairly extensive in order to effect the sophisticated strategy that the studies suggest. Whether or not that is a fair representation of these studies, most political scientists—particularly those in the judicial subfield—have assumed more bargaining and communication than actually transpire. This chapter argues that little bargaining on cert. transpires in the U.S. Supreme Court, and to the extent that it does, it takes a particular—some might say peculiar—form. This atypical behavior for a political institution is more comprehensible, however, when decision theory is consulted.

45. For an exception, see Joel Grossman, "Dissenting Blocs on the Warren Court: A Study in Judicial Role Behavior," *Journal of Politics* 30 (November 1968): 1068.

> *Perry:* Did your chambers act strategically in the cert. process?
> *Clerk:* Oh yes. (C53)

7 Strategy

With the exception of dissents from denial of certiorari, bargaining and attempts at persuasion to obtain a vote on cert. are rare. That is not to say, however, that the cert. process is devoid of strategy, simply that strategy usually occurs within chambers rather than between chambers. Unlike interchamber activity, however, where the behavior of one justice is much like that of any other, justices do differ in their willingness to engage in strategic behavior. The variations are both situational and related to justices' perceptions of their roles.[1] Some justices are more strategic than others, and the ones who are the most strategic are the ones we would expect to be. But as shall be argued later, all of the justices act strategically on cert. at times, and much of the time none of them acts strategically. Strategic behavior can take many forms but only the most obvious are discussed here. Also, of course, there are strategies by players outside the Court, but those efforts are discussed elsewhere.

Defensive Denials

A term I did not use initially—indeed I had never heard of it until I began my interviews—was used over and over again: "There were

---

1. See Doris Marie Provine, *Case Selection in the United States Supreme Court* (Chicago: University of Chicago Press, 1980), who argues that role perception limits strategic behavior. Also see James L. Gibson, "Judges' Role Orientations, Attitudes, and Decisions: An Interactive Model," *American Political Science Review* 72 (1978): 911–924.

these things that we called 'defensive denials'" (C9).[2] The words are almost self-explanatory. There are areas of law generally, and cases specifically, where a justice believes that if a case is reviewed, he will not like the outcome on the merits. Therefore, even if he believes the case is certworthy, and perhaps even believes that the ruling below is a horrible injustice, he still will vote to deny the case. The reasoning is, why make a bad situation worse? Recall that a denial of cert. has no precedential value, and refusal to take a case in no way signifies that the Supreme Court agrees with the ruling below. Difficult as it may be for a justice to let a ruling stand, by doing so he has let the precedent remain only for its immediate jurisdiction—for example, only the second circuit—rather than for the entire country.

During the informants' tenures on the Court, the "liberals" felt that the "conservative" justices were dedicated to undoing "important gains" achieved during the Warren era. Of course to the conservatives, these were the "evils and excesses" of the Warren era. Whichever, given the basically conservative majority, the "liberals" had more to worry about when a case was reviewed. As one clerk from one of the more liberal chambers noted:

> Justice A [a liberal] was more in the position of preserving law that was already made. His particular worry was seeing it step backwards. Whereas Justice C [a conservative] the year before took every Fourth Amendment case that walked in the door. (C59)

Another clerk observed:

> Justice A and Justice B [two liberals] didn't seem to want to accept any cases. (C1)

These fears would certainly be abetted by the fact that about two-thirds of all cases accepted for review are reversed. But as many have pointed out, the conservative revolution to overturn the Warren Court precedents never really materialized.[3] A few informants said that some

2. Though I had never heard the term "defensive denial," the concept is central to much of the political science literature that suggests that cert. votes are strategic.

3. For an excellent analysis, see Vincent Blasi, *The Burger Court: The Counter-Revolution That Wasn't* (New Haven: Yale University Press, 1983). For an earlier assessment, see Stephen L. Wasby, *Continuity and Change from the Warren to the Burger Court* (Pacific Palisades, Calif.: Goodyear, 1976). Recall, however, that I interviewed clerks who served during the October terms of 1976–1980, so for some of them, their tenure was before it was obvious that the counterrevolution had fizzled, and for all of them, it was prior to the arrival of O'Connor.

of the conservative justices misjudged votes. Early on, the conservatives aggressively brought up cases only to lose on the merits. This resulted in conservatives as well as liberals having to become more strategic in evaluating outcome on the merits. Reporting the use of defensive denials must be qualified, however. They are not used with wild abandon, contrary to what some of the political science literature suggests. But they do occur, and here I wish to document their use. Chapter 9 will discuss in more detail when and under what circumstances they are employed.

All of the justices acknowledged the existence of defensive denials. The first justice I interviewed described a defensive denial before I had heard the term, and before I brought up the issue. Incidentally, he was not a justice from one of the ideological wings of the Court, and he initiated the discussion:

> *Justice:*   . . . I might think the Nebraska Supreme Court made a horrible decision, but I wouldn't want to take the case, for if we take the case and affirm it, then it would become a precedent . . .
>
> *Perry:*   Actually this leads to something I wanted to ask later, but let me follow up on that now because I want to be sure I understand you. Do some justices vote strategically on cert.? For example, it is conceivable to me that Justice _____ would see a case that he believes ought to be granted, yet he is afraid that if he votes to grant cert. and brings the case up, that given the . . . personnel on the Court . . . in fact it might make things worse, so he would rather let it lie?
>
> *Justice:*   Oh, I think that does happen. Just as I have said with the Nebraska Supreme Court, some things might be better not to be taken.

When asked about defensive denials, another justice admitted their existence but seemed disdainful of them.

> Yes, I think Justice _____ does that. I can't say that I don't do it because there are perhaps things that I am defensively denying and don't realize it. Part of my interest is in the tribunal. I see the Court as a tribunal, and our case selection process should be less result oriented.

A third justice was a bit more blunt.

> *Justice:* Now there are plenty of strategic considerations, but
> I think those are really made in the individual chambers.
> *Perry:* Would one such strategy be defensive denials?
> *Justice:* Oh certainly that happens.

The next justice had a bit more to say. The topic came up in the
context of his fear that certain justices were wanting to weaken the
exclusionary rule.

> *Justice:* Take, for example, the policeman where a warrant is
> issued incorrectly, but he serves the warrant in good faith;
> he has no idea that he was serving a bad warrant. Is that
> something that ought to be excluded? In my opinion,
> whether or not it was intentional has nothing to do with it, I
> think it is the practice not the intent. My attitude on that is
> to deny all applications for review.
> *Perry:* That leads me to something else. I've heard many
> people talk about defensive denials . . .
> *Justice:* [Interrupting] Certainly, it's a standard of the way we
> behave, and it's a perfectly honorable standard. I think any-
> one who suggests that this is an objective institution is just
> wrong; the notion that we are objective is just fallacious.
> *Perry:* . . . One of the things I'd like to ask you since you
> have been on the Court for a while, and if you will excuse
> the terminology, you have been on the Warren Court and
> the Burger Court . . .
> *Justice:* [Interrupting] If you are going to ask me if I have
> more defensive denials now than when I was on the Warren
> Court, of course I do. I remember rarely doing it then.[4]

Obviously, he had calculated that taking any exclusionary rule case
was dangerous, so he voted to deny them all.

As the preceding quotation suggests, the strategy of defensive denials predates the current Court. Another justice told me:

> When I was in law school, Felix Frankfurter once came out to
> lecture and he said that he knew of cases of where four

---

4. The conversation with this justice about defensive denials continued and is reported
in a later chapter, where he qualifies their use.

wanted cert., but when the vote was taken, cert. was denied, because only three would be in dissent. The reason for this was practicality. The four were convinced that if they went to full argument they would lose, so they would not take this case and would try for another day. He made this as a flat statement in the classroom. I haven't seen that much of it on this Court.[5]

Clerks in all chambers were aware of defensive denials, but they varied in the extent to which they suggested them explicitly in their cert. memos or markups. Different ethics seemed to exist in different chambers, and to some extent, within chambers. In three of the chambers, from both sides of the ideological spectrum, clerks talked about defensive denials unabashedly and saw them as standard operating procedure for cases in certain areas. A rather curious thing happened with clerks from other chambers. Most of the clerks from the other six chambers, while acknowledging that defensive denials occurred, said that they were not a consideration in their chambers. Many of them made statements like, "My justice was not that ideological," or "Justice _____ thought he would be able to persuade the others," or "It was rare for Justice _____ to be in the minority position." And yet, when I interviewed their justices, the justices admitted doing it. Moreover, clerks in all chambers at times were concerned about outcome on the merits when evaluating certain cert. petitions, and such a calculation figured into their recommendation, but they rarely would call this a defensive denial. I suspect the reason for the discrepancy is that while some justices had large, "big issue" areas for which they would defensively deny, for example the exclusionary rule, other justices tended to deny defensively on particular cases. As a result, clerks from the latter chambers did not see what they were doing as the same thing.

The following clerks, from chambers that used defensive denials frequently, provide good examples of how defensive denials were seen and used.

5. Prior to this response there was a good lesson for me on interviewing. By the time I interviewed this justice, I had heard the term "defensive denial" many times and assumed that the term was used universally. Other justices knew exactly what I meant when I used the term. However, when I asked this justice about defensive denials, he looked very puzzled and asked me to repeat the question. Then I was puzzled, because I could not understand why he was confused. After I posed the question again, he launched on a long exposition of why it was rare and unnecessary to write in defense of a denial. Obviously, he is aware of the strategy of defensively denying, but evidently he does not use the terminology.

Sure, we have those, called "defensive denials." It was a real worry of whether or not we were likely to win on the merits. (C11)

Justice _____ and Justice _____ often don't vote cert. because they know they can't get the votes to win if the case is granted cert. (C7)

I think in some cases considerations like that have become second nature with some of the justices. (C20)

The fact that certain justices would defensively deny was of course not a secret. As one clerk from a chamber not predisposed to deny defensively noted:

Well, Justice A and Justice B voted to deny a lot of cases my year. Everyone seemed to believe that they were afraid that if the Court took it that a disaster would follow with the new Court. I think that is particularly true on the liberal side. I never really felt that Justice C [his justice] did that, though he was often in the minority on cert. votes. The liberals just felt that the court was against them. (C24)

The best way to effect a defensive denial, of course, is by never having to say anything. Note the implications of the procedure of using a discuss list.

I think if he knew that they had a majority, he might feel it is better not to let them decide and not to let the case go through. One of the things he could do is not let it show up on the discuss list. Then it didn't have a chance of getting mentioned. You just wouldn't want to rock the boat. (C13)

Though defensive denials are clearly used strategically, they are not some powerful secret strategy. Everyone knows that justices may use them, so that limits their effectiveness. A clerk pointed out their limitations.

Perry: In terms of what you just said, I understand that there are things called defensive denials.
Clerk: Oh yeah. Obviously you have heard the term.
Perry: Yes.

> *Clerk:*   I didn't attempt to apply them or think about them
> that way. I never did recommend defensive denials. It was
> usually obvious he wasn't going to take it. I might say, "you
> may worry how this would come out." I guess I see the role
> of the Court as that it has to decide important topics. If you
> try a defensive denial on the most political cases, the Court
> was not going to pay attention to your defensive denial any-
> how. It's going to be granted so it would be ineffective. If
> the problem is serious it is also going to get granted. A de-
> fensive denial doesn't always work the same way. A defen-
> sive denial is inconceivable in a death case, for example. By
> its very definition the thing you are worried about is people
> being executed, so to deny cert. is counterproductive. But
> that's not true with an equally bright line like in an obscen-
> ity case.   (C40)

And, as another clerk pointed out, sometimes one does not have the
luxury of defensively denying without looking suspicious, particularly
if a dissent from denial is circulated.

> For example, if Justice A and Justice B [moderates] were
> going to dissent from a denial on a liberal cause, it's awkward
> if Justice C and Justice D [liberals] are not there to form the
> four. People are going to ask why C and D are not on. It is
> easier for the clerk to say, "This is a hot potato, don't take this
> case," if there is no dissent; but if there is a dissent from
> someone else, then C and D probably would need to go
> along.[6] There is a different dynamic operating.   (C47)

Even though everyone knows that justices have the tool of defensive
denials, which limits their general effectiveness, it is not always obvious
that on a particular case a justice is trying to effect one. That is,
sometimes a justice might make jurisprudential arguments against
taking a case—for example arguing that there is a messy fact
situation—when in fact, it is the potential outcome that motivates his
objection. This ploy does not mean that the justice is being disingenuous. There are many reasons to deny cert., and the best strategy to
use in getting another justice to go along with his position would be

6. This illustrates nicely Ulmer's argument that justices act strategically at cert. except
that they will attempt to hide their bias. S. Sidney Ulmer, "Selecting Caes for Supreme
Court Review: An Underdog Model," *American Political Science Review* 72 (September
1978): 902–909.

to make arguments that would appeal to that colleague. Nevertheless, his primary concern is the outcome.

Capital cases seemed to be the only category of cases that were off limits to defensive denials per se, at least in terms of attempts to avoid discussion. Recall that all capital cases are put on the discuss list, and that Brennan and Marshall would dissent on all capital cases. Acting truly strategically, Brennan and Marshall might have preferred to pass over some capital cases in order to get a better case for their desired doctrinal outcome, but they did not do this. They dissent on all such cases. Yet several informants said that there were distinctions among capital cases, and that Brennan and Marshall pushed harder on some than on others.

Evidently the justices can defensively deny even when it is tough to do so.

> *Perry:* Does a defensive denial still work in a case even when the justice is outraged? In other words, if he sees a horrible case and it really upsets him, is he still willing to deny defensively?
>
> *Clerk:* No question, because it is better to have it just in a lower court than having it affirmed by the Supreme Court. (C42)

Defensive denials were talked about in all sorts of areas, but they came up most often on Fourth Amendment concerns and obscenity cases. When asked about defensive denials, one clerk said.

> That's absolutely true. Our assumption was that we wouldn't vote on a Fourth Amendment case because we didn't want Justice _____ and Justice _____ to get a hold of it. Justices would be fairly stupid to take a case knowing you would lose. It would be only natural not to take a case unless he thought he could win. I know that was Justice _____ [his justice's] concern. I don't think anyone is like that—where they wouldn't take it into consideration. (C16)

And from two other clerks:

> [Cert.] is generally not a vote on the merits. Although, for awhile I do know on some obscenity cases Justice _____ knew that they would lose five to four. [The four] knew they would lose, therefore, they began not voting for cert. (C13)

> Criminal cases are an area where he's more likely to have de-
> fensive denials. He doesn't have much faith in the Court tak-
> ing on criminal cases. Although again this is where he judged
> wrongly because in our year the Court really extended some
> of the rights of criminals. (C26)

Defensive denials, then, are used selectively but unabashedly in some
chambers. As suggested earlier, however, many clerks feel that defensive denials are somehow improper or unseemly, sometimes even by
those whose own justices do it.

> *Clerk:*   That's basically what we look for and in some ways it
> was influenced by an estimation of whether or not we had
> the votes. I mean there are certain risks involved bringing
> your case up.
> *Perry:*   I've heard this referred to as defensive denials.
> *Clerk:*   Well, I think Justice A [his justice] was less inclined to
> do that than others. I mean he is a very principled guy.
> *Perry:*   Let me ask you about that. Why would you assume
> that a defensive denial would not be principled?
> *Clerk:*   Formally, if a case should be granted because of an
> issue, it should be granted without any regard to who would
> win. Justice B engaged in very few defensive denials. I
> mean [he] would vote to grant a case even if he thought it
> was right. (C56)

And from another clerk:

> Then there was the matter of defensive denials. I didn't really
> get into it because I don't believe in them. I believe that if an
> important case deserves to be heard and decided, that it ought
> to be decided, and the Supreme Court is too political an insti-
> tution anyway to get into things like defensive denials, so I
> tend to resist them. But nevertheless Justice _____ [his jus-
> tice] believed in them. (C26)

These last two quotations bring to mind the discussion in the preceding chapter about clerks being uncomfortable when behavior was
perceived as being "political." But for the same reasons proffered in
the evaluation of horse trading, the ethical dilemma about defensive
denials also seems unjustified so long as it is neither the role nor the
practice of the Court to accept all cases that justices think are wrongly
decided. Unquestionably and unapologetically, clerks and justices en-

gage in strategic behavior in opinion writing. That seems perfectly appropriate to them. Yet for some, strategy at the case selection stage does not.

It is interesting that every justice denounced and denied any log-rolling on cert., but they all admitted that defensive denials occur. Most justices view defensive denials as an acceptable strategy; logroll-ing is an unacceptable strategy to them all. Yet both activities could be seen as efforts that sacrifice a short-term outcome in order to achieve a more desirable long-term goal. The primary distinction is that log-rolling involves two justices whereas a defensive denial involves one. The different normative assessments of these behaviors—one accept-able, the other despicable—is probably the result of socialization and role perception by the justices. Judges are strongly socialized not to allow outside influence. Of course persuasion is acceptable (though its forms are highly constrained), but influence is not. One should make up one's own mind. Horse trading may be seen in terms of influence, whereas a defensive denial comes about as a result of an individual judge's evaluation of a situation. In terms of principle, I smell roses, but justices obviously see the two forms of strategic behavior as very different.

In any event, defensive denials are the exception. That is a very important point and bears emphasizing. Nevertheless, they are signif-icant, because when they occur, it is often in the most contentious areas. Moreover, defensive denials help explain some of the "contra-dictions" in the decision process that are discussed later.

Aggressive Grants

If justices attempt to keep cases from being decided for strategic reasons, do they also reach out and take cases based on strategic calculations? The expression "defensive denial" came from my infor-mants. No common term emerged to describe the opposite phenom-enon, so I invented one—"aggressive grants."[7] I would ask my infor-mants something to the effect:

> You have described denying defensively. Does the opposite
> happen? Are there aggressive grants? That is, do justices
> sometimes reach out to take a case that is not the best candi-

7. A more precise term might have been "offensive grants," but I did not use that term for various reasons. One was that I feared it would strongly suggest calculating behavior, an implication that might engender defensive, textbook responses.

date for cert., because they have calculated that it has certain
characteristics that would make it particularly good for developing doctrine in a certain way, and the characteristics make it
more likely to win on the merits even though it might not be
the best case to take?

Obviously justices grant cases when they think an issue needs resolution, or an area needs clarification. Or at times the justices will reach
to decide a case that is unimportant in the grand scheme of things
because the result is seen as egregious.[8] The aggressive grant question,
however, was asked in the context of *strategically reaching* to solve a case
to further or alter doctrine. As with defensive denials, all justices
admitted that aggressive grants occur, but they seemed to differ in
terms of how comfortable they felt about admitting it. Two justices
responded to my question as follows: "I suppose that is true," and,
"Sure there is." One justice answered this way:

> I am not sure I like your term "aggressive grant," but I think
> what you have described certainly happens . . . [but] unless
> my colleagues are more Machiavellian than I think, waiting
> for some little case to come out of [the] Justice [Department]
> to construe the agenda, a lot of it is just reaction to cases.

And another justice said:

> A consequence of reaching out is that sometimes it hurts the
> Court's credibility.

A third justice spoke of aggressive grants more favorably:

> Because clerks change from year to year, they can't be fully
> aware of the particular areas that I'm interested in, and cases
> that I'm looking for. Let me give you an example. The opin-
> ion of _____ v. _____, which I wrote . . . I had spent several
> terms looking for a case that presented this issue pretty well.
> I think _____ was one of the most important cases we have
> done in the ____ years I've been on the Court. I mean it set in
> team the whole progeny of _____ cases. I think that [doctrine
> as it developed] is extremely important. That's the sort of
> thing I do sometimes. I look for cases.

8. "Egregious" cases are discussed in Chapter 8.

One justice remarked:

> If, for example, . . . I'm interested in overturning the exclu-
> sionary rule, it's my particular interest, I'm going to be look-
> ing for cases for that.

Necessary editing robs many of the preceding quotations of the sense
of "strategic reaching," that is, trying to get a case that would allow a
certain doctrinal outcome and would be one that would be likely to
win. Nevertheless, that was the point that was being made. Finally, one
justice analyzed aggressive grants this way:

> Yes, that goes on, but any efforts at that are overwhelmed by
> the mass of work. You may be successful on one out of fifty.

The basic response to the question about aggressive grants by all
informants was that yes, it occurs, but it is unlikely to be successful.
As has been discussed earlier and will be further discussed later, there
is a huge presumption against granting a case. As one justice put it:

> Arguments in favor of a grant are far harder to present than
> arguments against. The person trying to get a case to be taken
> is a laboring oar against the conference's disposition to deny.
> With arguments against [granting], you don't really need to
> spend time pointing out reasons why.

Anytime there is a recommendation to grant, the case comes under
close scrutiny. This close inspection makes it much more difficult to
"get away with" recommending a grant for strategic reasons. One can
defensively deny in most cases without raising suspicion. When there
is a vote to deny, one usually does not have to justify one's vote. In
fact, the case may not even make the discuss list. However, recommending a grant involves an entirely different dynamic. A strategic
grant usually requires making one's case in nonstrategic terms in order
to convince the brethren. In other words, one must argue why this
particular case is the best one to take for reasons other than that it
would lead to a desired outcome. Obviously, that cannot be done
credibly with just any case, no matter how desirable the fact situation
is in terms of getting the desired outcome. Aggressive grants, therefore, are quite difficult to achieve.

There are times when all (or most) of the justices agree that they
are looking for a case to achieve a desired outcome. One justice's
comments in this regard were interesting:

> Sometimes the Court says now is the time to deal with an is-
> sue. I'm thinking of *Miranda* . . . I don't mean *Miranda,* I
> mean *Gideon.* Now Abe Fortas is a friend of mine, and a lot of
> people gave him credit for the victory, but the Court was
> ready for that case, and a third-rate lawyer from Yonkers
> could have won it. To a degree, the Court was ready for
> *Brown*—same way with one man, one vote. The Court had a
> hard time approaching this issue, then all of a sudden, it be-
> came something else for the states to say that the Constitution
> didn't say anything about these voting procedures. Maybe that
> was true somewhat in the abortion case.

If this justice's assessments are correct, his account differs from those
that suggest that the Court had to wrestle with these cases with much
anxiety and intense deliberation over the correct outcome. This justice
seems to argue that the outcomes were foregone conclusions, and
everyone on the Court knew it at the time the case was selected; indeed,
the case was selected to reach the desired outcome. From what one
can glean from history and doctrinal development, this probably was
true for *Gideon* and perhaps *Brown,* too. The records on the apportionment and abortion cases seem less obvious in support of his assertion. In any event, there are probably few times when the Court as a
whole aggressively grants.

Gideon type cases notwithstanding, the relative ease of defensive
denials compared to the difficulty of aggressive grants has interesting
implications. It suggests that it will be far easier to maintain the status
quo than it will be to change, particularly on a closely divided court.
This might help explain the failure of the conservative counterrevolution. The traditional explanation sees two of the Nixon appointees,
Powell and Blackmun, unwilling to go along with Burger and Rehnquist on some of the most divisive cases. That is observable and is
undoubtedly a partial explanation for the failure of the counterrevolution. There may be other factors that also played a role. Perhaps
even the most conservative justices were not as committed to overturning as much of the Warren Court's legacy as politicians and the
media believed. And perhaps some of the justices have a stronger
affinity for *stare decisis* than was commonly assumed, regardless of the
implications for their own philosophy. In addition to these traditional
explanations, however, there may also be a systemic one. The failure
of the counterrevolution may have something to do with the bias in
the cert. process against change, particularly when there is a divided
Court. All justices can see, and are probably fairly resistant to, attempts
to manipulate the agenda strategically. This resistance would be par-

ticularly true when several justices are known to be less ideological, less result-oriented, and more "judge-like." Whether this is a good or bad thing depends on whom one is talking to. Some admire these justices for their lack of an agenda and their less ideological, less result-oriented approach. Others criticize them for not having a consistent ideology or vision of the constitutional order—something that should differentiate a justice from a judge. The merits of that debate aside, the point is that the presence of "judge-like" justices, whatever their ideological leanings, makes strategic manipulation at cert. more difficult. Once a case is given plenary consideration, conservative but "judge-like" justices may indeed vote with conservative ideologues on the merits. But the primary factor governing their cert. behavior is usually certworthiness in some jurisprudential sense rather than a strategy for outcome on the merits and some ultimate doctrinal stance. From the perspective of the justices who do have an agenda and are willing to act strategically on cert., the attitude of the "judge-like" justices is bad news, because the cases that can muster a grant are not necessarily the best ones strategically to achieve a desired outcome. For example, they might not be the cases most likely to pick up a swing justice.

There is an irony here. The rule of four was developed to make agenda access relatively easy and to assure that there would not be a tyranny of the majority when it comes to setting the agenda. "Relatively easy" does not mean that a case should have easy access. It means that making it onto the agenda should be easier than trying to command a majority opinion. For a case to have its day in court, the requirement is less stringent than in institutions that require majority consent for setting the agenda, or that concentrate agenda power in the hands of a few. Yet practically speaking, other norms have developed on the Court so that the process makes access extraordinarily difficult. The irony is that implicit in the rule of four is the notion that a "policy minority" should at least be able to get a case argued with the hope that a fifth justice could be persuaded on the merits. Yet the presumption against granting, which results in resistance to strategic manipulation of the agenda, works against a "policy minority" getting the chance to put their best case forward, which might enable them to pick up the swing justice. The formal rules, then, allow for a freer access to the decision agenda than in other institutions, and much is frequently made of this, particularly in textbooks and sometimes by the justices. But the reality is that other norms mitigate against access, making it extraordinarily difficult, and easier access does not lead to a substantially improved ability for a minority to structure the agenda to its favor. The point should not be overstated. Obviously requiring only four votes is better than requiring five, and one need only observe the current Court to realize that the importance of one justice is frequently dispositive. Nevertheless, we cannot assume that significantly greater access to the Court's decision agenda is achieved simply because a formal rule allows less than a majority to set the agenda.

Whether this inability to "manipulate the agenda strategically" is a good thing or a bad thing turns largely on one's concept of the role of the Supreme Court. Whatever one's position, however, "strategic manipulation" need not connote something sinister. It can mean something as simple as putting one's best case forward. Still, such a concept was seen as unseemly by many of the informants. There is a fairly strong normative presumption by many that the case selection process should be nonteleological. If a case "deserves" or "does not deserve" to be heard, it should be granted or denied without respect to outcome. Nevertheless, all justices and clerks engage in strategic behavior on cert. sometimes. When and how often this occurs are discussed later.

Invitations and RSVP's

One strategy is related to aggressive grants, though it is not the same thing. The Court need not simply wait for cases to knock at its door. As is well known, justices often send out signals; they invite cases. When asked, justices acknowledged that they do this. Though in response to a different question, one justice's comments are apropos here.

> *Perry:* If we read a textbook account of the Supreme Court, it is described as a reactive rather than proactive institution. By that I mean the classical explanation is that the Supreme Court has to wait for cases to come to it. And yet by what you've just said, it sounds as if in some ways you have some freedom in setting the agenda.
>
> *Justice:* The Supreme Court really does have to wait for cases to come to it—it is basically reactive. But to be honest, that may exist more in theory than in practice. Some justices, I think, wait eagerly for cases to come. That was particularly true in the earlier days that I was on the Court, and less true of the current Court. In fact, I am not really sure that anyone currently has agendas as when I was first on the Court.
>
> *Perry:* Well some people have suggested that Justice _____ has an agenda and that he is actively seeking certain cases.

Justice: [He sat back in his chair and looked up at the ceiling, paused for a moment, then smiled and said] Justice _____ is a very competent, agreeable justice. He does have a very strong view of _____ . . . Perhaps he does encourage cases and wait for them. I must say that my view is that the Court ought to be a more passive institution—perhaps naively and wrongly—but I think it is basically there to facilitate justice. But I think there are some justices who may have more of an agenda.

When asked specifically about inviting cases, one justice had the following to say:

Perry: How do you invite cases?
Justice: What do you mean?
Perry: If a justice wants to hear a case in a certain area, doesn't he sometimes make that known?
Justice: Yes. He says something [in an opinion] that might indicate that the Court would be willing to hear a case which brought up certain issues. We say this is something that we are not deciding here, but that it is something that the Court might want to resolve . . . I think generally that people are sometimes aware of what the Court or a justice might be interested in.

The first part of the justice's response confirms something that has always been assumed, but his latter statement was interesting and deserves some comment. Most of the bar are probably not aware of what the Court or individual justices might be interested in. Granted, there are some issues that any casual observer knows will be taken up sooner or later, though one cannot predict which particular case will be selected to resolve the issue. And, perhaps, one can guess the interest of certain justices in certain issues. Or when the Court practically issues a printed invitation, one learns of the Court's interest. Undoubtedly some people, such as the solicitor general, a few New York and D.C. attorneys who argue with some frequency in the Court, and some Court watchers, have a sense of the Court's, or an individual justice's, interest. But most of the nation's best attorneys are not likely to be aware of the types of cases that might interest many of the justices. And if they guessed, they would often be wrong. Several clerks suggested that when they began clerking for their justice, they assumed they knew some of his interests, either from knowing something about the justice's background, or from having observed him from the perspective of clerking on a court of appeals. Many times they turned out to be wrong. Not only was their justice not predisposed to taking the cases that they thought he would, but they also found that he was interested in things they would never have imagined. If the invitation is not clear, there may not be the desired RSVP's.

Having said all this, one often does not have to guess at the justice's interests because signals are sent. The trick is simply to find the signals. This usually requires watching the Court more closely than most attorneys have time to do, but some signals are pretty evident. Cases are invited through written opinions, as the justice suggested above; and our old friends, dissents from denials of certiorari, serve as an excellent place to find invitations. Obviously, the fact that a case was denied is discouraging, but often the dissent signals what it might take for a similar case to get a grant.[9]

Deciding whether or not justices bargain, influence, or act strategically is an issue of perspective. The cert. process is political, and odd as it may seem, that is a point that needs to be made. The process is quite often characterized, particularly by lawyers, as routine and relatively free of strategy. But by any other name, much of the behavior that occurs is still political. Equally important, however, is the fact that just because there are sometimes attempts to achieve certain ends, these attempts differ in many ways from the ones we are used to and might expect from observations of other political institutions. Other times, they look much the same. Horse trading and logrolling do not occur. Persuasion and threats do, although they occur in a limited and particular form. Agenda coalitions are not formed and nourished explicitly, but coalitions are sometimes assumed based on anticipated reactions. There is strategy involved in some cert. decisions, but depending on one's perspective, it looks very much, or very little, like strategy in other political institutions.

Undoubtedly the boundaries and forms of acceptable political behavior on the Court result from perceptions of what is and is not proper behavior for justices.[10] Inevitably, it seems to me, constraints on political behavior in a political institution, real or imagined, exogenous or endogenous, are going to bring about behavior that appears suboptimal, peculiar, and contradictory. This is not necessarily a crit-

9. See Peter Linzer, "The Meaning of Certiorari Denials," *Columbia Law Review* 79 (November 1979): 1227–1305.

10. Again, others have made this point. It is best articulated by Provine, *Case Selection.* See also Harold Spaeth and Gregory Rathjen, "Denying Access in Plenary Cases: The Burger Court," in S. Sidney Ulmer, ed., *Courts, Law, and Judicial Process* (New York: Free Press, 1981), p. 265.

icism, nor is it unique to the Court. We probably want our presidents and members of Congress to be both political and above politics. Likewise our justices. Nevertheless, constraints lead to behavior that is nonconstant. In this instance, as shall be argued later, it leads to an almost dichotomized pattern of decision making.

I shall not today attempt to define the kinds of material I understand to be [hard-core pornography]. I could never succeed in intelligibly doing so. But I know it when I see it.

Justice Potter Stewart

It is really hard to know what makes up this broth of the cert. process . . . Some cases are ones you can just smell as grants.

U.S. Supreme Court Justice

8 Certworthiness

Until now, I have tried to finesse precisely what it is that makes a case certworthy. The question can no longer be avoided. Unfortunately, neither can it be answered with much precision. Would that I could; my consulting fees would easily ameliorate the problem of an academic salary. But no one can predict with much certainty whether or not a certain case will be taken. One can predict in a trivial sense. Since so few cases are granted, one can predict denial and be right 95 percent of the time. Moreover, there are some cases that one can predict easily, such as when a state court declares a federal law unconstitutional, or when the solicitor general is the petitioner. But for most cases, meaningful prediction is a faulty enterprise. Still, the criteria for certworthiness are not quite as mysterious, serendipitous, or dependent upon one's olfactory skills as the quotations that began this work and this chapter suggest.[1] As a result of empirical work done by others, combined with what is reported below and seen in the light of the decision process, we can generalize far more intelligently, though we still cannot predict with any precision.

Earlier Studies

Despite some instability in results, we have learned that several things are associated with case selection. For example, we know with a high

---

1. The first epigraph is from Stewart's concurring opinion in Jacobellis v. Ohio, 378 U.S. 184, 197. The second is from a personal interview with a justice.

degree of certainty that when the federal government seeks review, the chances of a case being taken are quite high.[2] Studies have resulted in differing assessments of the importance of other criteria, such as dissension on the court below and the presence of a civil liberties issue.[3] An amicus brief on cert. increases the likelihood of a grant.[4] Conflict in the circuit courts has been shown to be important.[5] Scholars have demonstrated that cert. votes are related to votes on the merits.[6] Similarly, though not precisely the same thing, scholars have suggested that justices cast cert. votes on an ideological basis and are more likely to reverse lower court decisions that they think are wrongly decided.[7]

2. See Chapter 5. Several scholars have demonstrated the importance of the federal government in case selection. As examples, see Joseph Tanenhaus, Marvin Schick, Matthew Muraskin, and Daniel Rosen, "The Supreme Court's Certiorari Jurisdiction: Cue Theory," in Glendon Schubert, ed., *Judicial Decision Making* (New York: Free Press, 1963); S. Sidney Ulmer, William Hintze, and Louise Kirklosky, "The Decision to Grant or Deny Certiorari: Further Consideration of Cue Theory," *Law and Society Review* (May 1972): 637–643; Virginia Armstrong and Charles A. Johnson, "Certiorari Decision Making by the Warren and Burger Courts: Is Cue Theory Time Bound?" *Polity* 15 (1982): 141–150.

3. See previous note; see also Doris Marie Provine, *Case Selection in the United States Supreme Court* (Chicago: University of Chicago Press, 1980).

4. See H. W. Perry, Jr., "Indices and Signals in the Certiorari Process," paper prepared for the Midwest Political Science Association Meeting, April 9–11, 1986. See also Gregory A. Caldeira and John R. Wright, "Organized Interests and Agenda Setting in the U.S. Supreme Court," *American Political Science Review* 82 (December 1988): 1109–1127.

5. See, e.g., Samuel Estreicher and John Sexton, *Redefining the Supreme Court's Role: A Theory of Managing the Federal Judicial Process* (New Haven: Yale University Press, 1986); Floyd Feeney, "Conflicts Involving Federal Law: A Review of Cases Presented to the Supreme Court," in Commission on Revision of the Federal Court Appellate System, *Structure and Internal Procedures: Recommendations for Change* (Washington, D.C.: Government Printing Office, 1975); S. Sidney Ulmer, "Conflict with Supreme Court Precedent and the Granting of Plenary Review," *Journal of Politics* 45 (1983): 474–477; S. Sidney Ulmer, "The Supreme Court's Certiorari Decisions: Conflict as a Predictive Variable," *American Political Science Review* 78 (December 1984): 901–911.

6. See, e.g., Lawrence Baum, "Decisions to Grant and Deny Hearings in the California Supreme Court: Patterns in Court and Individual Behavior," *Santa Clara Law Review* 16 (1976): 713–744; Lawrence Baum, "Policy Goals in Judicial Gatekeeping: A Proximity Model of Discretionary Jurisdiction," *American Journal of Political Science* 21 (February 1977): 13–33; Lawrence Baum, "Judicial Demand-Screening and Decisions on the Merits: A Second Look," *American Politics Quarterly* 7 (January 1979): 109–119; Ulmer, "Further Consideration of Cue Theory."

7. Armstrong and Johnson, "Is Cue Theory Time Bound?" Baum, "Gatekeeping"; Baum, "Screening"; Jan Palmer, "An Econometric Analysis of the U.S. Supreme Court's Certiorari Decisions," *Public Choice* 39 (1982): 387–398; Provine, *Case Selection*; Donald Songer, "Concern for Policy Outputs as a Cue for Supreme Court Decisions on Certiorari," *Journal of Politics* 41 (November 1979): 1185–1194; S. Sidney Ulmer, "Selecting Cases for Supreme Court Review: An Underdog Model," *American Political Science Review* 72 (September 1978): 902–909.

Furthermore, some scholars have argued that cert. votes are not only related to votes on the merits, but that justices calculate likely outcomes on the merits and vote accordingly.[8]

Earlier studies have provided objective evidence that several factors are related to a grant of certiorari. It remains to be seen what those engaged in the decision making claim to be their criteria for certworthiness. Before examining certworthiness per se, however, the discussion must be put in context. Some of what is discussed in the following contextual sections has been said or alluded to before but deserves extended consideration here.

Presumption against a Grant

Approximately 95 percent of all petitions are denied. This statistic, the burgeoning docket, and other factors have led to something I term the "presumption against a grant." Certworthiness can be understood only when seen in context of this mind-set. The statements of several clerks are demonstrative:

> I have talked about this with my former co-clerks. We saw our role as clerks to find every reason possible to deny cert. petitions. If the justice were interested in the area, he'd probably grant anyway. We'd try to show where it may have problems. (C10)

> Of course there is also the rule that anything that is avoidable should be avoided. (C33)

> There is enormous pressure not to take a case . . . there is an institutionalized inertia not to grant cert. (C5)

One justice demonstrated his willingness to be guided by the presumption:

> If a case is arguable as to whether or not it should be a grant, I try to form the reasons for denial.

8. See, e.g., Saul Brenner, "The New Certiorari Game," *Journal of Politics* 41 (1979): 649–655; Glendon Schubert, "The Certiorari Game," in *Quantitative Analysis of Judicial Behavior* (New York: Free Press, 1959); Glendon Schubert, "Policy without Law: An Extension of the Certiorari Game," *Stanford Law Review* 14 (March 1962): 284–327; Ulmer, "Underdog Model."

One clerk put it more graphically:

> There is a great presumption on the Court that on its face, a
> case just won't be heard . . . There is really almost a siege
> mentality. You almost get to hate the guy who brings the cert.
> petitions around. He is really a nice guy, but he gets abuse all
> the time. You have to screen down to [so few] argument days,
> so there is a strong presumption for not hearing cases . . .
> Today the backdrop is: "is this one of the 160 most pressing
> cases of the year? Show me." (C11)

Informants differ over the cause of, and justification for, the presumption. Some argue, as suggested in the last quotation, that the small amount of available argument time in the face of so many petitions requires it. Others disagree, saying that there simply are not that many certworthy cases. Indeed, they argue that not only is every worthy case heard, but in fact, the Court takes far too many cases, many of which do not belong in the Supreme Court. Therefore, the presumption is justifiable substantively, irrespective of caseload. Whatever one's belief about the cause, or justification, no one denies that a strong presumption against granting exists. It may not be irrebutable, but it is redoubtable.

As suggested in the earlier discussion of aggressive grants, the presumption has conservative implications (that is, it tends to reinforce the status quo). Moreover, the decision process is not geared to check the presumption but reinforce it. Granted, it takes most clerks time to learn the presumption, and even after they do, they continue to recommend more cases than the justices take. But all the procedural rigmarole involved in researching and writing cert. memos does little to brake the momentum for denying. Therefore, the way the clerks view their role—either as surrogates or as detectives to flesh out the issues—really may not matter very much given the presumption. Except when a clerk knows that her justice is looking for cases, or when the clerk has a particular interest in a case herself, there is a huge predisposition to recommend a denial, regardless of how she sees her role.

One could imagine the process working differently. Knowing that the justices are predisposed to deny, the clerks' role could be seen as one to make every effort to "save" a case and let the justices bear the presumption. Of course going overboard, making heroic arguments as to why almost every case "might" be certworthy, would render clerks of little assistance to their justices. But surely there is some middle ground. There could exist a different presumption. Except for obviously uncertworthy cases, which constitute a large number, the presumption could be more positive from the clerk's perspective.[9] In any event, the overwhelming existence of such a strong presumption must be understood before one can understand and evaluate the process and the likelihood of a case's acceptance.

Finally, recall that not only is there a presumption against a grant on the part of the clerks, but there is an incentive to recommend a denial, because to recommend a grant requires "guts," not to mention much more work. No clerk would recommend a denial simply to avoid work, but there is little incentive not to recommend a denial. Along this line, one clerk made a statement that nicely ends this section and introduces the next.

> I would check jurisdictional questions to see if they were actually on time. Usually that was the Clerk [of the Court]'s responsibility, but every once in awhile somewhere he might have missed something. Maybe a holiday came in there or something. Of course, that was always unfortunate as far as the petitioner was concerned, but it was usually to our delight if we could find that.

Case Fungibility

As the previous quotation suggests, and as I have noted so many times in this book, the Court basically sees itself not as a place to right wrongs in individual cases but as a place to clarify the law. There is an irony here. Justices see it as improper to negotiate over granting particular cases because the fate of the individuals should not be bargained; yet they see most cases as unimportant in and of themselves. There are exceptions. With a case such as *U.S. v. Nixon*, it is the result for the litigant that is all-important. And as discussed below, there are those individual cases that the justices see as egregious. But generally, individual cases are seen as fungible; it is the issue that the case raises that is important, not the case itself. This came to my attention when the first few informants said something that confused me:

9. I am not arguing that is how it should be. In fact, I have sympathy with the argument that the Court is taking too many cases, and that it ought to spend more time (and interchamber communication) on those cases that it takes rather than on cert. petitions.

> *Clerk:* You see, it really didn't matter if the Court made a mistake in not taking a case. It is better to let it have a little extra time, because if we didn't grant cert., the case will come up again.
>
> *Perry:* Do you mean the case will come back up again, or the issue?
>
> *Clerk:* Oh no, the issue will be back up again, so it doesn't matter if it is not taken. The exception would be with those few great cases of public interest. (C2)

Justices did it too. One told me, "A case will come back if it is really important." It is remarkable how many of my informants used "case" and "issue" interchangeably. The fungibility of terminology is an indication of the fungibility of cases.

It is important to understand what I mean when I use the word "fungible" because it has various meanings. Cases are fungible in that, in Webster's words, one may be used in the place of another in the satisfaction of an obligation. To say that cases are fungible is not to suggest that an individual case is of no importance, or that differences between cases do not matter. Indeed, much of this chapter argues precisely the opposite. Nevertheless, it is the issue, not the case that is primary. As with the denial presumption, one must also understand this perception of fungibility in order to comprehend determinations of certworthiness. One clerk's comments justify the perception and illustrate the mind-set.

> It's going to come up again if it's really an important issue. In fact a test to see if an issue is really important is to see if it comes up again . . . I can say I never really feared that if we don't take it now or miss this one, that we won't have the chance to decide it again. (C24)

Is Certworthiness a Tautology?

Fundamentally, the definition of "certworthy" is tautological; a case is certworthy because four justices say it is certworthy. As discussed in Chapter 2, the criteria given by the justices are vague, nonbinding, and not very helpful; and, despite their grumbling about attorneys petitioning frivolous cases, justices do not want lawyers or anyone else to know precisely what it is that makes a case certworthy. Sometimes the justices will grant cert. solely because they believe that the result below was egregious, something that they continually suggest does not make a case certworthy. Yet even though certworthiness is ultimately subjective, changing, and undefinable, there are criteria for cert. that are usually important and usually dispositive, so the notion of a tautology for most cases is really only true in some theoretical sense.

Uncertworthiness

Given the presumption against a grant, it makes sense first to examine those things that make a case uncertworthy. It is also easier. As one justice told me, "I would put it that you know it when you don't see it." Often the converse of things making a case uncertworthy make it certworthy and vice versa. The criteria for the two categories, however, are not mirror images.

Frivolousness

The one thing said most frequently and consistently in the interviews was that "a large number of cases are frivolous." Most informants would agree on which cases these would be and on the criteria that make a case frivolous. First, there are the cases that might be called absurd. A good example:

> [There was] a case once that said "it was unconstitutional because my wife got up out of bed and left me alone on Christmas Eve." (C43)

Another clerk proffered:

> Then there's that certain proportion of just nut cases. Often a lot of them are pro se or some of the lawyers have just gone off the deep end. It's a case about traffic tickets in the Supreme Court. (C8)

A third clerk estimated the number of absurd cases:

> About 10 percent of the petitions raised issues which just didn't make any sense at all. They really had incompetent lawyers. They were just filing a petition that didn't make any sense. (C3)

After "absurd" cases, three categories of cases were repeatedly described as frivolous: fact-specific cases, insufficient evidence cases, and diversity cases. They are discussed in turn.

When asked for examples of frivolous cases, one justice responded:

> *Justice:* Factual issues. For example, whether or not the light was green. That doesn't have any business being in the Supreme Court. Or a case, no matter how much money is involved, if it has very little impact on others. Even if it is litigation involving a billion dollars. They have had a trial, and they have had an appellate Court rule on it . . .
>
> *Perry:* . . . Now I want to be clear about what you mean when you say frivolous . . . A law professor at Yale [not one of my informants] suggested to me that the definition of a frivolous case is a case that the justices are not interested in. A good lawyer could find an issue in any case.
>
> *Justice:* Well, that is interesting. There might be something to that though a lot of them are simply factual situations and simply do not belong in the Supreme Court.

One clerk gave a cogent explanation of what it means for a case to be "fact-specific."

> The buzz words in the pool memos were "fact-specific." By that I mean that it wasn't necessarily challenging the law, but it had to do with the facts of the case. Fourth Amendment cases were a particular example of this. For example, the law might say you have to get a warrant except when there are exigent circumstances and there might be a petition that would say there were not exigent circumstances. This really isn't a question of law, it's a question of whether or not the law applied specifically to facts in this case. (C8)

Though this informant's description of a fact-specific case was particularly good, his choice of an example may not have been. Fourth Amendment doctrine surely is one of the most confused areas of law, and it is an area where the Court has often drawn unpersuasive distinctions that seem to turn only on the facts. Such cases might be the best example to sustain the law professor's contention that all cases in the hands of a good lawyer can raise an interesting issue. Nevertheless, in most instances the Court does not want to take a case when resolving it adds nothing to doctrine but turns on the facts of the particular case. As one clerk said, "To say it was fact-specific was the kiss of death" (C38).

Related to fact-specific cases are cases involving claims of insufficiency of evidence.

> Many of the petitions were ones where they were trying to make the argument that the evidence was insufficient to support the findings . . . The Court really doesn't sit there to decide whether the evidence is sufficient. (C3)

Such cases constitute a large number of those petitioned. An interchange with a clerk went as follows:

> *Perry:*   What do you mean by "frivolous"?
> *Clerk:*   For example, in the criminal area. If the case is simply one of insufficiency of evidence. If you read *U.S. Law Week,* you find case after case described as insufficiency of evidence to find the verdict. That is not a case that belongs in the Supreme Court.
> *Perry:*   Can you give me other examples of frivolous cases?
> *Clerk:*   Diversity cases. (C5)

Like fact-specific cases, insufficient evidence cases are considered frivolous and receive only cursory attention.

Diversity cases, the third commonly mentioned category, usually raise issues that involve an interpretation of state law, but because of special circumstances (usually the litigants being from different states), the case is brought in federal court. When asked for an example of an obvious denial, one justice said:

> A diversity case. When the Court of Appeals didn't appear to understand the law of Arkansas. But that is clearly not the job of the [U.S.] Supreme Court. It is the responsibility of the Supreme Court of the State of Arkansas.

Many informants cited diversity cases as a category of frivolous cases per se.

Undoubtedly there are some crackpot or incompetent lawyers who petition absurd cases. Sometimes, however, lawyers intentionally petition a case that they know has no chance of review. Doing this may be for the client's benefit. One reason is to delay a final judgment. One former clerk who at the time of the interview worked for a major law firm said:

I have a petition before the Court now. The case clearly isn't certworthy, but it will delay [my client's] going to jail. (C5)

Another clerk gave a different reason for delaying tactics:

This is done particularly by insurance companies. They are seeking a delay because of the interest rates. They make more money by going ahead and protracting the litigation because they don't have to pay out over the time while its being litigated, and if they catch it right, an appeal late enough in the term, then it may be the next term, as much as nine months, before the case is [disposed of]. There are not really that large a number of diversity cases, but frankly, there were more than I expected. This is not a case of where it is done by stupid lawyers; they know exactly what they are doing. (C8)

One clerk, however, also from a big firm, argued that petitioning obviously frivolous cases was usually not in the client's interest.

A lot of lawyers bilk their clients. It's just inconceivable to me. I mean their clients pay $20,000 or whatever it costs to carry through and do a cert. petition to raise a legal question, and there is just no legal question there. A lot of big firms and good lawyers will do this. It is not necessarily their fault because clients are involved. The law firm does not exactly have the freedom to choose what it wants to appeal. But I don't think they try to dissuade their clients enough. If a client wants to take a case all the way to the Supreme Court, the lawyer just does it. But some very well known law firms send out some awful shoddy petitions . . . Not being a lawyer, you may not realize this, but lawyers can really be disturbing in terms of professional codes. (C11)

One need not be a lawyer to know to plead the Fifth on that last statement. Nevertheless, a clerk quoted earlier had a different perspective on the question of petitioning when there is little hope:

Another class of cases deals with many of the type this law firm does. Big corporations can often afford lawyers to do all the litigation even though they know there's a one-in-a-million shot that their case will get granted. If it would, however, and if a judgment would be found in their favor, it would be so worth it that they're usually willing to say, "what the heck,"

and go ahead and pay the lawyer's fees to take a shot at
it. (C8)

The Supreme Court actually can punish attorneys for petitioning frivolous cases, but this is a sanction rarely used.[10] Given the screening
process, it is much easier simply to deny cert. than to get involved in
trying to determine if a lawyer has acted irresponsibly. The justices
realize this. As one told me:

> I don't blame them for doing it. We don't give them any real
> incentive not to try . . . Some of them do it simply for delay-
> ing tactics. And given the rules we have given them, there is
> no reason for them not to do it.

Sanctions and legal ethics are interesting but beside the point for
our purposes save one thing. Earlier I suggested that control of the
workload "crisis" is somewhat in the Court's hands. The Court could
impose sanctions that would discourage frivolous litigants. They
choose not to do so. The more relevant point to our discussion is that
there are many cases that are obviously uncertworthy and can be so
adjudged very quickly by a clerk. To the uninitiated, clerk or layman,
the petition looks very complicated, but usually by reading the "Questions Presented," the experienced law clerk can tell immediately that
the case is uncertworthy.

Clear Denies

There are certain types of cases that, though not frivolous in the sense
just described, clerks come to treat as frivolous, particularly in terms
of preparing a memo, because they learn that either their boss, or the
Court as a whole, is simply unwilling to grant them. They are "clear
denies." Obviously, for nonpool clerks a wider variety of cases are seen
as clear denies because they are working only for one justice. However,
there was one issue during the tenure of the informants that all justices
had decided not to grant, and everyone knew it. There were several
other issues that most justices would always vote to deny, so their clerks
treated them as clear denies. Discussed here are only the examples
reported most frequently when I asked for an example of a clear deny.

10. The Court did issue penalties in a few cases in the early 1980s, leading some to
speculate that maybe the use of sanctions was about to begin. The Court has not seen
fit to continue the practice in any meaningful way.

First, the one everyone knew. At the time of the interviews, there was one issue on which the circuit courts of appeals had split; it was an important issue, it had been around for some time, and much had been written on it. In other words, cases posing this issue often fulfilled the normal criteria for certworthiness but invariably were denied. Practically every informant cited this as an example of learning—that as a clerk you learn that there are certain things the justices are just not interested in, period. The issue: ineffective assistance of counsel.

> Sometimes there are just certain cases they refuse to take. For example, a case dealing with the competency of counsel. The circuits have split on it, it has been split at federal and state level, and yet the Court just won't take it. (C2)

It did not take clerks long to learn that the justices had no interest in taking one of these cases. One clerk noted:

> There is a classical answer—effectiveness of counsel. Every summer there is some clerk who writes a memo saying, "This is just terrible. Look at all these different standards. The Court has got to do something." And the Court just as routinely denies these. (C31)

And as two other clerks said:

> All clerks get upset at the effectiveness of counsel and then they learn that the justices just aren't interested in that. (C61)

> Those were pretty generally a no-memo case. (C49)

One justice seemed amused that clerks always had to learn this lesson.

> Adequacy of counsel is a real favorite of law clerks. Someone will come in and say this is just terrible. All these different standards exist. But what we justices have seen is that the competency level [required in the various circuits] is just about the same. The standout is the second circuit. They have this idea of farce or mockery. But as we look at the second circuit, we don't see much difference. In every case in the second circuit, it is based on more than that.

This justice went on to give another example:

> Then of course another favorite of the clerks is the Allen
> charge. I always kid my clerks about this. I tell them that it
> was written by Oliver Wendell Holmes, Jr., and they don't
> want to be the ones to knock out his last opinion. Generally
> on these if it is a bad case, there are other issues too. In these
> criminal cases there are fine distinctions, but the jury will
> come out with the same result.[11]

The Allen charge was not talked about as much as effective counsel,
but several did mention it. To quote one clerk:

> There is something called the Allen charge. I don't really
> know where it got its name, but I guess it had something to
> do with someone named Allen. It has to do with when the
> jurors are out to deliberate. There are certain things the
> judge can tell them when they can't come to a decision to try
> to force them to get their act together. On the other hand,
> you don't want to intimidate them if someone is holding out
> on a verdict. The justices have just considered it best to leave
> these types of things to the trial judge's discretion.

Effectiveness of counsel and Allen charge cases might be considered
uncertworthy for various reasons. One interesting reason is discussed
later, but with respect to the present topic, a common explanation was
that these cases are essentially fact-bound. Effective counsel depends
on the facts of the particular case. About all the Court could do would
be to come down with some prophylactic rule, and if it did, it is not
clear that it would change results in any of the circuits. As one justice
put it:

> We have a conflict on effectiveness of counsel. They have all
> come into line pretty much. If the second circuit gets a bad
> case, I think they can apply other standards and go off their
> standard. If we took a case, it would have to sound strange. If
> Clarence Darrow had tried a case . . . the Court might grant
> and affirm, but I think if they ever got a bad case, they would
> probably come in line.

11. Allen v. U.S., 164 U.S. 492 (1896). I guess part of the joke was that this opinion
was written before Oliver Wendell Holmes was even appointed to the Court.

Finally, one clerk repeated a rumor about why effectiveness of counsel cases were not taken.

> There were stories or rumors that went around the Court that there was a pact made at the time of *Gideon,* which gave a right to counsel, that they wouldn't try to second-guess as to what then was "effective" counsel. (C48)

Apocryphal or true, the point is that clerks knew that justices considered these cases clear denies.[12]

The second most frequent example of clear denies for some justices were tax cases. There are special tax courts in the United States, and tax cases are usually extraordinarily complex. Several justices have come to believe that tax cases generally are not worth the Court's time or effort, and that it is better to leave the questions to the specialized tax courts. All justices do not agree, but an overwhelming number of the clerks I interviewed did. They hated tax cases, even those who worked for justices who liked tax cases. The typical response, is reflected in the following clerks' statements:

> Justice _____ thinks that the Court just should never deal with tax cases. Tax cases ought to be left to the more specialized courts that can deal with them. The Supreme Court isn't that competent unless it deals with a constitutional issue [implicated in a tax issue], or maybe if there is just a complete breakdown with a split in the circuits. But if it is purely an issue of interpretation of a tax statute, he just thinks that the Supreme Court ought not to deal with it. (C16)

> No one wanted tax or patent cases. They are technically very difficult. The Court really doesn't have the expertise developed to deal with them. They wouldn't grant them unless there was just a clear split in the circuits, and we clerks were essentially instructed to work very hard to show why in fact there was no split in circuits. (C3)

12. Since the time of the interviews, the Court has looked at the counsel issue, but the point here is that clerks knew for their Court the issue was a clear deny.

One justice, assessed it this way:

> Some people on the Court are either comfortable or ex-
> tremely uncomfortable with tax cases. Justice A is comfortable
> with them. Justice B claims to be. Justice C is probably the
> most uncomfortable with them. Justice D to an extent, and so
> forth. [The justice then wanted to go off the record to discuss
> the various justices.] . . . I don't mind working on tax cases,
> but I certainly don't go out and look for them. We have
> enough to do, although I am impressed with their importance
> in the federal area.

This justice, however, was out of sync with most of his brethren who
felt that tax issues were generally unimportant.

For virtually the same reasons, patent cases were clear denies for
many justices.

> In certain areas the justices don't do very well. When they
> take patent cases, they do a terrible job.   (C9)

And finally one clerk, describing his nonpool cert. memo, said:

> There are certain cases that you can deal with very quickly.
> We were instructed [to deny] when it was something on pat-
> ents . . . On the novelty of patents we would write, "it is just
> another case like the cow shit case [a case involving a patent]
> —deny."

Certain cases, then, are seen as clear denies because of their subject
area. From the clerk's standpoint, they can be treated as frivolous.
From the observer's vantage, however, there is a distinction, because
today's clear deny may not be tomorrow's, if there is a change in
personnel. Those cases seen as frivolous, however, will probably remain so irrespective of personnel.

Percolation

Justices like the smell of well-percolated cases. A case that has not
percolated through various courts will usually be considered uncertworthy. The concept is one well known in jurisprudence. The Supreme Court exists primarily to clarify the law. Once it speaks, however, its interpretation is final, so justices want to make sure that when

they do speak, they can do so as intelligently as possible.[13] It is good jurisprudence and makes good sense to put off rendering an interpretation as long as possible—or more precisely, as long as the benefits of avoidance outweigh the problems—so that the Court can benefit from analysis by others. As one clerk said:

> The Court does not want to start considering a federal question without having other courts look at it. There needs to be some procedural rigor established by having other courts look at it. They do not want to look at a claim in the abstract. What they want to do is review how other courts have looked at this issue.

The "others" may be lower court judges, law professors in law reviews, or various other commentators. But when has an issue percolated enough, and when must a case be taken despite a desire for more percolation? When outlining considerations for cert., one clerk said:

> Fifth, is it ripe? Now I am really misusing a term of art here, but what I mean is, is it time for consideration. What is the harm in terms of what it does for uncertainty of the law by not taking this case now? What is the harm for waiting and letting the courts of appeals flesh out the issue more. It is better if you can come in with a large body of experience of people who have considered it. (C23)

Another clerk assessed the choice this way:

> The Court is aware that when they rule on [a given issue], it will be pretty final, and they can't come back five years later and reverse very easily. So as a result, this should percolate even more and get law review articles written and more lower court opinions before they have to make a final decision. On the other hand, if the issue is one that is really making a mess of the federal court system, and people are getting very different results depending on which court they go to, then even though the justices might want to see law review articles and court decisions, they really have to balance between letting the problem go unsolved and allowing it to percolate, versus

---

13. The Supreme Court is the final interpreter of the Constitution. Of course if it rules on a statute, Congress can always amend the statute.

needing to settle it. That judgment is fairly subjective . . . If it
is not a very important issue and there is no reason to worry
about a lot of percolating, then you might want to go ahead
and settle it; but on the other hand, if it is not very important,
the Court might say, "Well, we are not going to have to deal
with this so there is no reason to worry about it, so let's see if
it works itself out."   (C35)

Another clerk suggested:

If it was an issue where you didn't have to educate the Court
about it, you might take it, versus looking up and saying,
"Hey, this is a novel issue. Let's let a few other courts address
this to see what might come out."   (C62)

A justice's education about an issue may not come solely from Court
experience. As one clerk said:

The justice may say, "you know when I was practicing law I
had a case just like that and that is just not right. We need to
get that cleared up." I think though that . . . the presumption
is not to take the case, and then if it is taken, it is probably
just because it hits the justice in the right way.   (C10)

We shall have a further opportunity to see how a justice's pre-Court
experience affects his cert. behavior. For now it is safe to say that if
the justices feel confident about an issue, and a court below botches it,
it might behoove them to nip the problem in the bud rather than allow
additional percolation.

Sometimes if a court below would interpret a statute incorrectly, the justices would say we better stop it now.   (C1)

When I asked one justice how he knew if a case had percolated
enough, his response was not very helpful.

That's easy. When you have the first decision as the only decision, you don't take it. But after you get other decisions, then
you do.

A discussion with another justice:

> *Perry:* . . . I have often heard about the need to let an issue
> . . .
> *Justice:* [Interrupting]—percolate?
> *Perry:* Yes. But how does one know when it has percolated
> enough?
> *Justice:* That is driven by time. If, for example, the Third
> Circuit has a ruling that seems to create a conflict, we will
> let it percolate to see if the conflict will work itself out. Con-
> flicts often work themselves out, particularly if the conflict is
> within a circuit, we will let them decide *en banc*. But we are
> better informed if the issue has been considered by several
> courts of appeals, although some issues don't fit that mold.

A third justice's response was more instructive. Moreover, his statement raises interesting auxiliary points that shall be discussed later—
most notably, the importance of the judges below:

> That is really just my own judgment. There are no black and
> white rules. We might differ on that. But the first time that an
> issue is resolved is no time to take it—certainly if it is in a
> court that is less respected and we know a case is being de-
> cided elsewhere. So it is both the number of judges and cases,
> and the character of the judges who have talked about the
> issue. Plus the extent to which others have talked about it in
> other forums. So there are really a lot of factors, but what
> finally makes one decide is hard to say.

Not only does the Court want to allow percolation before it addresses
an issue, but often after it decides a case, it wants to allow its own
decision to percolate in the courts below before it looks at the area
again. The Court is in some ways the ultimate incremental institution,
preferring to take a small step at a time.

> The Court had decided to stay away from certain areas. For
> example, they decided to stay away from double jeopardy
> cases. In double jeopardy, they had decided several cases the
> year before, and they wanted to see how it was beginning to
> work its way out. (C24)

It is probably easier to determine when a case has not percolated
enough than when it has, and it is clear that an inadequately percolated

issue renders a case uncertworthy unless there is perceived to be an overriding necessity to resolve the issue or the particular case immediately. Given the presumption against granting, issues are usually seen as in need of more percolation.

Bad Facts (Vehicle)

Another commonly agreed upon criterion that renders a case uncertworthy is if it is a "bad vehicle" or has "bad facts." The expressions were used interchangeably for the most part, and again, they were the informants' terms, not mine. Good/bad facts or a good/bad vehicle actually can mean several things. Later, when examining the positive, certworthy side under "good vehicle," we shall see that the expression is sometimes used to mean something very different from the meaning discussed here.[14]

As my very first informant said, "It is important to find a case that presents the issue clearly." Virtually all succeeding informants said the same thing. Putting it in the negative, a justice said, "Some of the cases we turn down if they are too messy. They have bad facts." A general rule in jurisprudence is that a case is to be resolved on the narrowest grounds possible. For example, if a case can be resolved on statutory rather than constitutional grounds, it should be so decided. Likewise, if procedural issues dispose of a case, the primary issue will never be reached. Bad facts often prevent reaching the primary issue. Such a disposition is not problematic at a lower court, but when the Supreme Court takes a case, the purpose is to solve some important issue, not simply resolve the instant dispute. As suggested earlier, the Court at times runs roughshod over jurisprudential constraints and resolves an issue that properly should not be reached, but generally speaking, the jurisprudential rule is followed. Bad facts are not always obvious, else the Court would not take such cases. Cases that are taken with bad facts are often those that are digged, or that wind up being decided on some very narrow ground. And, of course, facts are bad to greater and lesser degrees. Much of the clerks' screening function is to look for bad fact/vehicle problems. As one clerk said:

> The law clerk would review each case for technical problems which might cause a case ultimately not to be decided on the merits. There are sometimes procedural problems in cases . . .

14. I shall use "bad facts" here rather than "bad vehicle" to help keep separate the "good vehicle" concept, which I discuss later.

sometimes even the litigant was not aware of them, and other times of course, the litigants would try and obfuscate the problem. (C23)

And from a justice:

> Rushing at an issue you might later find that the relevant issue is surrounded by other issues. You must be careful to see that the facts surround the issue in such a way that you can get to it.

There are reasons for wanting an issue presented clearly other than its accessibility. It is an old saw: hard cases make bad law. One clerk elaborated on the reasoning behind the rubric:

> When the facts are complicated, then their decision is less legal and more factual. They want a case . . . where they can establish a principle of law pretty cleanly. The more the facts complicate the case, it's less legal and more factual. (C46)

The clerk makes the point well. One of the principal tools of advocacy is to try to distinguish one case from another. To the extent that a principle of law can be argued to rest on a particular fact situation, and a messy or complex fact situation makes such arguments easier, later cases have more of a justification to argue that the rule set down does not apply to them. They can be more easily distinguished on the facts. The goal of clarifying the law has been subverted. As one clerk noted:

> The justices like cases with simple facts—very simple and very clean—that is the type of case they want. And also if the decision below was clear; that's of interest to them. One reason that they want a clear opinion below is that it helps assure them that once they get into the case they do not run into any surprises, particularly with regard to the facts.

The term "bad facts" sometimes refers to a situation in a particular case irrespective of whether the facts would make issuing a principle of law more difficult. A justice illustrated:

> For example, if you take cases raising the burden of proof in termination of parental rights, that is an issue that could go on for a couple of years. But it would be tragic if it meant a

trial would be held up and it meant that a child would have to live with what you perceive to be an unfit parent for a couple of years because you are taking the case. To clear up burden of proof, you might be willing to let that one go.

Many informants discussed this interpretation of "bad facts," but perhaps one clerk put it best:

> For example, if they are going to want to rule on an insanity case, they wouldn't want to use Charles Manson to make a decision on that issue. (C12)

Bad facts, therefore, can mean different things, but one thing it almost always means is cert. denied. As one clerk put it, "there is no reason to take a case with bad facts" (C5). To sustain such an attitude, however, presupposes that cases are fungible and that a better case will come along.

The Pipeline

No one wants to take a case with bad facts. Bad and good, however, are relative terms. When assessing whether or not a case is a good vehicle, the decision must be made in terms of "is a better case likely?" It was argued earlier that no one worries about rejecting a case for fear that the issue will not again present itself. If it does not, that suggests that the issue is not all that important, or there is no need for resolution by the Supreme Court. If an issue is to be decided, however, one does worry some about passing over a case that may be the best vehicle that will be presented to resolve the issue. At the outset, it should be stated that no one worries about this very much because of the overwhelming assumption that the issue will keep presenting itself if it is important. Nevertheless, once the Court decides that the time has come to resolve the issue, then the time frame shortens for a good case to appear, and the pool of cases is smaller. It often helps to know if the issue will present itself again fairly soon. Cases not only percolate, according to my informants, they also "bubble up" and are "in the pipeline."[15]

15. The various metaphors get a bit confusing. "Inadequate percolation" means that an issue needs more examination by lower courts and others. When a case is "in the pipeline," it suggests that there is a particular case that is about to be appealed. Informants sometimes refer to both situations as "bubbling around down there."

Basically, when trying to decide whether or not to grant a case, if the Court is aware that cases presenting the issue are "bubbling around down there in the appeals courts" or are "in the pipeline," then there is a tendency to put off until tomorrow resolution of the issue. Allowing other courts to deal with it provides the benefits of percolation, and if the case at hand is less than a great vehicle, why not wait? Perhaps the next one will be better. The obvious question becomes, are the justices aware of what is in the pipeline?

The answers to that question differed, but the most common response was that justices and clerks are generally aware of what issues are bubbling around in the circuit courts but are rarely aware of specific cases. It is therefore difficult to make a judgment on a case today with any knowledge of a future case. An exception to this is when the justices know that an appeal of a particular issue is imminent. In such instances, they often will hold a case and not render a cert. decision until after the second case arrives. Often what happens then is that they will pick the best case and announce that they are holding the other awaiting the disposition of the chosen case.[16] But for most cases, the Court does not have the luxury of comparing one with another. If the justices are aware that the issue is bubbling around down there, then the general predisposition is to wait.

> *Perry:* . . . How do you learn that a better case is coming up?
> *Clerk:* I think justices often talk to other judges, and clerks always seem to have friends from law school clerking below, but really apart from what comes up on paper, there is not a great knowledge of what is down there. Having said that though, it did seem that people were often aware of a case that was coming up. (C33)

From the very next informant, however:

> *Perry:* One of my informants suggested to me that the justices might talk to judges or that clerks have friends clerking below and this might make them aware of what is going on.
> *Clerk:* I would be really surprised at that. I knew about two-thirds of the people clerking on the D.C. Circuit, and we

16. For Court watchers, when the disposition of a petition is not announced at the time one would normally expect, it is usually a good indication that the Court is going to resolve the issue that term, whether or not it does it with the particular case being held.

never would talk about anything like that. And a justice
would never talk with a judge on a case he has just decided.
There are too many propriety questions. (C34)

A justice had this to say:

> All clerks work on the cert. petitions, except for Brennan's,
> and they kind of have an underground communication net-
> work. Most all are alumni from courts of appeals, so they are
> informally aware of what cases are coming from all the cir-
> cuits. And of course, lawyers may mention what is down
> there. And you read the newspapers. There is no systematic
> searching for what is in the pipeline, but some of it is known.

The amount of talking that goes on obviously varies with individuals.
Apparently, though, there is not a particularly active information network, because people are too busy, and except for the D.C. Circuit,
too remote. Of course on a hot case or topic there may be some
discussion, but there is no consistent communication. Several informants suggested that the most common way to find out what is below
is from the litigants.

> *Clerk:*   I think the best way was for the litigants to let the
> Court know. Sometimes in *Law Week* you can see that cert.
> has been filed on a case, and that actually precedes the time
> the chambers get it because the chambers don't get it until a
> response has come in. (C34).

> *Clerk:*   Sometimes parties will tell you if this case is being liti-
> gated in district court somewhere. And other times, you just
> know it is likely to come up. (C25)

> *Clerk:*   I might say [in my cert. memo] a case is in the pipe-
> line, which might make this case unimportant.
> *Perry:*   How did you know if a case was in the pipeline?
> *Clerk:*   It mostly came from the papers [filed by
> counsel]. (C38)

Now, for a little free advice for attorneys. Informing the Court of
other cases in the pipeline is probably good strategy if it is done
correctly. If counsel is opposing cert., it is a very good idea to point
out in the opposition brief ("opps.") that another court is considering
this issue, and so the Supreme Court should pass on this case and wait

until the other court has had a chance to consider it. Taking the case now would be premature; the Court should wait for the benefits of more percolation. Especially effective would be a demonstration that the case in the pipeline presents a better fact situation, a cleaner case, and so on. One clerk agreed:

> It is really smart when opposing cert. to say there are all kinds of other cases coming up and that you could decide this issue if you wanted to, but you don't want to decide it here in this particular case. (C10)

Petitioner might want to show why this case is particularly good *vis à vis* the cases that are bubbling around below. And, depending on how many lower courts are wrestling with the issue, petitioner might be able to convince the Court that it needs to take the issue now to help the lower courts, demonstrating, of course, why this case is a particularly good vehicle. Such a strategy is a double-edged sword. Pointing out that there are many cases in the pipeline usually has the effect of making the Court wait. But if counsel has reason to believe that the Court has decided to decide the issue, then demonstrating why this is a good vehicle compared to cases in the pipeline is probably wise. Many attorneys know to make the "need to help lower courts and this is a good vehicle" claim, but they rarely do it by looking ahead to cases in the pipeline. The claim is usually made in the abstract. The petition usually focuses on demonstrating why cases already decided are in conflict with the present case. The clerks, meanwhile, are working diligently to show that seeming conflicts are distinguishable. But if it can be demonstrated that the issue is unavoidable, that it will have to be resolved very soon citing real cases rather than a hypothetical parade of horribles, that this case is the best to use, and that future cases have problems, then the Court might be convinced. On balance, peering into the pipeline probably aids the respondent more than the petitioner. The wise attorney will have to decide whether or not looking in the pipeline is beneficial for the instant case, but it is probably a tactic that is underused. Generally speaking, however, awareness that cases are in the pipeline tends to make a case uncertworthy.

Intractableness

The causes of uncertworthiness are varied. For example, the reason not to take tax cases differs from the reason for summary rejection of ineffective counsel cases. One underlying justification for not taking certain cases, however, is particularly interesting, and is the focus of this section. There are some cases and issues of law that the justices see as "intractable."

> *Perry:* Are there times that cases are certworthy by all the criteria, yet the Court does not take them?
>
> *Justice:* Some things are just intractable. Like child custody. If the Court took a case like this, what does the Constitution say about child custody? The Court would be fragmented and even though it might be a perfectly certworthy case, this is one where the Court would wind up so fragmented that it really wouldn't help anybody. We really don't know what to do. Or, for example, how does the Court determine ineffective counsel. The claim is often made, but the Supreme Court really can't add anything. The conflict which exists is really in the verbalization of what effective counsel really is, and there is no real reason for the Court to take this . . . What we do a lot is grant a case and once we get into it, we will realize that it is so intractable and such a mess that there is nothing that we can add or really do with it, and so we would choose to write the opinion on as narrow grounds as possible.

One sentence in the above quotation from this justice, the first I interviewed, intrigued me and led me to ask a question of most of my other informants. The sentence was, "We really don't know what to do." This caused me to wonder if inability to perceive a solution would lead to a case being denied cert. Though I came to inquire about this, frequently the informants would mention it without having been asked. It often would come up when discussing ineffective assistance of counsel, but it would also come up in other contexts. In one such situation where I had not asked the question and we were talking about something completely different, one clerk said:

> I think [a denial] might happen often simply because a justice doesn't know what the answer is. (C61)

From two others:

> There must be sometimes when they're thinking "what will I do with this?" If he can't articulate a sensible rule, it must lead to some hesitation. (C52)

One looks to see if the question is clearly presented. How clearly the question is presented might determine how available a solution is. (C58)

Many suggested intractability in the context of effectiveness of counsel:

They don't take cases that they don't understand . . . Well what are they going to do with it? How do you decide competence, and then you go on and what would they do? Would you go back and retry cases where there is a claim of incompetent counsel? I am not sure they really know what to do with the case, and it would cause such a mess to decide it, that they just bite the bullet and refuse to hear the case. (C2)

There is nothing they really . . . can do . . . I just understood that this was something that the Court wasn't going to take, although when I was on the D.C. Circuit, I certainly saw what the problem was. (C29).

A justice had this to say:

One area that the Court has refused to deal with is incompetency of counsel. But I think the reason there is that the courts of appeals and the highest courts of the states—while the rules are confused—they have a pretty good handle on what is going on there. We have the feeling if we got in there we would probably just mess it all up.

When I asked one justice directly if the inability to see a solution to an intractable problem led to a denial, he responded: "I suppose it plays a part." Intractability was not limited to effective counsel, though that was the example used the most. One clerk explained:

Each justice has an area that he thinks is intractable. He thinks that either the Court doesn't know what to do and they would just get it and mess it up, or he doesn't know what to do; or before on this issue they have had a bunch of 5-4 splits with people going every way and wrangling it. Each has their own category. (C38)

Informants were asked if a case were likely to have a badly split opinion would that diminish its chances for cert., although at the time I did not see that as relating to "no solution," per se. If the Court desired unanimity or at least clear positions from the majority, then perhaps forecasting that there was no way to achieve such an end could be seen as a problem without a satisfactory solution. Yet to my surprise, there did not seem to be much worry about fractured opinions. One justice, quoted earlier in this regard, suggested that Chief Justice Warren was too concerned about achieving unanimity in *Brown*. The justice thought dissents were healthier. Another justice seemed concerned about the splits, but he did not seem to think it made much difference on cert.

> *Justice:*   . . . But I think there is some concern that we're splitting in all these different ways.
>
> *Perry:*   Do you think it is because of personalities [I meant to say "personnel"], or is it because the justices aren't talking enough?
>
> *Justice:*   No, I think it comes down to, do you go along on one of these issues? And then someone says, "I just can't go along with it."
>
> *Perry:*   When you are discussing cert., does anyone ever say, "If we take this case we're going to go off eight different ways"?
>
> *Justice:*   Yes, that happens. That will come up in discussion. Splits are always unfortunate but they have their reasons. I am concerned about the 4-4-1, or 4-2-3 splits. That's one obvious difference between the Warren Court and the current Court . . . I know scholars are upset. One of the ways to avoid splitting in this way is not to take a case.
>
> *Perry:*   Is that happening?
>
> *Justice:*   No. I really don't think so. What's happening is that sometimes you never know how you're going to go until that first draft of the opinion is written . . . But you can do any amount of talking and then finally come down and realize you just can't join an opinion and write your own. In some ways that's the height of collegiality.

In many ways this was a rather confusing answer that really did not address my question. It probably was my fault for having accidentally said "personalities" rather than "personnel," and so it elicited a somewhat defensive answer. Nevertheless, there is enough there to suggest that if a case at the outset is thought to be potentially fractious, that is sometimes considered in the cert. decision, although such an assessment is evidently not dispositive.

Some informants did not think that the lack of an available solution played a role in a cert. decision. One clerk assessed it this way:

> That sounds odd. I didn't see that in my chambers. A member may wait for the membership to change on the Court. For example, a justice might have tried one or two cases and the Court went off eight different ways and they were not able to agree on a rationale. So after trying a couple of cases he may vote to deny cert. because he knows that there is no way to bring them together on this and to get a majority rationale. (C30)

Finally, one clerk put the "intractability/lack of solution" question in what is probably its proper perspective:

> I think that is right in some sense, but on the other hand I can think of lots of examples that the Supreme Court has plunged into where they knew there wasn't a solution. They knew that there certainly wasn't an easy solution, and they probably knew it at the outset. (C48)

Undoubtedly, there are times when the Court chooses or feels compelled to take a case when it does not have a clear notion of how the problem will be solved. But if it has a strong reason to believe at the outset that the problem is intractable, it will avoid taking the case if at all possible.

Such a notion should sound familiar to the social scientist.[17] In his study of agenda setting in government, John Kingdon argues that "the chances for a problem to rise on the decision agenda are dramatically increased if a solution is attached."[18] Paul Light makes a similar argument with regard to the President's agenda. Those agencies or departments that have available alternatives and well-developed solutions are advantaged in seeking a spot on a President's domestic agenda.[19] For the Court, a solution may come from many places. A justice may believe that he knows the solution. And as suggested ear-

17. See, e.g., Michael D. Cohen, James G. March, and Johan P. Olsen, "A Garbage Can Model of Organizational Choice," *Administrative Science Quarterly* 17 (March 1972): 1–25.

18. John W. Kingdon, *Agendas, Alternatives, and Public Policies* (Boston: Little, Brown, 1984), p. 150.

19. Paul C. Light, *The President's Agenda: Domestic Policy Choice from Kennedy to Carter* (Baltimore: The Johns Hopkins University Press, 1982), pp. 147–149.

lier, one of the reasons for percolation is to allow alternatives and solutions to develop. Good lawyers offer solutions in their briefs, as well. Parenthetically, some more free advice to attorneys. It may be too late to wait to offer the solution in the briefs. If the problem is perceived as being intractable, then the time to offer the solution is in the petition, despite justices' protestations that petitions should focus solely on why the case is important. An example might be to show the Court that it need only take an incremental step and then show what that step might be. Or perhaps petitioner could suggest that all that is needed is a summary disposition.

There has been much criticism about the quality of the current Court's opinions. Some say this is because the Court is taking too many cases and not devoting enough time to craft careful opinions. Others argue that the Court is intellectually lacking. If the criticism of the quality of opinions has merit, perhaps the explanation is that brilliant solutions are not available. It may not be the workload per se, but rather that the Court is taking cases too soon. They are not allowing enough percolation, which offers them a good solution—or at least a giant step toward such a solution. Or maybe the lack of intellectual leadership has less to do with the justices and more to do with the fact there are not as many Learned Hands on the courts of appeals offering creative solutions. Or maybe the workload on the courts of appeals is so burdensome that it does not allow its judges to design creative solutions. Or perhaps the plank is in the eye of the law professors, who always "tut tut" about the lack of intellectual leadership on the Court—they loved to point out that there were no intellectuals (read "former professors") on the Burger Court. Perhaps it is they who are not offering quality solutions in law review articles or treatises. I am not arguing that any of these *is* the cause of the decline in the quality of Supreme Court opinions. I do not have the data, the desire, or the dexterity to address these hypotheses, including the premise that Supreme Court opinions are generally worse today. I am prepared to argue, and I doubt that anyone would disagree, that the availability of alternatives or solutions leads generally to better decisions. Where they come from—an intellectual on the Court, more time, better appeals judges—may not matter so much as that they are available.

In sum, to the extent that the availability of a solution, or lack thereof, is observable at the cert. stage, it probably affects case selection. Perhaps it is not so much that an attached solution puts something on the Court's agenda as that the lack of a solution keeps it off.

The first portion of this chapter has dealt with things that make a case uncertworthy, such as bad facts, inadequate percolation, intractability, and others. At times, of course, the Court takes cases with these undesirable characteristics. That is how the informants know so much about them, and why they see them so negatively. But there are times when the Court is forced to take a case, or more precisely, justices feel they cannot avoid taking it, because of the presence of other factors that might make a case certworthy. Of course, the best of all worlds is to have the positive factors without the negative. We now turn to those positive things and examine the other side of the coin: what makes a case certworthy.

Criteria for Cert.

Before we begin the task, one of the rare moments occurs when it is necessary to make a distinction between cert. and appeals. Most of what is said with regard to certworthiness applies to both appeals and certs. Appeals were treated basically as if they were certs. There was one category of appeals, however, that were guaranteed review in law and in fact: when a federal law had been declared unconstitutional. Most informants would agree with this justice: "We nearly always will take a case when a federal judge declares a federal law unconstitutional." Equally suspect were cases where a state judge declared a federal law unconstitutional. The only quibble anyone would have with the justice's statement is the qualification. This exception aside, we may now turn to the things that make a case certworthy.

The first thing that must be said is that no one generalizable characteristic makes a case obviously certworthy in the same way that a fact-bound case is uncertworthy.

> *Perry:* You have talked about what makes a petition a clear deny. Now could you tell me what makes a petition an obvious grant.
> *Clerk:* I am not sure there really ever is such a thing as an obvious grant. Now there are some where it is obvious the Court is going to grant it, but that doesn't make it an obvious grant.

It only takes one thing to make a case uncertworthy. It takes a combination of things to make a case certworthy. This concept is crucial to understanding the decision model that is offered in the next chapter. It is not precisely correct to discuss this process in terms of necessary and sufficient conditions, but it is helpful to think of it that way. Several things are necessary to make a case certworthy, none of which alone is sufficient.[20] It should be noted that the quotations here are responses to various questions. As shall be demonstrated graphically in the next chapter, certworthiness is almost invariably a combination of factors, so the statements reported here should be seen in that context.

Circuit Conflict

Comments from two justices:

> *Justice:* A conflict among federal courts is important, particularly. Every now and then we will take a case that is a conflict among states. Many times it is not about state law but about federal law. State law doesn't make much difference up here.

> *Perry:* Could you tell me what would make a case an obvious grant?
> *Justice:* Conflict among the circuits might.

"Might." Few things are said without qualification when it comes to certworthiness, but I shall do so now. Without a doubt, the single most important generalizable factor in assessing certworthiness is the existence of a conflict or "split" in the circuits. The overwhelming majority of my informants, indeed almost all, listed this as the first and most important thing that they looked for in a petition.

When asked what they looked for in a cert. petition, the following clerks gave responses similar to almost all of my informants':

> First, a conflict. Then you had to see if there really was a conflict . . . I really do believe that a conflict is the reason that most cases are taken. In some ways it is the driving force. (C39)

> If there's a genuine conflict, that's the single most important factor, though alone it's not enough. (C52)

> First, is there a conflict. Those really dominated and were clearly the most important reason for taking cert. (C32)

---

20. The problem with describing it this way is that the "necessary" things are not truly necessary because some cases are granted in their absence, but standing alone they are not sufficient conditions either. Explication must await the next chapter.

A justice said the following:

> Some cases obviously should be granted cert. For example, if
> there is a clear conflict between circuits in interpreting the in-
> ternal revenue code so that the tax code is being administered
> differently in different parts of the country—that is simply
> intolerable. The Supreme Court must grant cert. so that the
> tax law is administered uniformly over the United States. You
> could make this decision without even going into the merits of
> the case. I don't think that anybody would disagree that to
> hear this case is a proper function of the Supreme Court.

But witness what one of his brethren said:

> Naturally, I would look for conflicts, although I don't see if
> there is a conflict involving some obscure provision of the In-
> ternal Revenue Code that means the nation is going to go to
> hell. I am really looking for more important issues.

The two justices' comments are not necessarily contradictory. All justices believe that a conflict must involve an important issue. But the
justices vary somewhat on their willingness to tolerate a conflict. As
one justice told me:

> One thing I hear around the conference table more and more
> is that "something is a 'tolerable' conflict," or "there is a con-
> flict out there but . . ." Justice A will say let's consider this but
> [several years later], although the date is getting pushed back
> a bit. Justice B and I are both concerned about this. He more
> than I. We see it as a job of the Court to resolve federal con-
> flicts. It is intolerable to have a certain law for the people in
> the Second Circuit and something else for people in the
> Eighth. Sometimes I join Justice B's dissents. I don't always
> join because I think his notion of conflict is rather strained.
> But I don't believe that we should have the First Circuit say-
> ing something and another interpretation in the Ninth Cir-
> cuit. But sometimes there are just so many hours in a day.

Justice B is at one extreme believing virtually every conflict should be
taken as long as the issue is not completely trivial. The justice just
quoted is fairly close to Justice B's position. The following justice,
however, is probably the justice at the opposite extreme:

Now as for what I look for, that is really my appraisal of importance. I would say that a conflict is neither necessary nor sufficient to get a case granted. For example, you have cases like the Iranian assets case or Bakke where the importance just cries out. But also there are cases where the conflict is clear, but I don't think it is important enough for us to deal with it. Justice B is strong on conflicts. He not only believes that we should resolve federal conflicts, but he believes it extends to state courts. I think his views are based partly on his understanding of the Court's commitment to Congress at the time of the Judiciary Act of 1925, but I disagree with his understanding.

I don't know if you are familiar with a motion for a judgment notwithstanding a verdict. It means the judge can set aside the verdict or the judgment regardless of the verdict of the jury. In one circuit they reversed a district court's refusal to set aside—I don't remember the exact situation—because there they looked at the defendant's testimony as well as the plaintiff's. Whereas in other circuits they look at only the plaintiff's testimony, and in another circuit it is even something else, so there are different standards. But if we ever get a conflict on this, unless there is something more important raised, there is nothing inherently unfair in any of these methods. There are no significant differences. It is not that much different from what different state courts might have. We certainly don't feel the need to go in and make them uniform in this big country. So I don't think the difference is significant, and what is happening in all circuits is basically fair. Now Justice B would certainly take a different view on something like that.

And of course lots of times that a conflict is alleged, there is not really even a conflict. So I look for conflicts, but it is certainly not controlling. I look more for the character of the issue and the need for resolution. Whether or not an issue is ripe.

These statements highlight the differences among the justices with regard to conflicts, but the remarks of the last justice must be put in context. He, too, sees conflicts as very important, and his comments were a reaction to the extreme position of Justice B. In fact, determining whether or not there is a split is one of his clerk's primary responsibilities as it is for all clerks. Justice B is known by all clerks to want to resolve virtually all legitimate conflicts. Since Justice B is a member of the cert. pool, much of the pool memo is involved in analyzing whether or not there is, in fact, a real conflict. Though Justice B is at the extreme, all justices are interested in circuit splits and think they are one of the most important things to establish certworthiness.

The importance of a conflict should be no surprise. It is one of the only explicit criteria for certworthiness given in the Rules of the Court. Moreover, it is a proxy for or is indicative of other important criteria. It indicates that an issue is of sufficient importance that it has arisen in different places, and the disposition is not obvious. But there are conflicts, and there are conflicts. They vary not only in terms of the importance of the issue but also in the extent to which there is a conflict. Determining whether or not a conflict exists is often subjective. Sometimes a conflict is quite evident. As one clerk noted:

> The clearest example is when a judge in another circuit says, "I understand what the First Circuit has held, and I disagree." If this involved an important issue, it would be a clear grant of cert. (C29)

Usually, however, judges do not announce that they are in conflict with another circuit. It is up to the petitioning attorney, and the law clerk, to determine if in fact a conflict exists. Clerks spend a great deal of time trying to "distinguish" the rulings to show that there is not necessarily a conflict. When the conflict is head-on, however, it is usually referred to as a "square conflict." Interestingly, the computer age may be having some effect on jurisprudence. One clerk noted:

> Before LEXIS came in, sometimes the circuits didn't know what each other were doing all that fast. (C29)

At times there may technically be a conflict, but it is not a live conflict. Perhaps the Third Circuit ruled one way thirty years ago, but today the Fourth Circuit goes another way. In this instance, the justices, even Justice B, would wait to see if the conflict is really alive. If it is an issue that only comes up every thirty years, then it is seen as not important enough for Supreme Court attention. There are also times that even though a conflict exists, there is reason to believe it may resolve itself.

> If the justices agree with what a circuit court of appeals is doing and maybe some of the district courts are going the other way, they will wait to grant cert. Or if one circuit goes one way and seven circuits then go another, they will kind of

hope that the first circuit will change and go along with what the other seven have done. (C48)

Another clerk agreed, though he used a slightly different example:

> In one respect, it mattered who generated the bloody conflict. If it was from a panel that was really undistinguished, there was an attitude that the system would probably cleanse itself, either by being resolved *en banc* within the circuit, or all other circuits would go the other way showing how erroneous they had been, and they would conform. (C63)

Once again, note the importance of the judges below as an index.

All things being equal, justices would prefer to let circuit splits percolate, allowing as many circuits to examine the issue as possible. But as has been suggested, often the cost is too high. Different treatment according to where one lives may be seen as intolerable and too unjust. Or delay may be unduly expensive and burdensome. If the Department of Health and Human Services must have several different procedures depending upon the circuit, then the Court is reneging on its responsibility to clarify the law. Sometimes it is obvious that the Court must resolve the issue at once. Other times, "necessity" is more of a judgment call. One clerk gave an example of a case that was obviously certworthy despite little percolation.

> There was a case my term that I think was called the Whirl-pool Case. It had to do with mine safety. There was some issue of if a worker felt his life were very much in danger, was he compelled to go into that situation. It was called something like whether or not you have to "walk into death." One court held one thing and a very influential judge elsewhere said something else. You had the SG soliciting cert. You could write this memo in one paragraph. This is the type of case I would call a bullet. (C29)

And sometimes the Court decides that it is wise to act early. As two clerks noted:

> You might have two circuit courts that are not squarely in conflict, but you have a feeling they are potentially, and you have district courts going all over the place. I might recommend that we take it now before a lot of problems occur or damage is done. (C34)

> [Usually you wait but] if it is a hard enough question and you
> realize you are eventually going to have to deal with it, they
> will go ahead and take it. (C30)

As discussed earlier, stepping in early is probably related to the extent
to which the Court thinks it knows what it wants to do. In this regard,
the circuit courts are not always cooperative. One clerk explained:

> Sometimes they wait around for a split in circuits and one
> doesn't develop. They decide that the way the law's been set-
> tled by all the circuits is wrong and they step in. (C26)

At times, of course, a case is so important in and of itself that they
do not even pretend to wait for a split. One justice mentioned the
Iranian assets case as an example. A clerk gave another:

> Then there are other questions. No one really cares if there is
> a conflict. For example, the draft case last year. There was no
> conflict, but the Court was going to take it. (C8)

Once again, some advice for attorneys, although it is of use only to
institutional players. In lower courts, there is much talk about judge
shopping. To some extent there is also an ability to circuit shop. For
many entities, a case can be brought either in the D.C. Circuit or
another circuit, or in various circuits, and so one would normally
choose the most favorable circuit. Undoubtedly, litigants that have such
a choice do this, but perhaps what they should do is try to force a
circuit split. If there is reason to believe that the Supreme Court might
be even more hospitable to one's claim than a favorable circuit court,
it might be desirable to try to force a circuit split rather than trying
always to bring claims in the more favorable circuit. It is, of course, a
risky strategy, but one could well imagine it being worth the risk. The
strategy may also be used defensively. If the Supreme Court decides
in one's favor, then all circuits would have to come into line, protecting
the litigant from times when it cannot choose the circuit. Therefore,
seeking an inhospitable circuit might be wise in the long run. One
could certainly imagine other strategies.

A circuit split is not simply a formal criterion for cert.; it is probably
the single most important criterion, and those who wish to comprehend the cert. process must realize this. A circuit split is neither necessary nor sufficient, but it is almost both. Though some political
scientists had noted circuit conflict in their studies, none had incor-
porated it as a predictive variable to explain review. It remained for

Sidney Ulmer in 1984 to give this characteristic the importance that it deserved in the political science literature.[21] He argued: "I believe it is possible to go beyond the heavily caveated generalizations in the legal literature. The need to do so defines my research problem. I wish to know not just how many conflict cases are granted or denied certiorari, but whether such decisions are associated with the presence and absence of the conflict condition." Ulmer's article is an excellent example of how the use of intelligent empirical research can be used to test presumptions.[22] His article deals both with conflict with Supreme Court precedent and intercircuit conflict. For the latter, he finds that the presence of intercircuit conflict increases the explained variance from 18–23 percent for the Vinson and Warren Courts and 6 percent for the Burger court over the traditional variables used by political scientists.[23] Ulmer also concludes quite correctly that, "given the time pressures on the justices who screen certiorari petitions, this need implies a large role for law clerks in distinguishing genuine conflict cases from those where the claim is too tenuous to warrant the Court's attention."[24]

If anything, Ulmer understates the role of conflicts. Though many cases do not involve a conflict, it is, nevertheless, the first thing looked for. The underlying assumption is that most issues, if important, will arise in the various circuits. If there is no split, then usually there is no need for Supreme Court action. What Ulmer's data cannot tell us is why so many cases are denied where a conflict of some sort exists. My informants help fill in that gap. For example, an issue usually needs to be adequately percolated, or the opinion comes from an undistinguished panel.

21. Ulmer, "Conflict as a Predictive Variable."

22. I have only one criticism of this article. I wish that Ulmer had elaborated in more detail how he determined the existence of a genuine conflict. It is not that I doubt his results, because as he claims, his numbers are in the ballpark with others who have made such attempts. But as I have demonstrated, one of the primary responsibilities of clerks is to determine if a claimed conflict is genuine. And according to them, this is often a very difficult task. It usually cannot be done quickly in cases that are not frivolous. Indeed, originally I had planned to code for conflict in my data set, and ultimately I rejected doing so because I felt that to do it correctly would take an extraordinary amount of time. If Ulmer found that it can be done fairly quickly or easily, that would be valuable information, particularly in light of the indices and signals discussed in Chapter 5.

23. For the Burger Court, "inter-circuit conflict is only one-fourth as significant in explaining variance in decision as federal government as petitioning party" (Ulmer, "Conflict as a Predictive Variable," p. 909).

24. Ibid., p. 911.

Importance

When asked what they looked for to determine if a case were cert-worthy, informants almost invariably would say that first they looked to see if there were a circuit conflict, and then they looked to see if the conflict involved an important issue. Sometimes a case is so important that it must be granted whether or not there is a conflict, but important issues usually generate a conflict. Conflicts, however, do not always involve important issues. Like certworthiness, importance is ultimately subjective. Nevertheless, informants were asked how they determined importance.

Important cases are of several types. Some are important in and of themselves; that is, it is the resolution of the particular case, not necessarily the legal issue, that is important. Such cases usually are, as lawyers say, *sui generis,* or the only one of their kind, and they are cases that most anybody would recognize as important. Cases such as *U.S. v. Nixon,* or the Iranian assets case come to mind. In such cases, there has usually been little or no percolation of the legal issue, but there is a perception that the case is of sufficient importance that it deserves resolution by the U.S. Supreme Court. Flaws such as inadequate percolation and bad facts must be ignored.

A second category of cases are those that present issues that are important to the polity. The Supreme Court is sometimes called upon to decide issues that are of huge political and societal importance. Such issues are ones that most anyone would consider important. The issues presented in *Brown v. Board of Education, Roe v. Wade,* and *Bakke* are possible examples. They resolve or address important issues of law, but their importance clearly emanates from their impact on society. Here, the Court may have some freedom to pick the particular case to resolve the issue. The justices will try to take into account, for example, whether or not the case of discrimination against Linda Brown in Topeka is *the* one to resolve the momentous Constitutional issue of "separate but equal," or if a better vehicle is likely. Frequently on issues of great societal importance, the Court is offered several cases to choose from, though that certainly is not always the case. But the flexibility is limited by the belief that the issue must be resolved soon, which often precludes the luxury of waiting for more percolation, for the circuits to split, or for a better vehicle. I, and my informants, refer to both of the above two categories of cases—*sui generis* and cases of great societal importance—as cases of public importance.

A third category consists of cases that are important to the law. I refer to these cases as ones of legal importance. Clarification of a rule of evidence or some administrative procedure may be crucial to the functioning of the criminal justice system, or some federal agency, but the importance stems from confusion in the legal system. The confusion has usually been generated by conflicting or improper interpretations by courts. Such cases also present important issues and constitute the bulk of the Court's workload.

Obviously, the categories are not neatly separable. Some cases belong in all categories, and many belong jointly in the last two. Cases of public importance often present issues for which resolution is needed for the proper functioning of the legal system; and resolution of the law is, of course, ultimately important to the polity. But for heuristic purposes, types of "important" cases can be thought about separately. What constitutes an "important issue" in the Supreme Court may be a highly technical issue of law, or it might be an issue of profound societal importance. Incidentally, the distinction is not constitutional versus statutory. Resolution of what constitutes double jeopardy may be of great legal importance, and a statutory interpretation of the Civil Rights Act may generate profound societal impact and interest.

There is little to say about "importance" in the first two categories. Aside from issues of obvious societal importance, trying to determine what constitutes importance in the Supreme Court is quite difficult. I received many answers, but two common ones emerged. Importance is often determined by the breadth of effect rather than the depth. In other words, if a ruling below has a potential impact on large numbers of people, that helps establish importance. If it has a large impact on one corporation or individual, that alone does not make it important. A second though related criterion is the effect something has on the federal government. When the solicitor general claims that a ruling or policy has a large effect on the government, and he urges review, such a case is almost always believed to be important whether or not the justices immediately see the importance. Beyond these criteria, however, importance is in the nose of the beholder.

Perhaps the more interesting question is why a case is not accepted despite the presence of an obviously important issue? Some reasons for this have already been discussed; bad facts, inadequate percolation, or a better case in the pipeline. Other reasons will emerge later. Examined now is why obviously important cases without the typical flaws are sometimes rejected, and why flawed cases are taken despite strong reasons for rejection.

There are times when the Court is presented with an obviously important issue, a case is petitioned with good facts, perhaps the circuits have split, the issue is one that seems to cry for resolution by the Supreme Court, and yet the Court refuses to take the case. In other words, while there are no jurisprudential reasons not to take the case, evidently the justices believe there are prudential reasons to avoid it.

Every student of constitutional law knows the case *Loving v. Virginia*.[25] The case itself is really not very interesting because the conclusion is obvious. What is interesting is that it took the Court thirteen years after *Brown* to decide it. After *Brown,* the Court struck down discriminatory statutes right and left. However, until *Loving* one type of statute survived—anti-miscegenation statutes. The Court had the opportunity to overturn such statutes as early as 1955 in *Naim v. Naim*,[26] but it effectively dodged the issue there, and it refused to face it until 1967 in *Loving.* The common wisdom is that the Court saw this issue as too hot and simply not worth it. Overturning state anti-miscegenation statutes might be "the final straw," engendering such resistance that it could undo all that the Court was trying to accomplish in other areas of race relations. Whether or not this is the explanation, most would agree that the Court was intentionally dodging the issue. For purposes here, the questions are how often does this dodging occur, and how do the justices decide an issue needs to be ducked? Prior to the interviews, I assumed that this dodging occurred quite frequently. My informants suggest that it is rare. I had intended to ask the justices about dodging issues and had intended to use *Loving* as an example. The first justice, however, beat me to the punch.

> *Justice:*   Now, I do think that timing is important. For example, right after *Brown* came down, there was all this talk, particularly by a lot of Southern politicians, saying all sorts of things about this decision and what it did that it really didn't. Nevertheless, after the decision came down, the Court refused to hear a case that dealt with anti-miscegenation statutes in the South . . . Some thought that people were going to have to have mixed marriages, as if that were such a terrible thing. Anyway, the Court just returned that case and didn't decide it. Now I wasn't on the Court at that time, but I chuckled when they got rid of it without deciding it, because I was convinced that what motivated them was that they thought that this was just not the right time to deal with this case, and they just passed making a decision no matter how important it was.

25. 388 U.S. 1 (1967).
26. 350 U.S. 891 (1955) and 350 U.S. 985 (1956).

> *Perry:* When a justice makes a decision like that, what are his
> criteria? . . . What causes him to make that decision?
> *Justice:* I think that differs from justice to justice, and for
> whatever reasons, they just didn't think that they should
> hear that case. I don't ever remember doing that myself,
> but there may have been times that other justices on the
> Court may have wanted to delay something. Now it is true
> with the timing that I didn't take a case because I thought it
> hadn't worked its way out in the lower courts enough—we
> didn't have enough decisions on it at the lower levels. But I
> don't ever remember myself putting off a case because
> things were too hot.

Another justice when asked about avoidance of anti-miscegenation
cases and the Court's refusal to take cases that are too hot responded,
"You might have to talk with someone with a longer historical perspective." He avoided giving other examples except for ones that were
delayed for jurisprudential reasons. A third justice said that he could
not really remember avoiding cases, but then said:

> We ducked on the school prayer case—something versus New
> Jersey. We ducked it on standing grounds, so that happens.

I am not sure whether he meant "ducking" as I am using it here. I
tried to pursue the issue with him, but he was clearly unwilling, so I
dropped it. In fact, this was an issue that several of the justices seemed
rather uncomfortable discussing. Finally, one justice responded this
way:

> *Justice:* I am sure it happens sometimes, although my view
> very honestly is that I don't think that it is a proper func-
> tion for this Court to try to judge what the political conse-
> quences might be . . . I think it is better to acknowledge
> what argument there is on a controversial issue . . . there-
> fore, I am not really big on waiting to make a decision. I
> don't think a case should be declined to be heard because
> the Court decided that the country wasn't ready for some-
> thing, because I have real doubts about the ability of an
> isolated institution such as this to make this type of decision.
> *Perry:* You said, though, that you were sure it happens?
> *Justice:* Yes, but it is not typical.

I asked the miscegenation question of the clerks and they varied on the extent to which they saw the justices ducking issues. Some said that they could not remember such a case their term. Many thought it probably happened but that it was rare. One clerk put it this way:

> I think it happens more than once every twenty-five years, but not every term. They ducked the Vietnam issue. (C38)

There was one issue, however, that many informants said that the Court was consistently avoiding.

> Yes, I can think of an area—gay rights. The clerks were screaming in their cert. memos about how the Court needed to resolve this. We came to know that the justices were just not going to enter this area. (C62)

And from another clerk:

> I can remember one case my term—a sodomy conviction. It presented the question squarely. It was consensual behavior by adults, but they just weren't ready to take this case. I mean who wants to get into it? . . . The feeling was that, oh God, we really don't need this . . . People weren't getting prosecuted for it . . . If people were getting thrown into jail, that might have been something else. (C45)

There were other issues mentioned, but the area of gay rights was the most frequently mentioned.[27] One clerk gave an interesting analysis of what was going on. He felt that some of the more liberal justices were afraid to take the case because they thought that they would lose on the merits. In other words, they were defensively denying. Other justices did not even see it as an issue, having no doubt that states could prohibit such behavior. There were also some justices who felt, why get involved in such a messy, controversial issue, perhaps doing reputational damage to the Court, when no one was really being prosecuted? The clerk surmised that if people ever began getting prosecuted for private consensual behavior, then these justices would probably vote to grant. Since the time of the interviews, the Court has addressed the constitutionality of sodomy laws in in *Bowers v. Hard-*

---

27. Many informants said this without any prompting. If they initially said "no," I would ask, "well, what about the issue of gay rights?" to which many would then say "yes."

wick.[28] It is my guess that the justices took the case because the fact situation was precisely the one that would cause those justices who had preferred to avoid the issue to feel that they no longer could. The unlikely had happened. In a bizarre situation, Michael Hardwick was arrested in the privacy of his bedroom for homosexual sodomy. Why the Court finally decided to resolve this issue is not important here. Like Loving, the interesting thing is why they waited so long to resolve it, given that it was an important issue and that many cases had been previously offered that fit all the criteria for certworthiness. Apparently for some justices, the constitutionality of sodomy laws was seen as an issue that was highly provocative, and as in the case of anti-miscegenation statutes, they were simply willing to avoid it despite its importance.

There are, of course, those who believe there are virtues to the Supreme Court remaining passive on highly charged issues. That debate has been carried on for years by both lawyers and political scientists.[29] Wise or not, according to the justices, there seems to be little inclination to avoid issues because they are controversial. The justices, however, were not particularly forthcoming on this issue, and to the extent that they were, their answers may have been self-serving. There was one clerk who, despite having an obvious political philosophy and a debatable normative position, seemed to be correct in description.

> I think it would be extremely rare to have something like that in any given term. To the contrary. The Court, I think, has decided to step up to the bat and decide the bad ones. Actually in the last decade, the Court, I think has been too quick to decide these types of issues . . . Instead, I think they should let the democratic process take care of these controversial issues if at all possible . . . I have a strong sense that on this Court they feel there is a profound sense of responsibility to

28. Bowers v. Hardwick, 478 U.S. 186.

29. See for example, Gerald Gunther, "The Subtle Vices of the 'Passive Virtues,'" *Columbia Law Review* 64 (1964): 1, 11–12, disagreeing with Alexander Bickel. See Alexander Bickel, Foreword to "The Passive Virtues," 75 *Harvard Law Review* (1962): 40, and *The Least Dangerous Branch* (1962). Robert McCloskey, *The American Supreme Court* (Chicago: University of Chicago Press, 1960). See also Robert Dahl, "Decision-Making in a Democracy: The Supreme Court as a National Policy-Maker," *Journal of Public Law* 6 (1957): 279–295; Jonathan D. Casper, "The Supreme Court and National Policy-Making," *American Political Science Review* 70 (March 1976): 50–63; Richard Funston, "The Supreme Court and Critical Elections, *American Political Science Review* 69 (September 1975): 930–932. Of course virtually everything written about judicial review and the role of the Supreme Court addresses this issue.

try to tackle the hard cases and not back up. It has not served the Court or society well. (C53)

Let us now look at the flip side. Do justices ever get stampeded into resolving an issue because of public pressure? A conversation with one justice in this regard was particularly interesting, more for what he had to say about affirmative action than public pressure. He may have provided insight into how some of the justices have been thinking about affirmative action.

> *Perry:* Let me give you the reverse situation. Are there times
>   that a case might be taken that would normally not be
>   deemed certworthy, but because there is so much publicity
>   surrounding it, the Court feels that it has to take the case?
> *Justice:* Sure. The Iranian assets case was that way . . .
> *Perry:* Was *Bakke* an example of such a case? I have heard
>   that the record was messy and perhaps the Court should
>   have waited, but you felt the need to take it.
> *Justice:* I suppose that is true. At times the Court may feel
>   the public's demand on [affirmative action]. Though there
>   might be a strong argument in favor of postponing it, be-
>   cause if it turns out to be that the Constitution should be
>   color-blind, you could have allowed [affirmative action] to
>   go on and not have to come to that decision. You might be
>   able to bring about social change in the meantime.[30]

Another justice responded this way:

> *Justice:* Sometimes the people just demand that the Supreme
>   Court resolve an issue whether we really ought to or not.
>   That does affect us sometimes. We just feel that the Su-
>   preme Court has to decide.
> *Perry:* What would cause you to do that for one case and not
>   another?
> *Justice:* Once again, that would be relative to each justice. But
>   I think there are certain cases about which there is a lot of

---

30. This was really a rather remarkable statement. What the justice seemed to be saying was that if the Court eventually has to come to the point that affirmative action is impermissible because the Constitution commands color-blindness—and this justice seemed to think that that probably was what the Constitution commands—then by avoiding the case, the Court could allow all this remedial work to go on before it was forced to declare the policy unconstitutional.

public hue and cry, and we just feel that we have to take the
case. We are going to have to take it sooner or later.

Another justice, however, seemed to discount the effect of public
awareness. Indeed, the first part of his answer was rather surprising,
and I do not think he was simply being glib. When asked about public
"pressure" he responded:

> *Justice:* That is hard to answer, because I was not aware that
> the public was that aware of what the Supreme Court does.
> Are you thinking of any examples?
> *Perry:* One example may be the Iranian assets case.
> *Justice:* Oh well, I think there, well—I hadn't thought about
> that. What happened there is that had the Court of Appeals
> reached a same result as below, we probably wouldn't have
> taken it. But some district court somewhere came up and
> went the other way. Then we would have assets flowing out
> of some circuits and not others, and that was intolerable.

The Supreme Court may or may not, as Mr. Dooley said, read the
"illiction returns," but they do read the newspapers, and they do live
in Washington, and they undoubtedly know when the resolution of an
issue needs the imprimatur of the Supreme Court.

Most issues of societal importance, and many of legal importance,
are ones where the justices would agree that the issue is important.
They may disagree about whether a particular case is the correct one
to resolve the issue or whether the issue is ripe, but on an issue such
as affirmative action, or one where the solicitor general says resolution
of the legal issue is highly important for fair administration, there
would be little disagreement that the issue is important. Like any other
group, however, there are issues that some members see as very important while others see them as of little importance. Though there
are always idiosyncratic differences in judgment, perceptions of importance are often highly correlated with particular areas.

Areas

Provine has argued that there are some areas of interest to the entire
Court. Her observation is surely true. From my interviews, however,
I was struck by the fact that interest in areas was generally not universal. Each justice has areas of particular interest, or as one clerk put
it, "every justice has his hobby horse" (C5). Frequently, he sees cases

in these areas as extremely important, whereas his colleagues may feel quite differently. One justice described it this way:

> *Justice:* When personnel change on the Court there becomes new interest in new issues. For example, there was a time when four members simply weren't interested in hearing Securities and Exchange Commission cases. You want me to name names? Justice _____ just wasn't interested in hearing these. Now I believe the Court is more disposed to hearing those cases.
>
> *Perry:* So are you suggesting that certain justices favor certain areas of cases and that it is not really a question of whether a case is certworthy so much as whether or not a justice might be interested in it?
>
> *Justice:* Well, we all inherit from our past experiences certain things that we are interested in. And personnel has a great deal to do with the agenda.

Another justice, when asked if justices have areas of special interest that affect their cert. behavior responded, "there's no doubt about it." And from another justice, "that is absolutely true, absolutely true." One justice was somewhat more cautious in his response. He said, "I am sure it [does], but I am not even sure what those areas are for me." Later in the interview, when talking about what would cause an issue to be important that might not otherwise be seen as such, he said, "the strong interest of a justice would make it an important issue." The following quotations from justices provide an example.

> Another area is water rights. Those of us who do not come from the arid West do not seem to be as concerned about the problems. But three justices, O'Connor, Rehnquist, and White have grown up there, and in Rehnquist's case, practiced there, and they are intensely interested in these cases. But until O'Connor arrived, there were only two to try to convince us of the importance.

And from a Westerner:

> We now have three Westerners and we are very concerned about Western water rights and Indian cases. And you can tell by our votes for cert. that we are interested in them. You know it is sometimes hard to convince those from states with too much water why this is important . . . I think it is just

terrible the number of people who live in the East and have
made several trips to Europe but have never been west of the
Mississippi.

Of course, one need not interview at the Court to know what some
of the particular interests of some justices are. Everyone knows Marshall is and Brennan was especially concerned with capital cases; Blackmun worries about abortion; Powell was particularly attentive to the
problems of schools; Brennan had and Rehnquist has strong interest
in certain Fourth Amendment issues. One thing I heard repeatedly
was that all of the justices seemed to exhibit intense interest in First
Amendment issues of all types. But certain justices have developed
what might be considered unexpected areas of interest. Clerks frequently said that they were surprised to learn that a certain area was
of particular interest to their justice and, conversely, that their justice
was not particularly interested in areas they presumed he would be.
Erring on the side of caution prohibits me from giving specific examples of who is interested in what, but that is not important for the
argument here anyway. There were many examples of idiosyncratic
interests. Water rights was but one. A couple more examples should
suffice to make the point that there are areas where some justices have
a special interest and others do not. One justice said:

> There are two types of cases that I can think of that bear
> upon your inquiry. Tax cases . . . Another type may be Indian
> cases. The junior justice always gets the crud. As a junior jus-
> tice, I had my share of Indian cases. So has Justice _____ to
> an extent. We kid about saying we might vote to deny to avoid
> having to write an opinion on it. Actually, I think the Indian
> cases are kind of fascinating. It goes into history and you
> learn about it, and the way we abused some of the Indians,
> we, that is the U.S. government . . . But I think those are two
> areas where we are inclined to vote our background with a
> little bit of a bias.

And from another justice:

> Then of course there is the securities area. Justice _____ is
> intensely interested in the securities area, and Justice _____
> has some interest. Then there are the oil and gas cases, which
> some [think are very important and some] consider very dull.
> There are a lot of boring administrative agency cases . . . I

think there is an element of bias in the selection of those areas.

Several clerks of one justice spoke of his rather surprising interest in anything having to do with national security. This justice normally played a low-key role in cert., but evidently on these cases he became very aggressive.

Interest in an area can come from various places. As one justice suggested, all justices come to the Court as a product of their experiences. Said another: "We all have our own ideas of what is important that we bring to the Court with us." And as one clerk put it:

> For example, maybe . . . years ago he was on a board of directors and he starts thinking, "good Lord, if this had happened to us, we would all have been liable." (C21)

It is easy to understand Justice Marshall's interest in civil rights, or Justice Powell's interest in the problems of schools, from their activities prior to their appointment to the Supreme Court. In other instances, it is an interest that develops later, perhaps from some personal experience or from something that has happened on the Court. One frequent observation was that once a justice wrote a seminal opinion in an area, he usually became very interested when cases were petitioned in that area. The justice would often see himself as responsible for overseeing doctrine. Of course, his brethren were not always willing to concede that responsibility to him.

The point that different justices have different areas of interests may seem trite. It is not. Much of the discussion about certworthiness, particularly by lawyers and clerks, is cast in jurisprudential terms. Disagreements over certworthiness are often seen as differing judgments over issues such as whether a case is ripe or whether a conflict truly exists. Justices may have biases, but as good judges, they do not let them intrude upon their cert. judgment. To assert that differences in the perception of importance could be something so influenced by individual justices' predilections is to acknowledge legal realism just a little too much. I do not mean to suggest that lawyers naively believe that there are no politics on the Court. No one doubts that who is on the Court can make a great difference on the outcome on the merits, and that there are fierce ideological battles. Also, no one would deny some strategy on the part of justices even at cert. Yet somehow, the case selection process is seen as more pristine. Recall that even on the Court, negotiation is valued at the opinion-writing stage but disdained at cert.

Lest I be accused of setting up a straw man, witness the movement for a National Court of Appeals.[31] Though the proposal has taken various forms, basically it would create an intermediate court between the U.S. Courts of Appeals and the U.S. Supreme Court. The task of such a court would be to screen cases seeking review and certify those worthy of review to the Supreme Court. The court would determine the existence of legitimate circuit splits, importance, ripeness, justiciability, and so on. Several of the justices have favored the creation of such a court. The assumption that underlies such an organization is that another court can set the Supreme Court's agenda, because determination of what is certworthy is basically a legal decision. If, however, importance is so important for cert., and importance is frequently a function of an individual justice's interest in an area, then the cert. process is much more complex than is suggested by the proponents of a National Court of Appeals and by those who see certworthiness as mostly objective.

Prediction of cert. is so difficult in part because of these idiosyncratic interests in particular areas that lead some justices and not others to see certain issues as important. One can generalize to say that justices first look to see if there has been a circuit split, and then try to determine if the issue is important, but importance is highly subjective. There are some cases that most could agree are important, but there are others where one must have some familiarity with the interests of certain justices in order to determine if they would consider them important. Combine that with the need to determine if four justices would consider the issue important, and one can readily see the difficulty of the enterprise. This is not to say that such prediction is impossible. As with any empirical work, one must make assumptions and coding decisions that are surrogate measures for reality. And of course, one need not explain every case to have an empirically impressive model. Nevertheless, the importance of idiosyncratic views of importance indicates why this is such a formidable task.[32]

Another reason for focusing on the concept that each justice has particular areas of interest is that when cases involve these areas, we see a different decision calculus on cert. The justice usually knows how he wants doctrine to develop in the area, and he therefore acts stra-

31. See U.S. Senate, Hearings before the Subcommittee on Courts (of the Committee on the Judiciary), 98th Cong., 1st sess. on S. 645, "Court Improvements Act of 1983," March 11 and April 8, 1983, serial no. J-98-16.

32. It also explains why I determined that coding cert. petitions in a meaningful way with the hope of predicting grants would be too massive an undertaking for this project. When I coded and analyzed petitions, I had more modest purposes in mind.

tegically at the cert. decision. That is, a case is seen as certworthy if it is one where the justice thinks he will win on the merits, and if it allows him to move doctrine in the way he wishes. Such cases are referred to as "good vehicles" or they have "good facts." Typical of many statements was the following:

> But there were a few areas he had staked out a position . . .
> In my markup I might say something like, "this is good old x case again but this is really not the right case to try and set the balance you want to set." (C48)

Bad vehicles in this context mean that one might lose on the merits; or even if one won, it might take doctrine in a way that was undesirable. Therefore, if the justice cares strongly, a bad vehicle would lead to a defensive denial.

In sum, everyone says that a case must present an important issue for it to be certworthy, but determinations of importance are sometimes related to an individual justice's interest in an area, making the notion of importance even more subjective.

Egregiousness

Try as they might, justices cannot always resist acting as a court of last resort. Sometimes they will take a case that is a flagrant abuse of justice even though it presents no particularly interesting question of law. The term that was invariably used to describe such cases was "egregious." Everyone acknowledged that an egregious result below sometimes prompted review for an otherwise uncertworthy case, but no explanation emerged that one could use systematically to distinguish between those cases that the justices could hold their noses and ignore from those they could not. However, cases that are considered to be egregious come from two categories: those where a severe injustice occurred, and those where there has been a flagrant disregard for announced doctrine.

With regard to the first category—blatant injustice—one clerk's imprecise explanation was typical and is probably about the best one can give:

> They all kind of have these tug at the heart string cases . . . I mean the justices are human, and when they see something like that [a terrible injustice he had described], sometimes it strikes them. (C48)

The justices admitted their behavior without any better explanation.

> *Justice:* This is not a court to simply assure that justice is
> done. We cannot right all wrongs.
> *Perry:* Although [justices] always claim that, there always
> seem to be a few cases that the Court picks that, to an out-
> sider, the only justification for taking the case seems to be
> that you felt the result was so egregious.
> *Justice:* That's true. That happens. But not all that often.
> Basically we scc it not as a court of justice.

I was unable to determine what might commonly strike justices as
egregious. One justice said:

> I really think it is almost random. We are all influenced to a
> different degree about different things and when we happen
> to come together, it is almost random. There are times when I
> think the Court is simply correcting an error.[33]

Nor were the clerks able to figure out what might move the justices.
As one said about a client he was currently representing:

> I have a case now, and the Court granted cert. I have no idea
> why they did. I told my client there is a one in ten chance that
> they'd accept it, and the most we could hope for would be a
> summary reversal. I am glad they took it because . . . the
> decision below was clearly wrong . . . I think I will win, but
> they are just not predictable on these things . . . [When clerk-
> ing] we certainly saw cases where someone really got screwed

33. The justice then said, "This next is not really for public consumption," and
proceeded to tell me something very interesting about why he could overlook injustice
in many cases. I point this out here as a specific example of one of the dilemmas one
faces with this type of research. One realizes that in this situation, the academic does
not have the luxury of the journalist to quote "unnamed but reliable sources." Reporting
what he said would add a great deal of insight about this justice, and perhaps a lot
about decision processes at the Court generally. I, of course, honor his request for
confidentiality here as I do for other justices when they so requested. Most of the other
instances, however, were cases where a justice chose to say something less than flattering
about one of his brethren (the request for confidentiality often followed having made
the remark). The inability to report those types of remarks only makes for a less
interesting work; the omission occasioning this footnote is of a different sort, and the
consequences are more substantive.

below . . . and I would recommend that they take . . . and
often those were just not followed. (C19)

All this talk about egregious cases being granted must be kept in
perspective. The justices are not bleeding hearts. As one clerk noted:

> Sure that happens, but it happens rarely. Justice _____ would
> come in and say, "boy this is a shame, it is really wrong, but
> we just can't correct everything." I guess it just depends upon
> how incensed they are. (C35)

One cannot generalize about what type of injustice will strike a justice
as egregious; but I did hear from several sources that cases involving
children were frequently ones where justices were unwilling to let a
bad decision stand. One justice seemed to confirm that.

> There are some cases like that [egregious], and I think some-
> times that it turns on the kind of case. In the last few terms
> where we have had a parent/child illegitimacy issue—that may
> just have more appeal and cause you to take it than something
> on the Miller Act.

The second category of egregious cases has to do with flagrant
disregard for precedent. Interestingly, this was described to me only
by the clerks—perhaps because this is an artifact of the interview, that
is, the context in which the subject arose, or perhaps because justices
were unwilling to acknowledge their reactions to opinions below. The
clerks frequently talked about the need to "slap the wrist" of a judge
below. The following remark typifies the comments from many clerks.

> Yes, that is absolutely the case. It is a relatively small percent-
> age of cases, but when they have a sense of outrage at a mis-
> application of the law, they will take the case when it doesn't
> seem to be certworthy for other reasons. They will particularly
> do this when there is a cavalier disregard for a precedent by a
> lower court judge. Mostly these are handled by summary
> reversal. (C23)

Another clerk painted the picture more dramatically:

> Sometimes they take cases which may seem frivolous. For ex-
> ample, you know there are many more lower courts and lower
> judges, and there is fear on the Supreme Court, and I think

real fear, that these courts seem to think that they can just
ignore the Supreme Court because they know that the Court
simply can't take but a few cases. (C12)

Many Court observers have suggested that judges on Courts of Appeals often play a bit fast and loose with precedent, knowing that the
Supreme Court cannot possibly review all decisions. This charge was
leveled particularly at the Ninth Circuit prior to the Reagan appoint-
ments. Whether willful disregard is a common practice by judges, and
whether there is "real fear" by the justices causing them to take cases
periodically to stop such behavior, one cannot be sure. If a wrist slap
occurs, however, it is usually done by summary disposition.

By way of concluding this section on egregiousness, I quote one
justice's response when I asked him why he thought an increase in
summary dispositions was occurring:

> *Justice:*   The volume is so enormous. I think part of the rea-
> son the volume is so enormous is that we are not a court to
> correct errors, and a lot of these summary judgments are
> just correcting errors. My belief is if a guy got a fair shake,
> even if I believe it was wrong, we can't go around correcting
> all errors, and I think it's wrong to review these cases.
>
> *Perry:*   I know that you justices often say that this isn't a court
> to correct errors, but sometimes it seems that if there is
> something egregious . . .
>
> *Justice:*   [Interrupting] Yes I'm just as guilty as some of the
> others about doing that, but I'm certainly trying to restrain
> myself.

Is Cert. a Preliminary Judgment on the Merits?

An underlying theme of most political science literature on the Court's
case selection process is that cert. votes are a preliminary judgment on
the merits, and that justices vote strategically on cert. to effect the
desired outcome on the merits. Such criteria for certworthiness obviously differ from those enunciated thus far.

I queried my informant's extensively on this notion that cert. is a
preliminary vote on the merits. The basic answer that I was given was,
"sometimes." One justice put it this way:

> I think that is an overstatement. If there is a conflict in the
> circuits, that is something that we'd probably deal with. But no

matter how wrong a case may be, if it's only been held in one circuit, and we feel it really needs ventilation, then we will vote to deny. On the other hand, if a single district judge rules that a federal statute is unconstitutional, I think we owe it to Congress to review the case and see if, in fact, the statute they've passed is unconstitutional.

And from another justice:

> Some certs. are granted without any consideration of the merits. If there is a clear conflict we will all vote to grant it. And it is not uncommon to hear someone say when voting on cert. that "I vote to grant, but I have no idea where I will come out." Or you will hear someone else say that "the Ninth Circuit is dead wrong in this case; I'll vote to grant." Many times I've heard people say, particularly Justice _____, that this decision is dead wrong, but let's let it go.

A third justice's response.

> It is in some cases. As I have said before, one factor that leads one to grant cert. is the fact that an error has been committed, because no one feels the obligation to correct something that has been correctly decided. But I am aware of a number of cases where at the cert. stage someone will say that obviously this must be reversed and after argument he decides that he must affirm it.

From a fourth justice:

> I would say that they are sometimes tentative votes on the merits. Now I would say that there are certain cases that I would vote for, for example, if there was a clear split in the circuits, I would vote for cert. without even looking at the merits. But there are other cases I would have more of a notion what the merits were.

For a fifth justice, however, his assessment of the correctness of the decision below seems to play a much greater role. When asked what he looked for to determine certworthiness, this justice responded:

> Something of recurring importance. If it were just a sport, no matter how wrongly decided it isn't worth while. But if it were

recurring, then I would make a horseback assessment of if it were correctly decided. Whether or not it was correctly decided was clearly the most important thing.

And, at a later point in the interview when asked if a cert. vote was a preliminary vote on the merits, he answered:

> In a majority of cases, yes. In . . . cases dealing with a conflict of some sort, the vote may be eight or nine to grant, yet the decision will split 5-4. Generally when people vote to grant, they feel that it is because it is wrongly decided.

However, this justice, like the others, spoke elsewhere in the interview of the importance of a circuit split, a case being a good vehicle, and the other factors I have discussed.

It is important to understand what all of these justices are saying and what they are not. Much of the time, they make decisions irrespective of the merits, the best example being when there is a clear circuit split. Other times, whether or not the case below was correctly decided influences their decision on whether or not to take that case. Clearly the justices are more inclined to spend their time "correcting" rather than affirming. If one counts vacates with reversals, the Court reverses at a rate of about 65–75 percent. That is not saying, however, that when justices feel that a case is wrongly decided, they will vote to grant cert. As has been demonstrated, the justices have several criteria that must be fulfilled to deem a case certworthy. Moreover, even if one concedes that some cert. votes are preliminary votes on the merits, that does not imply that a cert. vote involves any strategy or "sophisticated" voting, a topic discussed in the next chapter.

I think anyone who suggests that this is an objective institution is just wrong; the notion that we are objective is just fallacious.

U.S. Supreme Court Justice

9 A Decision Model

The preceding quotation came in an interview after the justice had described the cert. process as not being particularly difficult to understand because it basically involved searching for objectively determinable criteria. Was this justice being duplicitous only to be caught by me, the wily interviewer? No. Was he a simpleton who did not understand the contradiction? Certainly not. Are his statements easily reconcilable? Not really. They are, however, good descriptions of what is going on. This chapter offers a way of understanding many of the apparent contradictions in the justices' words and their behavior.

A quotation from C. Herman Pritchett appeared earlier in this work. It bears repeating here, because we now return to a theme which motivates much of this work. "Again political scientists who have done so much to put the 'political' in 'political jurisprudence' need to emphasize that it is still 'jurisprudence' . . . Any accurate analysis of judicial behavior must have as a major purpose a full clarification of the unique limiting conditions under which judicial policy making proceeds."[1] As I interviewed clerks and justices, so much of what they said simply did not jibe with much of the literature by political scientists on cert. Recall that much of the literature sees cert. votes as strategic voting calculated to have a desired outcome on the merits. Consideration of legalistic concerns such as circuit splits, jurisdictional defects, desire for perco-

---

1. C. Herman Pritchett, "The Development of Judicial Research," in Joel Grossman and Joseph Tanenhaus, eds., *Frontiers of Judicial Research* (New York: Wiley, 1969), p. 42.

lation, and so on play little or no role in much political science, yet they were the central concerns and the predominant factors discussed by those who participate in the process.[2] Unless there was a wholesale attempt to defraud me, something was amiss. On the other hand, when I interviewed clerks and justices, contradictions, or at least confusions, emerged from the stories they were telling me. In the midst of their rather legalistic interpretation of the process, they would say things that sounded very much like the scenarios portrayed in the political science literature.

Early in the interviewing process I reasoned that either one side or the other of the story must not be based on reality. The descriptions were simply too disparate. But as the interviews continued and I began to contemplate the accounts, I came to realize that both types of explanations revealed some aspect of the truth, that the statements were not necessarily contradictory. The process is both political and jurisprudential, but in a way that is not simply an acknowledgment that all things legal are political, or that some of the Court's work is legal and some political. A model of decision making that reflects this conclusion follows. It did not come about as an attempt to force an accommodation, for I was prepared to reject one set of explanations out of hand. It comes, I think, from analysis of the interviews, and it fits nicely with the empirical findings of other scholars.

A Process Model

I posit that deciding whether or not to take a case is a modified lexicographic decision process, that is, a hierarchical process of decisional steps or gates through which a case must successfully pass before

2. As I have noted before, I am oversimplifying the political science literature, and yet I think the thrust of my assessment is valid. For a very important exception, see S. Sidney Ulmer, "The Supreme Court's Certiorari Decisions: Conflict as a Predictive Variable," *American Political Science Review* 78 (December 1984): "Beginning with the work of Tanenhaus, those who construct models of certiorari decision making (including this author) have utilized such predictors as issue, petitioning party, socioeconomic status of petitioning and opposing parties, the ideological direction of the decision in the lower court, and the liberal or conservative makeup of the Court itself. None has included conflict as a variable in his or her models. The present study has shown however, that conflict is highly germane to such models. It may now be suggested that in making up its plenary case agenda, the Court is significantly responsive to the legal-systemic variable—conflict—and less governed by case issue variables than one might have thought. From a theoretical standpoint, this may suggest a shift of focus to systemic factors if the predictive power of my theories or semi-theories is to be enhanced" (p. 910).

it will be accepted.[3] Failure to "pass a gate" will usually mean a case will be denied. Because it is not always denied, however, the model is not truly lexicographic, hence the modifier "modified." But it is close enough that heuristically it makes sense to describe it this way.

In Professor Lawrence Mohr's terms this is a "process" model as opposed to a "variance" model. In his excellent book *Explaining Organizational Behavior: The Limits and Possibilities of Theory and Research,*[4] Mohr distinguishes between what he calls "variance theory" and "process theory." Though his argument is far too complex to reconstruct here, basically he suggests that variance theories can be characterized as follows:

1. The precursor (X) is a necessary and sufficient condition for the outcome (Y).
2. A variance theory deals with variables.
3. A variance theory deals with efficient causes.
4. In variance theory, time ordering among the contributing (independent) variables is immaterial to the outcome.

Process theories, by contrast, are characterized this way:

1. The precursor (X) is a necessary condition for the outcome (Y).
2. A process theory deals with discrete states and events.
3. A process theory deals with final cause.
4. In process theory, time ordering among the contributing events is generally critical for the outcome.

I do not assert that I have a process "theory," because I cannot meet precisely the standard of necessity. But I do suggest that it is instructive to think about what others have done as variance models, whereas what I am doing is a process model. A variance model would suggest that the decision to take a case would depend upon the combination and "weights" of certain factors in a case. In other words, rather than a case passing or failing to pass a series of gates, each case contains reasons to take it and not to take it, and how these interact, combine, and are weighed against one another determines whether or not the case will be taken. It should be noted that a process model does not

3. For a formal definition of "lexicographic," see Hal R. Varian, *Microeconomic Analysis,* 2d ed. (New York: W. W. Norton, 1984).

4. Lawrence B. Mohr, *Explaining Organizational Behavior: The Limits and Possibilities of Theory and Research* (San Francisco: Jossey-Bass, 1982).

exclude the weighing of factors and the importance of combinations, but the decision process to take a case is primarily sequential, not additive. Incidentally, a particular research methodology does not necessarily lead to either a process or a variance model. Indeed, a good study may have aspects of both process and variance.

I posit not only that the decision process is a series of steps, but that there are two different sets of decisional steps; and, depending upon the case and the justice, a case traverses one channel or the other. The justice is not choosing between two decision processes. He begins the process, and the decision at one of the gates forces him into one mode or the other. What this means is that the decisional steps for one case may look very different from those used by the same justice to evaluate another case. Likewise, the same case may be treated differently by different justices. I call these channels "decision modes." This conceptualization offers a synthesis and a more helpful way of addressing the question of whether or not the justices act "politically" or "legally," "ideologically" or "judge-like."

I have named the two modes of decision making the "outcome mode" and the "jurisprudential mode." The names may be uncreative, but they are not unconsidered. They are the best I could come up with to describe the decision modes fairly well without carrying any more baggage or preconceptions about what they mean than is necessary. Briefly, if a justice cares strongly about the outcome of a case on the merits at the time of the cert. decision, then he will enter the outcome mode to decide whether or not to take the case. If, however, the justice does not feel particularly strongly about the outcome of a case on the merits, he enters the jurisprudential mode with all its attendant steps. The steps differ in the two modes. Oversimplifying at this point, when in the jurisprudential mode, the justice makes his decision based on legalistic, jurisprudential types of considerations such as whether or not there is a split in the federal circuit courts of appeals. In the outcome mode, while the justice does not ignore jurisprudential concerns, they do not dominate his decision process. Rather, it is dominated by strategic considerations related to the outcome of the case on the merits. Jurisprudential concerns play a rather different role in the calculus.

To suggest that sometimes justices feel constrained by jurisprudential factors, while at other times they act on their own predispositions in a strategic manner is nothing new. What this model adds is a bit more precision in defining when and how the "political" and "legal" natures of the justices interact—at least in the agenda-setting process.[5]

5. I agree with Doris Marie Provine, *Case Selection in the United States Supreme Court*

There are several things to notice about this model. First, the model is one of individual, not collective, decision making. Second, it is not the case that some justices are "jurisprudes" and others "outcomers." Each of them uses each mode, though they may use them with differing frequencies. Third, as stated, the names of these modes were well-considered. One should not assume that cases that trigger the outcome mode are necessarily those of great social import, ideologically laden, or with great public policy implications. Likewise, cases triggering the jurisprudential mode are not necessarily the ones that present only technical "legal" questions. *What triggers one mode or the other is simply the degree of concern about the outcome on the merits.* Fourth, the two different modes do not suggest that a justice is a Dr. Jekyll and Mr. Hyde.

It became clear early on in the interviewing that the decision process was one of decisional winnowing steps. Informant after informant described the process as one whereby "first you look for X, if X is not present than you can throw out the case. If X is present, then you look for Y . . ." The notion that there were two fairly distinguishable modes of decision making came somewhat later. A couple of things basically led to this conclusion. First was the fact that an informant would say something and mean one thing; later in the interview, he would use virtually the same words but mean something different. I noticed this first with the different meanings people ascribed to "good vehicle." In fact, when I asked one justice whether it meant a good fact situation or something that would help him win on the merits, he answered, "both." Follow-up, however, suggested that it meant different things at different times. Also, justices and clerks would be giving jurisprudential descriptions suggesting that the process was objective and then would proceed to describe situations where strategy was clearly the driving force. The discussion of defensive denials provides a good example.

> *Perry:* There is one thing I want to clarify. Does a defensive denial come only on issues that particularly concern a justice?
>
> *Justice:* I was just going to say that you need to use this idea of defensive denials with an awful lot of caveats. Defensive denials are the rarity. I've just given you an example; when

---

(Chicago: University of Chicago Press, 1980), except that I think she has the impetus backward. She sees justices acting strategically but tempered by their perception of a judge's role. I would argue that the strategic behavior in case selection is the exception, even among the justices we would consider the most "political."

you feel strongly about the Fourth Amendment as I do, I
would use it. I just think that whether or not something is
done in good faith is irrelevant to the Fourth Amendment
issue.

Perry: Would this suggest that on some cases you might well
know what the vote on the merits will be, at least you think
you know, but you really wouldn't care that much about
cert., where on others you'd be more strategic?

Justice: Yes . . .

It was clear that strategic considerations tended to be the exception
rather than the rule for all of the justices, though some justices were
clearly strategic more often than others.

Second, I started hearing things that challenged some of my preconceptions about the different justices. For example, I assumed that
some justices would be very strategic in the cert. process, whereas
other justices would exhibit "legalistic" behavior. I was quite surprised
to find out that, at times, the latter justices could and did act as
strategically in cert. decisions as the former. Conversely, at times, the
former were driven by jurisprudential-type concerns when I would
have expected fierce ideological behavior.

Witness the remarks of clerks from several different chambers where
one would expect the justice to be less ideological and more "judge-
like":

> Justice _____ was more judge-like than many of the others,
> although he does have a particular interest in [an area of law]
> . . . He might vote because he wants to develop the law in
> those areas. But on other areas his cert. vote was more
> neutral.

Or this clerk:

> Justice _____ I think more than others would vote more on if
> an issue need to be decided, although from time to time he
> did think in terms of an outcome consideration.

From the same chamber:

> I mean he believes so strongly in _____ [an opinion he wrote]
> that when a case [in that area] would come up he would look
> right at the merits to see if it was an attempt to undercut [his
> opinion].

And finally, one said about his justice:

> Certain buttons could be pushed. There were a narrow cate-
> gory of cases that he had very strong views on and he would
> come to a quick decision . . . One was a technical/legal area.
> The other was an area of public policy.

So in other words, for the cert. process, it does not make sense to
characterize some justices as "ideologues" and others as "judge-like,"
or as "activists" vs. "restraintists," "jurisprudes" vs. "outcomers."
Rather, they all exhibit at one time or another an outcome orientation
or a jurisprudential one; therefore, the interesting thing was to determine how the two orientations differed and what triggered them.

Figure 9.1 provides a graphic representation of the decision process.
As with any model, the attempt is to simplify without being simplistic.
Such a model does not mean that a justice or a clerk literally has a
checklist through which he consciously proceeds, though often it was
described in precisely such terms. It does suggest that there is a series
of hierarchical decisions.

Clearly, the first thing that the justices consider, and this determination is really made by the clerks, is whether or not a petition is
frivolous. The next critical juncture in the model is the extent to which
a justice cares strongly about the outcome on the merits. I shall skip
the discussion of this decision mode for now and move down the
jurisprudential channel.

Jurisprudential Mode

If the justice does not care strongly about the outcome of a case on
the merits, the next question asked is whether or not there is a split
in the circuits. Recall that most informants said that the first thing or
main thing they looked for, after frivolity, was a split in the circuits.
Much of the clerk's time is spent at this stage trying to determine if
there is actually a split. Frequently, it is obvious that no such split
exists, or at least the case being petitioned is sufficiently distinguishable
so that one can claim that an actual split has not developed. The
determination of no legitimate conflict usually leads to denial. If there
is not a legitimate conflict, in rare cases the Court agrees to resolve an
issue or a particular case if there is a strong need to do so. Almost
invariably, these are cases where the solicitor general pleads the need
for immediate action because delay would cost the federal government
vast amounts of money, or the extant decision might put current

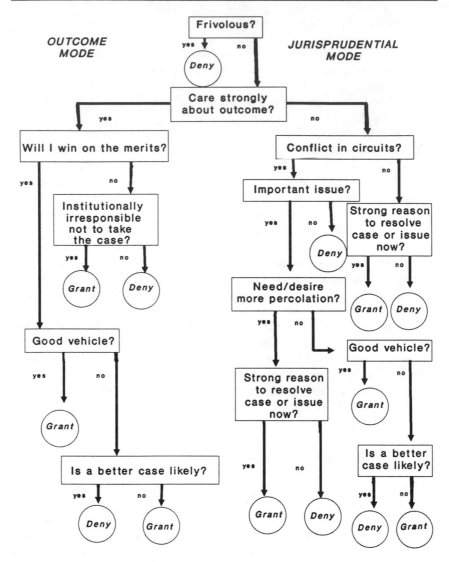

Figure 9.1   A decision model

governmental operating procedures in chaos. The Court would prefer to have the benefit of the consideration of as many circuits as possible, certainly more than one, before it renders an opinion, but in such cases that is not possible. It must be emphasized that such situations are rare, and the solicitor general carefully guards his reputation for an accurate assessment of a situation. As noted in the chapter on signaling, it is not in his interest to lead the Court astray.

The existence of a legitimate split does not assure that a case will be granted, however. The justice then asks whether or not the split is over an important issue. Recall from the discussion in the previous chapter that importance may mean several things, and different things to different justices in different situations.

If there is a legitimate conflict, and it involves an important issue, the next question that a justice considers is the need or desire for more "percolation." Though he desires more percolation, if there is a compelling reason to take the case at this time, he will usually vote to grant. But reasons are usually "compelling" only when the solicitor general says a decision is crucial. If no such argument is made, the case will be denied, to allow more percolation.

Even though there is a legitimate circuit split with several circuits having ruled, and there is no desire or need for additional percolation, the justice still asks if this particular case is a "good vehicle." In the jurisprudential mode, being a good vehicle is determined by such things as: is the issue clear and "squarely presented"? Is the record below clear? Is the fact situation nonambiguous? Can the primary issue be reached, or will some confounding issue have to be decided first, which would preclude a decision on the major issue? Are there potential problems such as standing or mootness? In other words, a justice considers procedural jurisprudential concerns to determine if the case is a good vehicle.

The jurisprudential mode is a series of fundamentally jurisprudential considerations. They are the types of things that one learns in law school. And as difficult as it is for us political scientists to accept at times, Supreme Court justices are very much lawyers who are trained and socialized in this vein, and they very much believe in the necessity and desirability of judges acting along such lines. Justices, too, have the idealized notion of what it means to be a dispassionate jurist, and they often try to act accordingly.

Outcome Mode

When a justice cares a lot about the outcome of a case on the merits, he seems to exhibit different behavior—behavior that is much more strategic and is more in line with the decision making portrayed by political scientists. Even though most of what my informants said was definitely in a jurisprudential mode, they would frequently say things like, "of course there are exceptions." This would usually be in re-

sponse to a question I asked on whether or not a vote on cert. could
be seen as a preliminary vote on the merits. The answer would usually
be "no," except that they were more predisposed to take cases that
they perceived to be wrongly decided than ones correctly decided. On
many cases, they had no predisposition, but even if they did, they did
not calculate in any strategic sense what the outcome on the merits
would be. To be sure, once the case was taken, there was an effort to
win. But the decision to grant cert. was not made on a strategic calculation of the outcome.

There are cases, however, where after frivolity, outcome is the driving force behind behavior on the cert. decision. Now this is not to say
that the justice has completely decided himself how all aspects of the
opinion should look. But if the area is that important to him, he
probably has a fairly well-developed idea of how doctrine should proceed; therefore, he has a good idea of how he will vote on the merits,
and he probably has a good idea of how his colleagues will vote. As
might be expected, those cases about which a justice would care
strongly are often ones of great importance. All the justices have very
strong feelings about issues such as affirmative action, obscenity, and
the exclusionary rule. But such intense concern about outcome is not
confined to cases of great societal importance. Indeed, the fervor may
be about a technical issue. Each justice seems to have certain areas,
large and small, where he feels strongly about how doctrine should
proceed or, for some reason, cares strongly about the outcome of a
particular case. It may well be something about which the rest of the
brethren are dispassionate. The "big issues" may not always lead to
the outcome mode. A justice might see an issue as one of great public
importance at one time, but later find that it has become a more
jurisprudential question for him. In other words, once a controversial area of law has become fairly well settled, the justice may become a jurisprude on the issue; *stare decisis* becomes more important.
Nevertheless, important issues usually continue to engender
outcome-oriented responses—even from the justices we think of
as being least ideological.

When entering the outcome decision mode, the first thing that the
justice does is try to make an assessment of whether or not he will win
on the merits. If he thinks he will not, he will vote to deny the case.
The one mitigating situation in this outcome-driven behavior would
be if it would be institutionally irresponsible not to take the case; for
example, if the SG convinces him that refusal to decide the issue now
would be disastrous, or if it is a decision where the Supreme Court
simply must act. An example of the latter might be something like the
Nixon tapes case. It is also possible that declining to decide a major

circuit split would at some point come to be seen as irresponsible. But in the outcome mode a justice, like everyone else, is very good at selective perception and is far more likely to avoid taking the case if he can do so in good conscience. He will at least try to wait for a better case. With the caveat of institutional irresponsibility, if the justice perceives that he will lose on the merits, the vote will be to deny. My informants frequently and openly referred to these cases as "defensive denials."

Much of the political science literature suggests a justice's decision process stops here—"If I can win, grant." A potential win on the merits is not enough to vote to grant, however. The next question that a justice asks is whether or not the case is a good vehicle. Here "good vehicle" means something different from what it did in the other mode. Good facts here might mean ones that would be most likely to pull a swing justice. Or good facts would be those that would allow the justice to move doctrine in the particular way he wanted. It might be quite possible to win the case, but it might not be the best way to get to one's ultimate goal. To be sure, jurisprudential factors are not irrelevant. For example, a messy fact situation might not serve one's cause. Even if the present case could be won, given the messy facts it might allow the next case to be distinguished on the facts in such a way that would make things worse. One might win the battle and lose the war. That said, messy facts or other jurisprudential problems certainly do not stop justices when they want to reach an issue. Every Court observer has seen the Court reach out to make a ruling, running roughshod over things such as standing, ripeness, or the policy of not reaching the Constitutional question if non-Constitutional issues are dispositive. And yet the same justice who does this—and they all do it one time or the other—will decry such behavior when his brethren do it, claiming that they are simply trying to reach a certain result. I suspect that the presence of a good vehicle is often just too good to pass up in a strategic sense, and this may help explain why we often see such cases being adjudicated despite their jurisprudential problems.

If a justice cares strongly about the outcome of a particular case, his calculations as to why a case is a good or bad vehicle may be complex and highly strategic. The particular fact situation might appeal to a swing vote; say, for example, it is a case of child abuse that so outrages another justice that it might pull his vote on the merits whereas a different fact situation might not. Even more strategically, if the case enables one justice to make his arguments for cert. in jurisprudential terms, though his motive is outcome, he may be better able to persuade another justice who happens to be a jurisprude on this issue. Undoubt-

edly, most arguments at conference to grant cert. are made in jurisprudential terms, likewise to deny. To the extent that this can be done
persuasively, it may allow one to avoid the appearance of being simply
result oriented, and it may disarm an opponent.[6] The factors, then,
of what constitutes a "good vehicle" in the outcome mode are not
wholly different from those in the jurisprudential mode, but they are
more complex and are largely driven by strategic considerations.

   If the present case is not a good vehicle, the question that remains
is, is a better case likely? If yes, vote to deny; if no, vote to grant and
hope for extraordinarily persuasive capabilities after the case has been
submitted for decision. One of the problems with some of the political
science literature is that it seems to suggest that if a justice can win on
the merits, he will want to take the case. Ironically, such an assumption
does not allow the justices to be political and strategic enough.

Living with Inconsistency

Would intelligent, diligent, honest justices allow themselves to have a
double standard for decision making? Before one answers that, it
should be pointed out that a double standard is not necessarily a bad
thing. It may well suggest flexibility. Should a justice always be a
"jurisprude"? Socialization in the law seems to suggest that being a
jurisprude is admirable, whereas being an outcomer is somehow
a necessary evil, which is, of course, poppycock.[7] Being "political" or
"strategic" should not connote anything unseemly. Recall the arguments in the chapters on bargaining and strategy. Moreover, having
two different methods of behavior is not bad *prima facie*. The justices
are not being disingenuous or schizophrenic, nor are they engaging
in self-delusion when they trumpet the virtues of jurisprudential considerations and "principled decision making" while at the same time
talking about things like defensive denials. Think of the standard
classroom exercise used to illustrate the Burkean dilemma. We all at
one time think that it is right, proper, and good for a representative
to be an instructed delegate, and at other times we insist that he or
she be a trustee. Not only is there not a definitive normative answer
to Burke, but empirically we see that representatives behave both ways

---

6. See S. Sidney Ulmer, "Selecting Cases for Supreme Court Review: An Underdog
Model," *American Political Science Review* 72 (September 1978): 902; Ulmer argues that
justices often are unwilling to appear unbiased to the brethren.

   7. Again, if there is a straw man here, it is not my doing. This pristine image comes
from my informants.

depending on circumstances.[8] Moreover, the dilemma usually does not actually arise and force a *conscious* decision to act one way or the other. Such would probably also be true of the Court.

Witness the President. Every beginning student of the presidency learns that the President wears different hats. At times we expect the President to be politically astute, and if he is not, he is often labeled a failure. Other times, we expect him to be above politics, and if he is not, he incurs our wrath.[9] The point is not that the public is fickle; rather, in order to do a good job, the President must often make decisions in different ways appropriate to the problem at hand.[10] The justices, too, must wear different hats—or should we say different robes? An institution such as the Supreme Court is an enigma to a democratic system, and the justices have always had to deal with tensions in this regard. The Supreme Court is the highest court in the land and as such must direct the legal system. To have a credible legal system where there is the rule of law rather than men suggests an adjudicative body that is "above politics" in some sense. At times the Court is called on to settle a rule of evidence, a technical tax statute. Other times, however, it has to step in and act as a relief pitcher for democracy and decide that separate cannot be equal. Given such different tasks, one should not only expect that the justices would make decisions in different ways, one should probably hope that they would.

Professor Judith Shklar has dealt with conflicting conceptions of the law brilliantly in her book *Legalism*. Though the context was different, her comments go straight to the heart of what I am arguing:

> Yet the quest for the holy grail of perfect, nonpolitical, aloof neutral law and legal decisions persists and remains a test for acceptability. It is also still often said that a politically oriented legal system spells the end of judicial legitimacy. In fact, although it is philosophically deeply annoying, human institutions survive because most of us can live comfortably with wholly contradictory beliefs. Most thoughtful citizens know

8. See John W. Kingdon, "Models of Legislative Voting," *Journal of Politics* 39 (August 1977): 563–595. See also his *Congressmen's Voting Decisions*, 2d ed. (New York: Harper and Row, 1981).

9. See Thomas E. Cronin, "The Presidency and Its Paradoxes," in Alan Shank, ed., *American Politics, Policies, and Priorities*, 3d ed. (Boston: Allyn and Bacon).

10. Mark A. Peterson, *Legislating Together: The White House and Capitol Hill from Eisenhower to Reagan* (Cambridge: Harvard University Press, 1990); Paul C. Light, *The President's Agenda: Domestic Policy Choice from Kennedy to Carter* (Baltimore: The Johns Hopkins University Press, 1982); Richard Neustadt, *Presidential Power: The Politics of Leadership from FDR to Carter* (New York: Macmillan).

that the courts act decisively in creating rules that promote political ends—to name only civil rights—of which they may approve. They also insist that the impartiality of judges and of the process as a whole requires a dispassionate, literal pursuit of rules carved in spiritual marble. Changes in these rules are to be made by legislative agencies, but never by the judiciary. All criticism and praise of judicial performances is couched in phrases drawn from this belief, which may seem ridiculous but is not at all socially or psychologically indefensible. Indeed, if we value flexibility and accept a degree of contradiction, this paradox may even seem highly functional and appropriate.[11]

By allowing the justices to act both as outcomers and jurisprudes, but not at the same time, the model provides a better understanding of the certiorari process in the United States Supreme Court. There is also reason to believe that the jurisprudential/outcome distinction is useful beyond case selection. Though this cannot be the forum, I am prepared to argue that it gets us much further in understanding attitudes and behavior on the Court generally than do our usual categories and ways of understanding justices: as political or legal, activist or restraintist, liberal or conservative, ideological or juristic. It also provides for a new way to address debates about interpretation. For example, it may do for the debate over "neutral principles" what good studies of congressional decision making have done for the Burkean dilemma.[12]

11. Judith Shklar, *Legalism: Law, Morals, and Political Trials* (Cambridge: Harvard University Press, 1986), x.
12. See Herbert Wechsler, "Toward Neutral Principles of Constitutional Law," 73 *Harvard Law Review* (1959), and the debate that article has spawned.

10 Conclusion

I began this book by claiming the need for a better understanding of how the U.S. Supreme Court's agenda is set and suggesting that this study would do that. That was a bit of oversell—or perhaps I should say I stretched my signaling credibility. To understand fully the Court's agenda, the net must be cast wider. One would need to examine many factors, such as changes in legislation and the existence of entrepreneurs for a cause, in short, why certain issues were being litigated in lower courts.[1] It was also promised that this study would examine and have something meaningful to say about the decision process used to select cases for review in the Supreme Court, which is the final stage of the agenda-setting process. That, I hope, has been accomplished. It is also my conceit that, while limited in some ways specifically to case selection, the book is really a window into decision making at the U.S. Supreme Court. This final chapter offers some brief concluding thoughts, or more precisely, some unanswered questions and possibilities raised by the conclusions that have already been drawn; and of course, it cries out for more and better research.

Let us address briefly the notion that behavior affecting the agenda-setting process is going on before the Court ever has to decide to

---

1. See Susan Lawrence, *The Poor in Court: The Legal Services Program and Supreme Court Decision Making*, (Princeton: Princeton University Press, 1990), for an excellent study of agenda setting as it related to the Legal Services Program. See also Frances K. Zemans, "Legal Mobilization: The Neglected Role of the Law in the Political System," *American Political Science Review* 77 (1983).

decide. Once upon a time, this book was to have contained a chapter entitled "The View from Down Under"—a full exposition of things learned from interviewing the solicitors general and their staffs and judges on the D.C. Circuit. Although I ultimately decided this would have to be the subject of another book, a few points should be made here. Crucial to the Court's agenda decision is what types of cases it is presented. "What types of cases" refers not to subject matter but to all the characteristics that make a case certworthy. The Supreme Court does have virtually any issue presented to it sooner or later, and it is free to pick or refuse a case at its own discretion, so it technically controls its own agenda. Moreover, it can send signals to invite cases. But given its own criteria for certworthiness, the Court's control is limited.

Certain repeat players know and understand the Court's criteria and are thus better able to act in a more sophisticated manner, which, in turn, enables them to play an important role in structuring the final agenda. The solicitor general is the best such player. He fiercely guards the deference he is shown by deciding what types of cases to present to the Court. But as I learned from my interviews with former solicitors general and their staffs, and as any political scientist should expect, the decision process used in that office is subject to all types of forces, of which signals from the Supreme Court is only one. The SG must contend with U.S. attorneys, governmental agencies, and sometimes, presidents. There is a system of communication within the solicitor general's office replete with indices and signals—some things manipulable, others not—that precedes petitioning the Court. Nevertheless, the SG is a formidable force in what ultimately becomes the agenda of the United States Supreme Court. Some in the Office of the Solicitor General, for example, boasted of leading the Court on double jeopardy doctrine by the order in which they chose to bring cases. As one put it, they got the Court to "duck its head a bit, then to bend over a little further until there had been a somersault, with the Court landing exactly where they had wanted it." In that instance, the staff member described a purposeful, strategic manipulation of the Court's agenda. In other areas, however, the SG's complained of the relative inability to control their own agenda. Understanding the decision process in the Office of the Solicitor General is a topic of interest in and of itself, but it would certainly be important to a complete understanding of the development of the Supreme Court's agenda.

One of the most remarkable things learned from interviewing judges on the D.C. Circuit was how little most of them know about the actual cert. process. Most of what they know comes from former law clerks who have gone on to clerk at the Supreme Court. The circuit judges often gave seemingly contradictory answers when it came to discussing their interest in whether or not one of their cases was reviewed. Their reaction is somewhat similar to that of the justices in the jurispruden-tial/outcome model. To oversimplify: at times they do not seem to care; other times they care a great deal. It is not only that they care, however, but that when they do care, they act quite strategically. Several of the judges noted that on some cases they wrote dissents in such a way as to try to attract the attention of one or more justices. Other times, they dissented without any attempt to gain review. I was also told of attempts to "certproof" a case. This was done by writing long, complicated opinions, resting the holding on various grounds. Such a case, of course, becomes a "bad vehicle." Justices want clean cases. In short, the communication between the lower courts and the Supreme Court is an interesting topic in itself. One could examine several aspects empirically. For example, one might want to observe the rate of review when particular judges write a dissent, controlling for important other factors. Hypotheses abound, but given what we now know about the decision process in the Court, we can formulate more intelligent hypotheses.

This book began with a bit of preachiness about political scientists, lawyers, and the undoubted importance of agenda setting. I return to the pulpit.

Scholars of the Court need to be more catholic and less parochial. Much of the behavior described in this work is not unique to the Court. This book does not attempt systematically to make many inter-institutional comparisons, but it suggests that attempts might prove profitable. For example, political scientists are always talking about, and trying to measure, the effects of salience or intensity on behavior. Issues of high salience or high intensity often lead to behavior that differs from the norm, be it by a voter or a member of Congress. Granted, just because high salience brings about different decision processes in voters, legislators, and justices does not mean that meaningful comparisons can be drawn, but it is worth a look.

Consider two other areas where the study of Supreme Court agenda setting might be informed by or contribute to the work of other scholars. What the Court faces in its agenda decisions is similar to what Jack Walker described for legislatures; that is, decisions are made on a continuum of issues, from required to discretionary.[2] If there are similarities that go beyond the superficial comparison, and I think there are, we might be better able to understand the behavior of

2. Jack L. Walker, "Setting the Agenda in the U.S. Senate: A Theory of Problem Selection," *British Journal of Political Science* 7 (October 1977): 423–445.

justices by looking at how members of Congress set their agenda and vice versa. Walker's required-to-discretionary continuum raises interesting questions about what makes decision makers see things as "required." In few political institutions are decisions actually required; it is that they are perceived to be. Are there generalizable criteria for predicting when decision makers in governmental institutions will feel that a decision is required? For example, are there similarities between budget making and the resolution of circuit splits? With such decisions, any action is perceived to be better than no action. Not to act would be seen as irresponsible, not only by the decision makers but also by many attentive publics. Moreover, there are ready solutions. Budgets can be changed incrementally, and a circuit split can be resolved one way or the other. When no obvious solution is available, are decision makers more likely to see an issue as discretionary? Many scholars are about the task of understanding decision criteria in other institutions, but their findings are rarely applied to the Court, and the work of judicial scholars informs their work even less.

In the context of my observation of justices acting as jurisprudes or outcomers, one might wish to examine Morris P. Fiorina's notion of legislators being maximizers or maintainers.[3] Though I grossly oversimplify, Fiorina suggests that individuals will act in certain ways. Maximizers will always try to maximize, maintainers maintain. I argue that all justices are both outcomers and jurisprudes and that different situations encourage different behavior. Assuming for the moment that Fiorina and I are both right, why the difference? Why are members of Congress "either/or," whereas justices are "both/and"? Is it that the comparison is faulty because Fiorina is talking about instrumental behavior given to achieve one goal, whereas I am talking about multiple goals at a different level of generality? Is it because I am dealing with agenda-setting decisions specifically? Is it something about the differences in courts and legislatures? Is it the difference between exogenous and endogenous forces? Does my observation of justices suggest that Fiorina is wrong and that all members of Congress will exhibit both maximizing and maintaining behavior depending on the actual decision? Or am I wrong, and justices should be seen as primarily jurisprudes or outcomers? Or, am I simply arguing that all justices are maintainers—balancing jurisprudential and strategic concerns? I make no pretense at answering these questions here, or even suggesting that they are good questions. It might be that the compar-

3. See Fiorina, *Representatives, Roll Calls, and Constituencies* (Lexington, Mass.: D.C. Heath, 1974).

ison is so flawed that it is ultimately of little use. That is not the point. The key word is "ultimately." Before commencing this study, I had thought a lot about the decision-making behavior of members of Congress, thanks to people like Fiorina, Ferejohn, Fenno, Kingdon, Polsby, Price, Shepsle, and others. It makes some sense to use what we know from those scholars—not just Court scholars—in trying to understand Court behavior. These suggestions are applicable to lawyers as well as political scientists. Likewise, the hope is that congressional scholars and others might profit by paying more attention to studies of courts— even if it is only to note why a comparison would be flawed. That alone would be instructive.

Political institutions come to collective decisions in different ways. A process that adds the sum of the parts with no ex post veto may produce very different results from one where the decision process is truly collegial. In the latter case, anticipated reactions and the level of personal knowledge and regard for one another might mitigate the differences, but they are still two quite different decision processes. One of the important contributions of theory is to demonstrate precisely how results might differ. I argue that the cert. process is a decision that adds the sum of the parts with very little discussion or anticipated reaction at the agenda-setting stage. Accepting or not accepting that argument as behavioral fact might lead to quite different theories to explain outcomes. Theories of group dynamics might explain far less about cert. than theories of individual decision making.[4]

Contrary to the suggestions of most political science literature, justices' cert. decisions are not simply strategic calculations to effect a desired policy or doctrinal outcome. Nor, however, is the cert. process simply one of a series of jurisprudential judgments with political desires continually submerged. It is a complex decision process that involves both of these descriptions, but standing alone, each does more to confuse than elucidate. I have tried to show some of the complexity. Other decision processes on the Court are different, and I do not argue that decision making on the merits proceeds in precisely the same way. I do believe, however, that this study suggests some things

---

4. This statement suggests that different behavior justifies using different types of theories. I have no problem with that, although I suspect some decision theorists might. When a group decision involves primarily the sum of individual decision processes, then explanations of individual decision making such as those provided by rational choice models might prove particularly useful. When group decisions involve significant group interaction and the opportunity for many intervening variables to affect the outcome, then perhaps many of the more organizational and empirically based decision theories are more satisfactory.

about behavior on the Court that go beyond case selection. For example, a body that acts so atomistically at the cert. stage probably does not become particularly collegial at the merits stage. Likewise the outcomer/jurisprude distinction probably operates in some form for decisions on the merits as well. The justices have, and should have, strong feelings about certain issues that they adjudicate. They also have an extraordinary belief in the importance of institutional maintenance—both the institution of the Court, and the institution of the judiciary as a group dedicated to judging in a fair and nonpartisan way. These beliefs and feelings pull in different ways. The way the justices resolve these countervailing tugs at cert. may not be all that different from what they do when deciding whether or not to join an opinion. Finally, signaling undoubtedly goes on in other facets of the Court's work. Identifying and separating the universal from the particular, the index from the signal, and identifying all the senders and receivers of signals would be worthwhile and lead to a broader understanding of decision making in the Court.

Deciding to decide in the U.S. Supreme Court is an important, understandable, generalizable process. The British empire may have been created in a fit of absent-mindedness; the agenda of the U.S. Supreme Court is not.

Appendix · Index

An Extended Discussion of Jurisdiction

As discussed in Chapter 2, it is impossible and not necessary to explore fully the questions of jurisdiction and procedure that surround case selection. Nevertheless, anyone who is serious about understanding how the Court selects cases must have at least a rudimentary understanding of these issues. As in Chapter 2, much of my discussion here comes from Stern and Gressman without specific citation.

The primary task of this appendix is to outline Supreme Court jurisdiction *during the time of the study*. The focus is on appeals and certiorari, and the appendix is so divided. Those categories are then divided to discuss federal courts and state courts because that is the way they are organized in the *U.S. Code,* and because the distinction between state courts and federal courts is so important. It must be remembered that the United States has a dual court system. State courts and federal courts function independently from one another to a large degree. The section on certiorari takes a slight detour to address briefly the history of the development of discretionary jurisdiction and the development of the federal court system because they are relevant to the Court's current understanding of its role.

On the following page, Table A.1 summarizes the appellate and certiorari jurisdiction. The reader may find it useful to refer to this table while reading the text.

Table A.1   Requirements for appeal and certiorari

FEDERAL COURT

Appeal	Certiorari
1. Act of Congress held *unconstitutional* in civil action; *or*	1. Any civil or criminal case in Court of Appeals, *before or after* judgment or decree
2. Court of Appeals *invalidates* state statute; *or*	
3. Decision by three-judge court	

STATE COURT

Appeal	Certiorari
1. Treaty or statute of the U.S. held *invalid*; *or*	1. Decision from highest possible court, and judgment is *final*; *and*:
2. State statute held *valid* when challenged as repugnant to U.S. Constitution, law, or treaty	a. Validity of state statute is drawn in question on grounds of repugnancy to U.S. Constitution, treaty, or statute; *or*
	b. Violation of a federal right claimed; *and*: (1) claim must have been asserted in state court, *and* (2) state decision not based on adequate and independent nonfederal grounds

Certiorari

Because certiorari jurisdiction is so important to the agenda-setting process of the Court, and because the history of its development helps one understand its current status, a brief and somewhat simplified history of the development of the Court's discretionary jurisdiction is in order. Excellent and thorough treatments of this history exist elsewhere.[1] My recounting is in no sense exhaustive, and it is derived primarily from secondary sources, with one exception.

1. See, e.g., Peter Linzer, "The Meaning of Certiorari Denials," *Columbia Law Review* 79 (November 1979). The seminal work is Felix Frankfurter and James M. Landis, *The Business of the Supreme Court: A Study in the Federal Judicial System* (New York: Macmillan, 1928). Robert Stern and Eugene Gressman, *Supreme Court Practice*, 5th ed. (Washington,

History of the Development of Discretionary Jurisdiction

I shall begin with the exception. On one of those days when even the thought of looking at another cert. petition seemed unbearable, I decided to try to find the earliest statutory mention of certiorari in Anglo-American law.[2] The first mention of certiorari that I could find in an act of Parliament[3] was in 1414, during the second year of the reign of King Henry V.

> Item, forasmuch as many men have been condemned in the courts of our lord the King, and in the courts of his progenitors, as well within the city of London, as in other cities and boroughs within the realm of England, and by the virtue of such condemnations have been committed to the prison of our lord the King, there to remain until they have made agreement to the plaintiffs to whom they were condemned; (2) after by their suggestion made in the chancery of our lord the King, they have had divers writs called *Certiorari*, and *Corpus cum causa*, out of the chancery of our said lord the King, directed to the sheriff, or keepers of the prisons where such persons condemned be holden, to have their bodies, with the cause of imprisonment with the condemned aforesaid, in the chancery, at the days contained in the said writs.[4]

D.C., Bureau of National Affairs, 1978), also traces some of the history. These works are the sources for most of my discussion in this section. Having said this, I have tried to spare the reader from an overuse of reference footnotes, but my debt to these authors is immense.

2. The value of such an exercise for this study might seem questionable, but it led to a wonderfully fun morning in the library, and since information was mined that might prove useful to some other scholar, I report it here. More important, this historical footnote adds some dimension to our current understanding of certiorari.

3. Since my expedition, I have recently come across an article by Jerome J. Hanus, "Certiorari and Policy-Making in English History," *American Journal of Legal History* 12 (1968): 63–94. Hanus, citing other scholars, suggests that the traditional phrasing of the writ was *certis de causis* and that it first appeared in 1272 in a letter from Henry III to the mayor and commonality of Bordeaux, but it can be presumed that it was used somewhat earlier (p. 74).

4. "Concerning writs of *Certiorari* or *Corpus cum causa*, granted for persons in execution," (act), 1414, 2 Henry 5, Stat. 1, ch. 2, in Danby Pickering, *The Statutes at Large*, vol. 3 (London: Cambridge University, 1762), pp. 10–11. The act goes on to read: "(3) after which writs, together with the body, and the cause of the condemnation, returned in the chancery aforesaid, the said persons so condemned have been delivered in the chancery aforesaid, by bail or by mainprise, against the assent and will of the said plaintiffs of the sums in the which they be condemned, against the law of the land; and so remain the said plaintiffs without remedy, in hindrance of the state of such plaintiffs,

The next mention of this writ was an act passed in 1432 under Henry VI, which sounds a bit more like its modern usage.

> (3) And imagining to defraud and make frustrate the said statute, do sue to remove such indictments and appeals out of the hands of the justices or commissioners aforesaid into the King's bench and elsewhere by *Certiorari* . . .
>
> (4). . . that if any such indictments taken, or to be taken, before any justices of peace, or before any other having power to take such indictments or appeals, or other justices or commissioners in any county, franchise or liberty of England, shall be removed before the King in his bench or elsewhere, by *Certiorari* or otherwise.[5]

The common law writ of certiorari continued to develop in British law basically as it began—a tool to ensure justice by allowing a superior court to remove proceedings from an inferior court. As defined in Bacon's abridgement in 1856:

> A certiorari is an original writ issuing out of Chancery, or the King's Bench, directed in the king's name, to the judges or officers of (a) inferior courts, commanding them to return the records of a cause depending before them, to the end the party may have the more sure and speedy justice before him, or such other justices as he shall assign to determine the cause . . .
>
> The Court of King's Bench hath a superintendency over all courts of an inferior criminal jurisdiction, and may by the plenitude of its power (a) award a *certiorari* to have any indictment removed and brought before itself; and where such *certiorari* is allowable, ought of right to award it at the instance of

---

and in defeating of the judgments given in the courts, aforesaid: (4) Our lord the King, willing herein to provide remedy, by the advice and assent aforesaid, and at the request of the foresaid commons, hath ordained and established, That if any such writ of *Certiorari*, or *Corpus cum causa*, be granted, or shall be granted at anytime hereafter, and upon the said writ if it be returned, that the prisoner which is so holden in prison is condemned by judgment given against him, that presently he shall be remanded, where he shall remain continually in prison according to the law and custom of the land, without being let to go by bail or by mainprise against the will of the said plaintiffs, until agreement be made to them of the sums so adjudged."

5. "What process shall be awarded upon indictments and appeals removed into the King's bench," (act) 1432, 10 Henry 6, Stat. 1, ch. 6, in Pickering, *The Statutes at Large*, III, 176–177.

the king, because every indictment is at the suit of the king, and he hath a (b) prerogative of suing in what court he pleases.[6]

Removal by certiorari could be limited by statute, however: "The Courts of Chancery and King's Bench may award a *certiorari* to remove the proceeding from and inferior courts, whether they be of an ancient or newly created jurisdiction, (a) unless the statute or charter, which creates them, exempts them from such jurisdiction."[7] Indeed in England, many such statutes exist that are concerned with limiting where the writ can issue.

The common law writ of certiorari in the American legal system developed in a way very similar to that of England. Any superior court in the United States could, by common law, issue extraordinary writs such as certiorari unless otherwise prohibited from doing so by statute. This was later codified to authorize all federal courts to "issue all writs necessary or appropriate in aid of their respective jurisdictions and agreeable to the usages and principles of law."[8] Such writs would include mandamus, prohibition, habeas corpus, and certiorari.[9]

The common law writ of certiorari is not the same as the writ of certiorari that brings most cases before the U.S. Supreme Court. It was the creation of "statutory certiorari" that revolutionized the Supreme Court's docket. Why then the preceding discussion of the common law writ? Three not entirely separate reasons: first, the common law writ is the underpinning of the statutory writ in the sense that the common law allowed superior courts to take and review cases on a discretionary basis to ensure that justice was done, as opposed to relying on an appeal by right. Second, it is arguable that the proponents of "statutory certiorari" did not feel that they were making a distinction between common law certiorari and statutory certiorari, a point discussed more below.[10] Third, writers do not always make clear

---

6. Matthew Bacon, *A New Abridgement of the Law*, vol. 2 (Philadelphia: T. and J. W. Johnson, 1856), pp. 162–163.

7. Ibid., p. 67.

8. 28 U.S.C. sec. 1651.

9. Stern and Gressman, *Supreme Court Practice*, p. 627.

10. There is potential for confusion here. The common law writ of certiorari is also technically provided for by statute in that it appears in Title 28, Section 1651, of the *U.S. Code*. Nevertheless, when referring to "statutory certiorari," people are not talking about the now codified common law writ. See J. Myron Jacobstein and Roy M. Mersky, *Fundamentals of Legal Research* (Mineola, N.Y.: Foundation Press, 1981), pp. 140–141, for an explanation of codification procedures and other useful information about the *U.S. Code*.

which certiorari they are talking about, something I found confusing in the course of my research; therefore, I hope my brief description of common law certiorari will be of some use to others who are not well-versed in the common law.

To understand the Court's current jurisdiction and the development of statutory certiorari, one must first understand a bit about the development of the federal judicial system.

Development of the Federal Judicial System

It is easy to forget that the Constitution creates only one federal court, the Supreme Court of the United States. Creation of other federal courts is left to the discretion of Congress.[11] Though it is hard to imagine such a system today, Congress could have left the adjudication of federal law to the state courts, only to be overseen by the U.S. Supreme Court. That of course did not happen. The First Judiciary Act of 1789 established the federal judicial system. It created thirteen district courts—two each in Virginia and Massachusetts and one in each of the other states. North Carolina and Rhode Island had not yet joined the Union. The country was divided into three circuits with each circuit court consisting of two Supreme Court justices and one district court judge. Basically, these circuit courts had different jurisdiction from the district courts; that is, they heard different types of cases.[12] For the most part, they did not serve as appellate courts between the district courts and the Supreme Court.[13] The layer of appellate courts between the district courts and the Supreme Court, as we know them today, was not created until some one hundred years later.

The circuit courts of 1789 imposed the much discussed burden of "circuit riding" upon the justices, which was particularly onerous because these were pre-railroad times. Travel was very difficult and time consuming, and at the time, there was only one chief justice and five associate justices. The Act of March 2, 1793, provided some relief from circuit riding by reducing from two to one the number of justices required to sit at each circuit, but the basic problem still existed. Ostensibly to relieve the justices of the burdensome circuit riding, the

11. United States Constitution, Article III, Section 1.

12. According to Frankfurter, *The Business of the Supreme Court* (p. 12), "Broadly speaking, to the circuit courts were allotted cases resting on the diversity of citizenship, while the district courts became the admiralty courts for the country."

13. There actually was some very limited appellate jurisdiction given to the circuit courts, but for all practical purposes they and the district courts were *nisi prius courts* (i.e., non-appellate courts). (Frankfurter, *The Business of the Supreme Court*, p. 13.)

Act of February 13, 1801, more commonly known as the Midnight Judges Act, created sixteen circuit judges. The act was short-lived. It was repealed on March 8, 1802. Recall that this was the act passed by the lame duck Federalist Congress that so raised the ire of Thomas Jefferson. The act was seen as an attempt to ensconce Federalists in power in an expanded federal judiciary.[14] Partly as a result of the politicization of this issue, the very real problems faced by the federal judiciary, including circuit riding, went unattended. The problem of circuit riding per se is not particularly important for our concerns except as it relates to another problem. The Supreme Court was increasingly falling behind in its work. In 1890, it opened its October term with a backlog of 1,800 cases.[15] Today's alleged workload problem of the Supreme Court is not an altogether new phenomenon.

Few lasting changes were made in the Supreme Court's appellate jurisdiction until the Circuit Courts of Appeal Act was passed in 1891. An Act of April 10, 1869,[16] had enabled justices to curtail circuit riding in practice if not theory, and the Act of March 3, 1875,[17] "vastly extended the domain of the federal courts."[18] But when the act of 1891 created circuit courts of appeals to perform strictly appellate functions, a major step was taken in beginning to reshape the appellate jurisdiction of the Supreme Court.[19] The act mandated that in certain areas the judgments of the circuit courts of appeal were to be final.[20] But the act added: "In any such case as hereinbefore made final in the circuit court of appeals it shall be competent for the Supreme Court to require, by certiorari or otherwise, any such case to be certified to the Supreme Court for its review and determination with the same power and authority in the case as if it had been carried by appeal or writ of error to the Supreme Court."[21] The House version of this bill had contained no mention of certiorari, and there is little in the legislative history to indicate why the Senate version did. The Senate version was accepted, however.[22]

14. Though similar, this Act of February 4, 1801, should not be confused with the Organic Act of the District of Columbia of February 27, 1801, which provided for the President to appoint justices of the peace for the District of Columbia. It was the latter act, of course, which gave rise to Marbury v. Madison.

15. Frankfurter, *The Business of the Supreme Court*, p. 86.

16. 16 Stat. 44.

17. 18 Stat. 470.

18. See Frankfurter, *The Business of the Supreme Court*, pp. 30, 87.

19. Linzer, "Certiorari Denials," p. 1232.

20. Ibid., p. 1233.

21. Act of March 3, 1891, 26 Stat. 826, sec. 6.

22. Linzer, "Certiorari Denials," pp. 1234–1235.

Though provided for by statute, this is still obviously the common law version of certiorari. As Linzer points out, the Supreme Court had used common law certiorari as early as 1806 in *Ex parte Burford* deriving its right to do so from the "All Writs Section" of the First Judiciary Act of 1789, the modern version of which is now codified at 28 U.S.C. sec. 1651, as discussed above.[23] However, Linzer argues, it was necessary to add the certiorari language here because "the All Writs section might not have been adequate to authorize certiorari where the circuit courts of appeals gave the 'final' word, since the Supreme Court would have had no jurisdiction and the writ apparently would not have been 'necessary for the exercise' of its jurisdiction."[24]

In 1914, certiorari was extended to certain state court judgments. This expansion of the Supreme Courts jurisdiction, was seen as a "safety valve for anomalous cases."[25] It was not viewed as a major expansion. Meanwhile, the Court's obligatory jurisdiction had been growing. Many categories of cases still had a direct appeal to the Supreme Court by appeal or writ of error, and the caseload problem was redeveloping. Of particular concern was the growing number of Federal Employers' Liability Act (FELA) cases. In 1916, the Webb Act addressed this problem by making the courts of appeals the place of final decision for FELA cases.[26] These cases usually did not need review by the Supreme Court. Once again, however, these "final" decisions still could be reviewed on certiorari in the Supreme Court. The Webb Act changed review by writ of error (mandatory review), to certiorari in several important categories. Linzer argues that this "made a profound change in the function of the writ of certiorari" because for "the first time a major area of undisputed national importance was subjected to the Supreme Court's discretion."[27] He continues: "One is tempted to ascribe a different view of certiorari to Congress here than that of an extraordinary remedy to be used when circuits disagree or when state courts did the rare act of striking down state statutes on federal grounds; now certiorari would govern many major cases as well."[28] Frankfurter agrees: "Here was a marked change of policy, albeit in form merely an extension of the principle of discretionary jurisdiction through *certiorari* derived from the Circuit Courts of Appeals Act. But the chief aim of this measure—to save the Supreme

23. Ibid., p. 1235, n. 60.
24. Ibid., p. 1236, n. 61.
25. Ibid., p. 1238.
26. 39 Stat. 726.
27. Linzer, "Certiorari Denials," p. 1239.
28. Ibid., p. 1240.

Court from the voluminous futilities of employers' liability litigation—was so compelling, that the important innovation of the Act went through Congress without serious consideration, certainly without debate."[29]

Finally, we come to the Act of February 13, 1925,[30] or the "Judges' Bill," which revolutionized the Court's appellate jurisdiction. The Judges' Bill was so named because it was literally drafted by Supreme Court justices. Reforming the judiciary was a passion of William Howard Taft. First as President, then as chief justice, he worked tirelessly toward this aim. Nowhere is this better seen than in his involvement with drafting and advocating the act of 1925. It was this act that established "statutory certiorari" as the preponderant method of review in the U.S. Supreme Court. After its enactment, few categories of obligatory jurisdiction remained. Though there have been changes over the years, this act remains the basis of the Court's modern day jurisdiction; therefore, we may proceed to the current situation.

Federal Courts

The Court's certiorari jurisdiction is found in Title 28 of the *U.S. Code*. For cases that are in the courts of appeals, Section 1254 provides review in the Supreme Court: "By writ of certiorari granted upon the petition of any party to any civil or criminal case, before or after rendition of judgment or decree." Note that this would include virtually every type of case in a federal court of appeals. Cases that have the right of appeal can petition for certiorari instead, but there is little incentive to do so. Appeals have a far greater chance of being taken than do certs., and if a case is not properly an appeal, the Court treats it as a cert. anyway.[31] Also note that certiorari can be granted before a final judgment, which is not true for cases in state courts. The Court rarely takes cases before final judgment, but there are occasions when it does. Its reason for doing so is usually the need for expedited review. The most notable recent example is *United States v. Nixon*.[32]

There is no review by certiorari from federal district courts. Practically speaking, in a case such as *Nixon*, it is almost as if cert. were

29. Frankfurter, *The Business of the Supreme Court*, p. 213.

30. 43 Stat. 936.

31. See sec. 2103.

32. 418 U.S. 683 (1974). Several scholars have criticized the Court for jumping in to resolve this case, believing that history and jurisprudence would have been better served if the Court of Appeals had been allowed to deal with the case first. That, of course, is a debatable proposition, and one with which I disagree.

petitioned from a judgment of the District Court, but technically a case must be properly in a court of appeals (which means that it must at least be docketed) before it can be taken.

State Courts

Section 1257 outlines jurisdiction over state courts.[33] Review of a state court judgment, whether on appeal or certiorari, can be taken only if the judgment is final, and if it is in the highest court in which a decision could be had. What constitutes "finality" and the "highest court" is fairly involved and is of little concern here.[34] What is important is that neither of these requirements exists for review of federal court decisions.

A final judgment of a state court could be reviewed on appeal, rather than certiorari, if it held a treaty or statute of the United States invalid or if a state law were upheld after having been challenged as unconstitutional. In short, if federal law loses against state law, there is a right of appeal; if state law loses then review is by certiorari.[35]

Finally, review by certiorari is permitted "where any title, right, privilege or immunity is specially set up or claimed under the Constitution, treaties or statutes of . . . the United States." If one has claimed a violation of some federal right even though one is in state court, one can petition for certiorari. Such cases constitute by far the most frequently exercised portion of the Supreme Court's jurisdiction over state courts.[36] However, the federal question must have been asserted in the state court, the state court must have passed upon the federal question, and the decision must not be based upon adequate and independent nonfederal grounds.[37] That is, it is too late to raise a

33. Section 1257 reads in relevant part: "Final judgments or decrees rendered by the highest court of a State in which a decision could be had, may be reviewed by the Supreme court as follows:

". . . (3) By writ of certiorari, where the validity of a treaty or statute of the United States is drawn in question or where the validity of a State statute is drawn in question on the ground of its being repugnant to the Constitution, treaties or laws of the United States, or where any title, right, privilege or immunity is specially set up or claimed under the Constitution, treaties or statutes of, or commission held or authority exercised under, the United States."

34. For an extended discussion, see Stern and Gressman, *Supreme Court Practice*, pp. 172–208.

35. More precisely, certiorari is permitted regardless of the outcome of a state court decision, but there would be little advantage for the United States to petition for cert. when it can go by appeal.

36. Stern and Gressman, *Supreme Court Practice*, p. 167.

37. Ibid., pp. 166–167.

federal question in a cert. petition if counsel did not raise it in the state court. And, when a state court's decision can rest upon nonfederal grounds, even if a federal question was addressed and incorrectly decided, the Supreme Court will not review the case.[38] As with "finality," determining what constitutes "adequate and independent nonfederal grounds" is a highly complex jurisdictional issue that need not be discussed here except to say that this jurisdictional hurdle prevents many cases from making it all the way to the Supreme Court.[39]

Appeals

A case properly on appeal theoretically has a right of review in the Supreme Court. Congress determines what cases qualify as appeals. Recall, however, that a major jurisdictional change in 1988 effectively eliminated appeals.[40] The discussion that follows is written in present tense though it concerns the law as it existed at the time of my interviews, which were prior to the 1988 changes.

Federal Courts

The first category of cases having the right of appeal is outlined in Section 1252 of Title 28 of the *U.S. Code*. This section provides for a direct appeal to the Supreme Court when any court of the United States (a federal court)[41] holds an act of Congress unconstitutional in any civil action, suit, or proceeding to which the United States or any of its agencies or officers or employees is a party.[42] To have the right

38. Ibid., pp. 230–231.
39. See ibid., pp. 230–245.
40. Public Law 100-352.
41. This might be an appropriate time to remind those who are not accustomed to reading about courts that when one says a court "of the United States" one means a federal court, whereas a court "in the United States" may include both state and federal courts.
42. Section 1252 reads in full: "Any party may appeal to the Supreme Court from an interlocutory or final judgment, decree or order of any court of the United States, the United States District Court for the District of the Canal Zone, the District Court of Guam and the District Court of the Virgin Islands and any court of record of Puerto Rico, holding an Act of Congress unconstitutional in any civil action, suit or proceeding to which the United States or any of its agencies, or any officer or employee thereof, as such officer or employee is a party.

"A party who has received notice of appeal under this section shall take any subsequent appeal or cross appeal to the Supreme Court. All appeals or cross appeals taken to other courts prior to such notice shall be treated as taken directly to the Supreme Court."

to appeal under Section 1252, then, the case must fulfill several criteria. Note that the statute says "any court," which means it would apply to both federal district courts and the courts of appeals, as well as any other federal court.

Section 1254 creates a second category of appeals.[43] When a federal court of appeals invalidates a state statute upon which a party is relying, the party can appeal to the Supreme Court; but the review is restricted to the federal questions presented, and such an appeal precludes a review by certiorari.[44] Finally, direct appeal lies to the Supreme Court from decisions by three-judge federal courts. This category requires more elaboration; first, just to understand it, but more important, because prior to 1976 (when some major jurisdictional changes were made) this category was responsible for a disproportionately high number of cases granted oral argument in the Supreme Court. As a result, it has been the subject of much discussion by Court observers both on and off the Court.

Most federal cases are heard first in a federal district court presided over by one federal district judge. Appeals are then usually made to the appropriate circuit court of appeals. From time to time, however, Congress has required that certain issues be tried by three-judge district courts, and when it has done so, it has invariably permitted direct appeal to the Supreme Court. The practice began with the enactment of the Three-Judge Court Act of 1910.[45] The act had been passed

43. Section 1254 reads in full (emphasis added): "Cases in the courts of appeals may be reviewed by the Supreme Court by the following methods:

"(1) By writ of certiorari granted upon the petition of any party to any civil or criminal case, before or after rendition of judgment or decree;

"(2) *By appeal* by a party relying on a State statute held by a court of appeals to be invalid as repugnant to the Constitution, treaties or laws of the United States, but such appeal shall preclude review by writ of certiorari at the instance of such appellant, and the review on appeal shall be restricted to the Federal questions presented;

"(3) By certification at any time by a court of appeals of any question of law in any civil or criminal case as to which instructions are desired, and upon such certification the Supreme Court may give binding instructions or require the entire record to be sent up for decision of the entire matter in controversy."

44. This is slightly misleading because under Section 2103 if an appeal is taken improvidently it is then treated as a writ of certiorari. Stern and Gressman argue (*Supreme Court Practice*, p. 68): "The preclusion clause in Sec. 1254(2) thus would seem to have effect only if the appeal were accepted by the Supreme Court, in which case, under the literal words of the statute, certiorari would not seem to lie to bring up issues other than those available on the appeal, although this has not been explicitly decided." They draw this conclusion from the Court's treatment of Bradford Electric Light Co. v. Clapper, 284 U.S. 221, 224, and El Paso v. Simmons, 379 U.S. 497, 501–503.

45. 36 Stat. 577, later codified in 28 U.S.C. sec. 2281.

largely as a result of the confluence of certain historical factors and a landmark Supreme Court decision. Around the turn of the century, big business and the railroads were expanding dramatically. In an attempt to exercise authority over these businesses, states began enacting regulatory statutes.[46] Meanwhile, in 1908, the Supreme Court held in *Ex parte Young*[47] that state officials could be enjoined by federal courts from enforcing unconstitutional state statutes. As injunctions began to issue from federal district judges, states became increasingly frustrated at their inability to enforce their own statutes. The situation was summarized in a report by the Senate Committee on the Judiciary: "Most controversial was the practice of many Federal judges of granting interlocutory injunctions on the strength of affidavits alone or of granting temporary restraining orders ex parte, i.e., without hearing or notice to the opposing side."[48] As a response, the three-judge, direct-appeal mechanism was born. Again quoting from the committee report:

> Congress enacted the Three-Judge Court Act (Act of June 18, 1910, ch. 309, Sec. 17, 36 Stat. 577) which prohibited a single Federal district court judge from issuing interlocutory injunctions against allegedly unconstitutional State statutes and required that cases seeking such injunctive relief be heard by a district court made up of three judges. The act also contained a provision for direct appeal to the Supreme Court in the belief that this would provide speedy review of these cases. The rationale of the act was that three judges would be less likely than one to exercise the Federal injunctive power imprudently. It was felt that the act would relieve the fears of the States that they would have important regulatory programs precipitously enjoined.[49]

Over the years, instances requiring the use of three-judge panels expanded, but these judicial Hydras eventually began to come under criticism. Many of the reasons to have such statutes had been rendered

---

46. S. Rep. no. 94-204, 94th Cong., 1st sess., 1975, p. 2.

47. 209 U.S. 123 (1908).

48. S. Rep. no. 94-204, p. 2.

49. Ibid. See Stern and Gressman, *Supreme Court Practice*, pp. 94–95, for a more complete history.

obsolete by judicial rules and changes in history.[50] Moreover, their existence was proving increasingly burdensome to the Supreme Court and to lower courts as well. Three-judge courts were required to have at least one circuit judge, which caused logistical difficulties. Also, utilizing three judges to hear one case had obvious ramifications for caseload problems at the lower levels. As for the Supreme Court, not only did the direct-appeal component exacerbate its workload problem,[51] but the three-judge arrangement was unsatisfactory for other reasons as well. Stern and Gressman point out that "a three-judge court was found to be ill-adapted for the trial of factual issues, the judges being reluctant to hold evidentiary trials and seeking instead to induce the parties to stipulate facts or otherwise short-cut any factual hearing. On direct appeal from such three-judge court determinations, the Supreme Court frequently found itself faced with an inadequate record."[52]

In the early 1970s, several statutes were passed repealing the requirement for a three-judge court in some situations. In 1976, Congress passed a law that severely restricted the use of three-judge panels, and it also redefined some of their operating procedures.[53] Only Sections 1253 and 2284 of Title 28, and four separate statutes, authorize the use of three-judge district courts and the direct appeal therefrom. Well, sort of. Be forewarned, this subject gets quite confusing.[54]

50. S.Rep. no. 94-204, pp. 7–8: "The original problems were largely obviated 2 years after the passage of the Three-Judge Court Act when the Federal Equity Rules were revised, extending to all injunctive cases much of the same protective procedures which the 1910 act had provided for by three-judge court proceedings." See also, Stern and Gressman, *Supreme Court Practice*, p. 101: "The fears emanating from the treatment of federal laws by single district judges were largely dissipated as the Court retreated from certain critical constitutional doctrines that had permitted easy invalidation; and the Court also revived earlier policies permitting the disposition of cases on constitutional grounds only in situations of strict necessity."

51. Stern and Gressman, *Supreme Court Practice*, p. 92: "The three-judge court appeals that survived summary treatment accounted for over 20 percent of the cases that the court heard orally after full briefing."

52. Ibid., pp. 92–93.

53. Public Law 94-381, 90 Stat. 1119.

54. At least it certainly confused me. I felt somewhat exonerated when I learned that the Court had referred to Section 1253 as "very awkwardly drafted" and containing "opaque terms and prolix syntax." Gonzalez v. Employees Credit Union, 419 U.S. 90, 95–97. Stern and Gressman argue (*Supreme Court Practice*, pp. 94–95) that Section 1253 was the result of earlier revisions of the Judicial Code. In a simplification of the code, 1253 was derived from three earlier statutes, but when those statutory mandates were repealed in 1975 and 1976, "1253 was shorn of the original reasons for its existence."

There are five statutory categories that require three-judge district courts. Four categories have "their own Act." The four acts (and their subsequent amended forms) are: the Civil Rights Act of 1964, the Voting Rights Act of 1965, the Regional Rail Reorganization Act, and the Presidential Election Campaign Fund Act. The authorization and requirements for direct appeal to the Supreme Court are found within each statute. The fifth category was inexplicably placed in Section 2284 of Title 28. This section supposedly concerns the composition and procedure for three-judge courts, but the section begins as follows: "A district court of three judges shall be convened when otherwise required by an act of Congress, or when an action is filed challenging the constitutionality of the apportionment of congressional districts or the apportionment of any statewide legislative body." So now we have a fifth statutory category, apportionment.

Section 1253 limits appeals from three-judge courts to orders that grant or deny interlocutory or permanent injunctions.[55] This seems straightforward enough except that the four separate acts establishing the four statutory categories already contain provisions governing their direct appeals, thereby rendering Section 1253 inapposite to them. The only remaining possible function for 1253, then, is to apply to the reapportionment cases. But Stern and Gressman argue that the intent of Congress was for reapportionment cases to have three-judge courts and to have direct appeal in all cases, not just those involving injunctions, and that the retention of 1253 was an oversight.[56] Nevertheless, because of section 1253, appeal in reapportionment cases seems to be limited to interlocutory and permanent injunctions.

In sum, appeals from three-judge district courts are an important category of the Supreme Court's obligatory jurisdiction, but their significance, or at least their number, is decreasing.

State Courts

An appeal lies to the Supreme Court from state courts in two instances: (1) when a treaty or statute of the United States is held invalid; and

---

55. Section 1253 reads in full: "Except as otherwise provided by law, any party may appeal to the Supreme Court from an order granting or denying, after notice and hearing, an interlocutory or permanent injunction in any civil action, suit or proceeding required by any Act of Congress to be heard and determined by a district court of three judges."

56. Stern and Gressman, *Supreme Court Practice*, pp. 112–113.

(2) when a state statute is held as valid after it has been challenged as being repugnant to the Constitution, treaties, or laws of the United States.[57] In both instances, however, the judgments or decrees must be final, and they must be rendered by the highest court in a state in which a decision could be had.[58]

57. Section 1257 reads in relevant part: "Final judgments or decrees rendered by the highest court of a State in which a decision could be had, may be reviewed by the Supreme court as follows:

"(1) By appeal, where is drawn in question the validity of a treaty or statute of the United States and the decision is against its validity.

"(2) By appeal where is drawn in question the validity of a statute of any state on the ground of its being repugnant to the Constitution, treaties or laws of the United States, and the decision is in favor of its validity."

Section 1258, applicable to Puerto Rico, is virtually identical to Section 1257 with regard to the basis for an appeal.

58. This does not always happen to be the highest court in the state per se; see, e.g., Thompson v. City of Louisville, 362 U.S. 199 (1960), which was taken from the Police Court of Louisville.

Index